Workshop on Computational Approaches to Analysis and Generation of Emotion in Text 2010

AA005801

Held at NAACL HLT 2010

Los Angeles, California, USA
5 June 2010

ISBN: 978-1-61738-671-8

Printed from e-media with permission by:

Curran Associates, Inc.
57 Morehouse Lane
Red Hook, NY 12571

Some format issues inherent in the e-media version may also appear in this print version.

Printed by Curran Associates, Inc. (2010)

For permission requests, please contact the Association for Computational Linguistics
at the address below.

Association for Computational Linguistics
209 N. Eighth Street
Stroudsburg, Pennsylvania 18360

Phone: 1-570-476-8006
Fax: 1-570-476-0860

acl@aclweb.org

Additional copies of this publication are available from:

Curran Associates, Inc.
57 Morehouse Lane
Red Hook, NY 12571 USA
Phone: 845-758-0400
Fax: 845-758-2634
Email: curran@proceedings.com
Web: www.proceedings.com

Introduction

The automatic detection of emotions in texts and the generation of texts that express emotions is important for applications such as natural language interfaces, e-learning environments, and educational or entertainment games. These aspects are also important in opinion mining and sentiment analysis, and in the larger area of affective computing.

This workshop provides a forum for discussion between leading names and researchers involved in processing emotions in the context of natural language understanding, natural language generation, or applications in which computational approaches to the processing of emotions are useful.

Topics of interest include, but are not limited to: emotion analysis in sentences and documents; classification of texts by emotion and mood; the generation of sentences that express emotions; emotion processing across different languages; the analysis of sentiment and opinion that contains emotional aspects; argumentation that includes emotions and opinions; emotion analysis in automatic speech transcripts; applications in which affective aspects are beneficial; other aspects of the computational treatment of emotion and affect.

We would like to thank all the authors who submitted papers for the hard work that went behind their submissions. We express our deepest gratitude to the committee members for their thorough reviews. We also thank the NAACL-HLT 2010 organizers for their help with administrative matters.

Organizers:

Diana Inkpen (Univeristy of Ottawa, Canada)
Carlo Strapparava (FBK-IRST, Trento, Italy)

Program Committee:

Cecilia Ovesdotter Alm(Cornell University, USA)
Carmen Banea (University of North Texas, USA)
Sabine Bergler (Concordia University, Canada)
Robert Dale (Macquarie University, Sydney, Australia)
Andrea Esuli (Consiglio Nazionale delle Ricerca, Italy)
Viola Ganter (EML Research gGmbH, Heidelberg, Germany)
Diman Ghazi (University of Ottawa, Canada)
Degen Huang (Dalian University of Technology, China)
Mitsuru Ishizuka (University of Tokyo, Japan)
Shahzad Khan (Whyz Technologies Inc., Ottawa, Canada)
Fazel Keshtkar (University of Ottawa, Canada)
Zornitsa Kozareva (University of Southern California / Information Sciences Institute, USA)
Saif Mohammad (National Research Council, Canada)
Alena Neviarouskaya (University of Tokyo, Japan)
Alexander Osherenko (University of Augsburg, Germany)
Fuji Ren (University of Tokushima, Japan)
Victoria Rubin (University of Western Ontario, Canada)
Stan Szpakowicz (University of Ottawa, Canada)
Theresa Wilson (University of Edinburgh, UK)
Maite Taboada (Simon Fraser University, Canada)

Invited Speaker: Oren Glickman (MoodBase.com),
Emotion Analysis as a Means of Categorizing Content

Table of Contents

Workshop Program

Saturday, June 5, 2010

9:00–9:10	Opening
9:10–10:00	Invited talk: Emotion analysis as a means of categorizing content, Oren Glickman
10:05–10:30	*Emotion Analysis Using Latent Affective Folding and Embedding* Jerome Bellegarda
10:30–11:00	Coffee Break
11:00–11:25	*Emotion Detection in Email Customer Care* Narendra Gupta, Mazin Gilbert and Giuseppe Di Fabbrizio
11:25–11:50	*Toward Plot Units: Automatic Affect State Analysis* Amit Goyal, Ellen Riloff, Hal Daume III and Nathan Gilbert
11:50–12:15	*Emotions Evoked by Common Words and Phrases: Using Mechanical Turk to Create an Emotion Lexicon* Saif Mohammad and Peter Turney
12:15–2:00	Lunch Break
2:00–2:25	*A Corpus-based Method for Extracting Paraphrases of Emotion Terms* Fazel Keshtkat and Diana Inkpen
2:25–2:50	*A Text-driven Rule-based System for Emotion Cause Detection* Sophia Yat Mei Lee, Ying Chen and Chu-Ren Huang
2:50–3:15	*Wishful Thinking - Finding suggestions and 'buy' wishes from product reviews* J Ramanand, Krishna Bhavsar and Niranjan Pedanekar
3:15–3:45	Coffee Break
3:45–4:10	*Evaluation of Unsupervised Emotion Models to Textual Affect Recognition* Sunghwan Mac Kim, Alessandro Valitutti and Rafael A. Calvo

Saturday, June 5, 2010 (continued)

Emotion Analysis Using Latent Affective Folding and Embedding

Jerome R. Bellegarda

Speech & Language Technologies
Apple Inc.
Cupertino, California 95014, USA
jerome @ apple.com

Abstract

Though data-driven in nature, emotion analysis based on latent semantic analysis still relies on some measure of expert knowledge in order to isolate the emotional keywords or keysets necessary to the construction of affective categories. This makes it vulnerable to any discrepancy between the ensuing taxonomy of affective states and the underlying domain of discourse. This paper proposes a more general strategy which leverages two distincts semantic levels, one that encapsulates the foundations of the domain considered, and one that specifically accounts for the overall affective fabric of the language. Exposing the emergent relationship between these two levels advantageously informs the emotion classification process. Empirical evidence suggests that this is a promising solution for automatic emotion detection in text.

1 Introduction

The automatic detection of emotions in text is a necessary pre-processing step in many different fields touching on affective computing (Picard, 1997), such as natural language interfaces (Cosatto et al., 2003), e-learning environments (Ryan et al., 2000), educational or entertainment games (Pivec and Kearney, 2007), opinion mining and sentiment analysis (Pang and Lee, 2008), humor recognition (Mihalcea and Strapparava, 2006), and security informatics (Abbasi, 2007). In the latter case, for example, it can be used for monitoring levels of hateful or violent rhetoric (perhaps in multilingual settings). More generally, emotion detection is of great interest in human-computer interaction: if a system determines that a user is upset or annoyed, for instance, it could switch to a different mode of interaction (Liscombe et al., 2005). And of course, it plays a critical role in the generation of expressive synthetic speech (Schröder, 2006).

Emphasis has traditionally been placed on the set of six "universal" emotions (Ekman, 1993): ANGER, DISGUST, FEAR, JOY, SADNESS, and SURPRISE (Alm et al., 2005; Liu et al., 2003; Subasic and Huettner, 2001). Emotion analysis is typically carried out using a simplified description of emotional states in a low-dimensional space, which normally comprises dimensions such as valence (positive/negative evalution), activation (stimulation of activity), and/or control (dominant/submissive power) (Mehrabian, 1995; Russell, 1980; Strapparava and Mihalcea, 2008). Classification proceeds based on an underlying emotional knowledge base, which strives to provide adequate distinctions between different emotions. This affective information can either be built entirely upon manually selected vocabulary as in (Whissell, 1989), or derived automatically from data based on expert knowledge of the most relevant features that can be extracted from the input text (Alm et al., 2005). In both cases, the resulting system tends to rely, for the most part, on a few thousand annotated "emotional keywords," the presence of which triggers the associated emotional label(s).

The drawback of such confined lexical affinity is that the analysis tends to be hampered by the bias inherent in the underlying taxonomy of emotional states. Because this taxonomy only supports simplified relationships between affective words and emo-

Proceedings of the NAACL HLT 2010 Workshop on Computational Approaches to Analysis and Generation of Emotion in Text, pages 1–9,
Los Angeles, California, June 2010.

tional categories, it often fails to meaningfully generalize beyond the relatively few core terms explicitly considered in its construction. This has sparked interest in data-driven approaches based on latent semantic analysis (LSA), a paradigm originally developed for information retrieval (Deerwester et al., 1990). Upon suitable training using a large corpus of texts, LSA allows a similarity score to be computed between generic terms and affective categories (Strapparava et al., 2006). This way, every word can automatically be assigned some fractional affective influence. Still, the affective categories themselves are usually specified with the help of a reference lexical database like WordNet (Fellbaum, 1998).

The purpose of this paper is to more broadly leverage the principle of latent semantics in emotion analysis. We cast the problem as a general application of *latent semantic mapping* (LSM), an extrapolation of LSA for modeling global relationships implicit in large volumes of data (Bellegarda, 2005; Bellegarda, 2008). More specifically, we use the LSM framework to describe two distinct semantic levels: one that encapsulates the foundations of the domain considered (e.g., broadcast news, email messages, SMS conversations, etc.), and one that specifically accounts for the overall affective fabric of the language. Then, we leverage these two descriptions to appropriately relate domain and affective levels, and thereby inform the emotion classification process. This *de facto* bypasses the need for any explicit external knowledge.

The paper is organized as follows. The next section provides some motivation for, and gives an overview of, the proposed latent affective framework. In Sections 3 and 4, we describe the two main alternatives considered, latent folding and latent embedding. In Section 5, we discuss the mechanics of emotion detection based on such latent affective processing. Finally, Section 6 reports the outcome of experimental evaluations conducted on the "Affective Text" portion of the SemEval-2007 corpus (Strapparava and Mihalcea, 2007).

2 Motivation and Overview

As alluded to above, lexical affinity alone fails to provide sufficient distinction between different emotions, in large part because only relatively few words have inherently clear, unambiguous emotional meaning. For example, *happy* and *sad* encapsulate JOY and SADNESS, respectively, in all conceivable scenarios. But is *thrilling* a marker of JOY or SURPRISE? Does *awful* capture SADNESS or DISGUST? It largely depends on contextual information: *thrilling* as a synonym for *uplifting* conveys JOY (as in *a thrilling speech*), while *thrilling* as a synonym for *amazing* may well mark SURPRISE (as in *a thrilling waterfall ride*); similarly, *awful* as a synonym for *grave* reflects SADNESS (as in *an awful car accident*), while *awful* as a synonym for *foul* is closer to DISGUST (as in *an awful smell*). The vast majority of words likewise carry multiple potential emotional connotations, with the degree of affective polysemy tightly linked to the granularity selected for the underlying taxonomy of emotions.

Data-driven approaches based on LSA purport to "individuate" such indirect affective words via inference mechanisms automatically derived in an unsupervised way from a large corpus of texts, such as the British National Corpus (Strapparava et al., 2006). By looking at document-level co-occurrences, contextual information is exploited to encapsulate semantic information into a relatively low dimensional vector space. Suitable affective categories are then constructed in that space by "folding in" either the specific word denoting the emotion, or its associated synset (say, from WordNet), or even the entire set of words in all synsets that can be labelled with that emotion (Strapparava and Mihalcea, 2008). This is typically done by placing the relevant word(s) into a "pseudo-document," and map it into the space as if it were a real one (Deerwester et al., 1990). Finally, the global emotional affinity of a given input text is determined by computing similarities between all pseudo-documents. The resulting framework is depicted in Fig. 1.

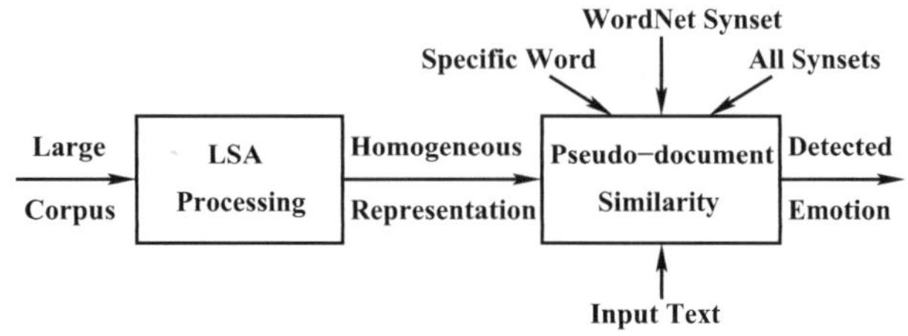

Figure 1: *Typical LSA-Based Emotion Analysis.*

This solution is attractive, if for no other reason than it allows every word to automatically be assigned some fractional affective influence. However, it suffers from two limitations which may well prove deleterious in practical situations. First, the inherent lack of supervision routinely leads to a latent semantic space which is not particularly representative of the underlying domain of discourse. And second, the construction of the affective categories still relies heavily on pre-defined lexical affinity, potentially resulting in an unwarranted bias in the taxonomy of affective states.

The first limitation impinges on the effectiveness of any LSA-based approach, which is known to vary substantially based on the size and quality of the training data (Bellegarda, 2008; Mohler and Mihalcea, 2009). In the present case, any discrepancy between latent semantic space and domain of discourse may distort the position of certain words in the space, which could in turn lead to subsequent sub-optimal affective weight assignment. For instance, in the examples above, the word *smell* is considerably more critical to the resolution of *awful* as a marker of DISGUST than the word *car*. But that fact may never be uncovered if the only pertinent documents in the training corpus happen to be about expensive fragrances and automobiles. Thus, it is highly desirable to derive the latent semantic space using data representative of the application considered. This points to a modicum of supervision.

The second limitation is tied to the difficulty of coming up with an *a priori* affective description that will work universally. Stipulating the affective categories using only the specific word denoting the emotion is likely to be less robust than using the set of words in all synsets labelled with that emotion. On the other hand, the latter may well expose some inherent ambiguities resulting from affective polysemy. This is compounded by the relatively small number of words for which an affective distribution is even available. For example, the well-known General Inquirer content analysis system (Stone, 1997) lists only about 2000 words with positive outlook and 2000 words with negative outlook. There are exactly 1281 words inventoried in the affective extension of WordNet (Strapparava and Mihalcea, 2008), and the affective word list from (Johnson–Laird and Oatley, 1989) comprises less than 1000 words. This considerably complicates the construction of reliable affective categories in the latent space.

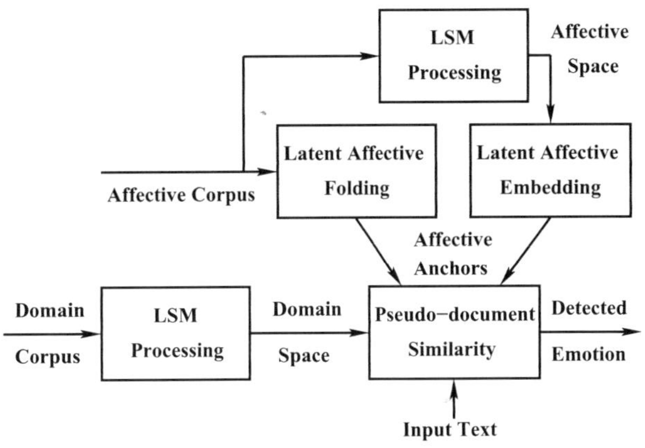

Figure 2: *Proposed Latent Affective Framework.*

To address the two limitations above, we propose to more broadly leverage the LSM paradigm (Bellegarda, 2005; Bellegarda, 2008), following the overall framework depicted in Fig. 2. Compared to Fig. 1, we inject some supervision at two separate levels: not only regarding the particular domain considered, but also how the affective categories themselves are defined. The first task is to exploit a suitable training collection to encapsulate into a (domain) latent semantic space the general foundations of the domain at hand. Next, we leverage a separate affective corpus, such as mood-annotated blog entries from LiveJournal.com (Strapparava and Mihalcea, 2008), to serve as a descriptive blueprint for the construction of affective categories.

This blueprint is then folded into the domain space in one of two ways. The easiest approach, called latent affective folding, is simply to superimpose *affective anchors* inferred in the space for every affective category. This is largely analogous to what happens in Fig. 1, with a crucial difference regarding the representation of affective categories: in latent affective folding, it is derived from a corpus of texts as opposed to a pre-specified keyword or keyset. This is likely to help making the categories more robust, but may not satisfactorily resolve subtle distinctions between emotional connotations. This technique is described in detail in the next section.

The second approach, called latent affective embedding, is to extract a distinct LSM representation

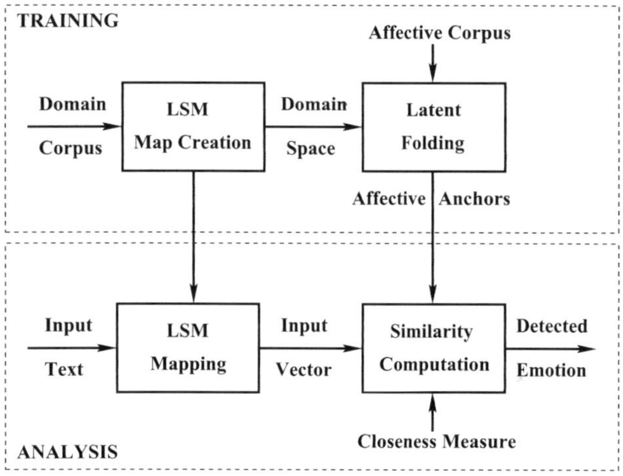

Figure 3: *Emotion Analysis Using Latent Folding.*

from the affective corpus, to encapsulate all prior affective information into a separate (affective) latent semantic space. In this space, affective anchors can be computed directly, instead of inferred after folding, presumably leading to a more accurate positioning. Domain and affective LSM spaces can then be related to each other via a mapping derived from words that are common to both. This way, the affective anchors can be precisely embedded into the domain space. This technique is described in detail in Section 4.

In both cases, the input text is mapped into the domain space as before. Emotion classification then follows from assessing how closely it aligns with each affective anchor.

3 Latent Affective Folding

Expanding the basic framework of Fig. 2 to take into account the two separate phases of training and analysis, latent affective folding proceeds as illustrated in Fig. 3.

Let $\mathcal{T}_1$, $|\mathcal{T}_1| = N_1$, be a collection of training texts (be they sentences, paragraphs, or documents) reflecting the domain of interest, and $\mathcal{V}_1$, $|\mathcal{V}_1| = M_1$, the associated set of all words (possibly augmented with some strategic word pairs, triplets, etc., as appropriate) observed in this collection. Generally, M_1 is on the order of several tens of thousands, while N_1 may be as high as a million.

We first construct a $(M_1 \times N_1)$ matrix W_1, whose elements w_{ij} suitably reflect the extent to which each word $w_i \in \mathcal{V}_1$ appeared in each text $t_j \in \mathcal{T}_1$.

From (Bellegarda, 2008), a reasonable expression for w_{ij} is:

$$w_{i,j} = (1 - \varepsilon_i)\,\frac{c_{i,j}}{n_j}\,, \qquad (1)$$

where $c_{i,j}$ is the number of times w_i occurs in text t_j, n_j is the total number of words present in this text, and ε_i is the normalized entropy of w_i in $\mathcal{V}_1$. The global weighting implied by $1 - \varepsilon_i$ reflects the fact that two words appearing with the same count in a particular text do not necessarily convey the same amount of information; this is subordinated to the distribution of words in the entire set $\mathcal{V}_1$.

We then perform a singular value decomposition (SVD) of W_1 as (Bellegarda, 2008):

$$W_1 = U_1\, S_1\, V_1^{\,T}\,, \qquad (2)$$

where U_1 is the $(M_1 \times R_1)$ left singular matrix with row vectors $u_{1,i}$ $(1 \leq i \leq M_1)$, S_1 is the $(R_1 \times R_1)$ diagonal matrix of singular values $s_{1,1} \geq s_{1,2} \geq \ldots \geq s_{1,R_1} > 0$, V_1 is the $(N_1 \times R_1)$ right singular matrix with row vectors $v_{1,j}$ $(1 \leq j \leq N_1)$, $R_1 \ll M_1, N_1$ is the order of the decomposition, and ^{T} denotes matrix transposition.

As is well known, both left and right singular matrices U_1 and V_1 are column-orthonormal, i.e., $U_1^T U_1 = V_1^T V_1 = I_{R_1}$ (the identity matrix of order R_1). Thus, the column vectors of U_1 and V_1 each define an orthornormal basis for the space of dimension R_1 spanned by the $u_{1,i}$'s and $v_{1,j}$'s. We refer to this space as the *latent semantic space* $\mathcal{L}_1$. The (rank-R_1) decomposition (2) encapsulates a mapping between the set of words w_i and texts t_j and (after apropriate scaling by the singular values) the set of R_1-dimensional vectors $y_{1,i} = u_{1,i}S_1$ and $z_{1,j} = v_{1,j}S_1$.

The basic idea behind (2) is that the rank-R_1 decomposition captures the major structural associations in W_1 and ignores higher order effects. Hence, the relative positions of the input words in the space $\mathcal{L}_1$ reflect a parsimonious encoding of the semantic concepts used in the domain considered. This means that any new text mapped onto a vector "close" (in some suitable metric) to a particular set of words can be expected to be closely related to the concept encapsulated by this set. If each of these words is then scored in terms of their affective affinity, this offers a way to automatically predict the overall emotional affinity of the text.

In order to do so, we need to isolate regions in that space which are representative of the underlying taxonomy of emotions considered. The centroid of each such region is the *affective anchor* associated with that basic emotion. Affective anchors are superimposed onto the space $\mathcal{L}_1$ on the basis of the affective corpus available.

Let $\mathcal{T}_2$, $|\mathcal{T}_2| = N_2$, represent a separate collection of mood-annotated texts (again they could be sentences, paragraphs, or documents), representative of the desired categories of emotions (such as JOY and SADNESS), and $\mathcal{V}_2$, $|\mathcal{V}_2| = M_2$, the associated set of words or expressions observed in this collection. As such affective data may be more difficult to gather than regular texts (especially in annotated form), in practice $N_2 < N_1$.

Further let $\mathcal{V}_{12}$, $|\mathcal{V}_{12}| = M_{12}$, represent the intersection between $\mathcal{V}_1$ and $\mathcal{V}_2$. We will denote the representations of these words in $\mathcal{L}_1$ by $\lambda_{1,k}$ $(1 \leq k \leq M_{12})$.

Clearly, it is possible to form, for each $1 \leq \ell \leq L$, where L is the number of distinct emotions considered, each subset $\mathcal{V}_{12}^{(\ell)}$ of all entries from $\mathcal{V}_{12}$ which is aligned with a particular emotion.[1] We can then compute:

$$\hat{z}_{1,\ell} = \frac{1}{|\mathcal{V}_{12}^{(\ell)}|} \sum_{\mathcal{V}_{12}^{(\ell)}} \lambda_{1,k} \, , \tag{3}$$

as the affective anchor of emotion ℓ $(1 \leq \ell \leq L)$ in the domain space. The notation $\hat{z}_{1,\ell}$ is chosen to underscore the connection with $z_{1,j}$: in essence, $\hat{z}_{1,\ell}$ represents the (fictitious) text in the domain space that would be perfectly aligned with emotion ℓ, had it been seen the training collection $\mathcal{T}_1$. Comparing the representation of an input text to each of these anchors therefore leads to a quantitative assessment for the overall emotional affinity of the text.

A potential drawback of this approach is that (3) is patently sensitive to the distribution of words within $\mathcal{T}_2$, which may be quite different from the distribution of words within $\mathcal{T}_1$. In such a case, "folding in" the affective anchors as described above may well introduce a bias in the position of the anchors in the domain space. This could in turn lead to an inability to satisfactorily resolve subtle distinctions between emotional connotations.

[1]Note that one entry could conceivably contribute to several such subsets.

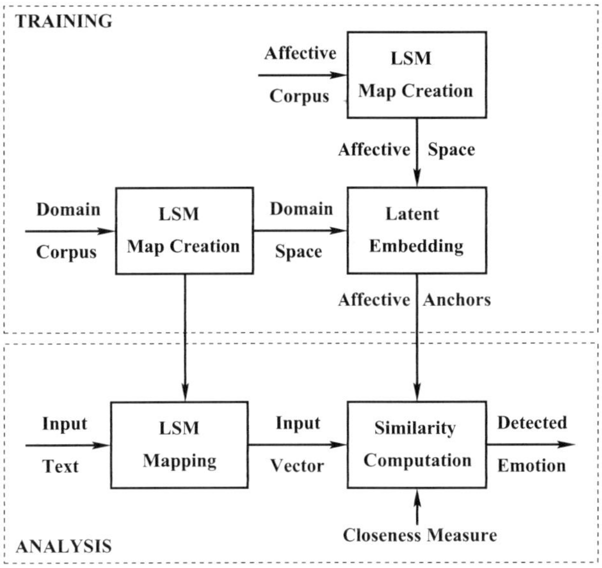

Figure 4: *Emotion Analysis Using Latent Embedding.*

4 Latent Affective Embedding

To remedy this situation, a natural solution is to build a separate LSM space from the affective training data. Referring back to the basic framework of Fig. 2 and taking into account the two separate phases of training and analysis as in Fig. 3, latent affective embedding proceeds as illustrated in Fig. 4.

The first task is to group all N_2 documents present in $\mathcal{T}_2$ into L bins, one for each of the emotions considered. Then we can construct a $(M_2 \times L)$ matrix W_2, whose elements $w'_{k,\ell}$ suitably reflect the extent to which each word or expression $w'_k \in \mathcal{V}_2$ appeared in each affective category c_ℓ, $1 \leq \ell \leq L$. This leads to:

$$w'_{k,\ell} = (1 - \varepsilon'_k) \, \frac{c'_{k,\ell}}{n'_\ell} \, , \tag{4}$$

with $c'_{k,\ell}$, n'_ℓ, and ε'_k following definitions analogous to (1), albeit with domain texts replaced by affective categories.

We then perform the SVD of W_2 in a similar vein as (2):

$$W_2 = U_2 \, S_2 \, V_2^T \, , \tag{5}$$

where all definitions are analogous. As before, both left and right singular matrices U_2 and V_2 are column-orthonormal, and their column vectors each define an orthornormal basis for the space of dimension R_2 spanned by the $u_{2,k}$'s and $v_{2,\ell}$'s. We refer to this space as the *latent affective space* $\mathcal{L}_2$. The (rank-R_2) decomposition (5) encapsulates a mapping between the set of words w'_k and categories c_ℓ and (after apropriate scaling by the singular values) the set of R_2-dimensional vectors $y_{2,k} = u_{2,k}S_2$ and $z_{2,\ell} = v_{2,\ell}S_2$.

Thus, each vector $z_{2,\ell}$ can be viewed as the centroid of an emotion in $\mathcal{L}_2$, or, said another way, an affective anchor in the affective space. Since their relative positions reflect a parsimonious encoding of the affective annotations observed in the emotion corpus, these affective anchors now properly take into account any accidental skew in the distribution of words which contribute to them. All that remains to do is map them back to the domain space.

This is done on the basis of words that are common to both the affective space and the domain space, i.e., the words in $\mathcal{V}_{12}$. Since these words were denoted by $\lambda_{1,k}$ in $\mathcal{L}_1$, we similarly denote them by $\lambda_{2,k}$ $(1 \leq k \leq M_{12})$ in $\mathcal{L}_2$.

Now let μ_1, μ_2 and Σ_1, Σ_2 denote the mean vector and covariance matrix for all observations $\lambda_{1,k}$ and $\lambda_{2,k}$ in the two spaces, respectively. We first transform each feature vector as:

$$\bar{\lambda}_{1,k} = \Sigma_1^{-1/2}\,(\lambda_{1,k} - \mu_1)\,, \tag{6}$$

$$\bar{\lambda}_{2,k} = \Sigma_2^{-1/2}\,(\lambda_{2,k} - \mu_2)\,, \tag{7}$$

so that the resulting sets $\{\bar{\lambda}_{1,k}\}$ and $\{\bar{\lambda}_{2,k}\}$ each have zero mean and identity covariance matrix.

For this purpose, the inverse square root of each covariance matrix can be obtained as:

$$\Sigma^{-1/2} = Q\Delta^{-1/2}Q^T\,, \tag{8}$$

where Q is the eigenvector matrix of the covariance matrix Σ, and Δ is the diagonal matrix of corresponding eigenvalues. This applies to both domain and affective data.

We next relate each vector $\bar{\lambda}_{2,k}$ in the affective space to the corresponding vector $\bar{\lambda}_{1,k}$ in the domain space. For a relative measure of how the two spaces are correlated with each other, as accumulated on a common word basis, we first project $\bar{\lambda}_{1,k}$ into the unit sphere of same dimension as $\bar{\lambda}_{2,k}$, i.e., $R_2 = \min(R_1, R_2)$. We then compute the (normalized) cross-covariance matrix between the two unit sphere representations, specified as:

$$K_{12} = \sum_{k=1}^{M_{12}} P\bar{\lambda}_{1,k}P^T\bar{\lambda}_{2,k}^T\,, \tag{9}$$

where P is the R_1 to R_2 projection matrix. Note that K_{12} is typically full rank as long as $M_{12} > R_2^2$. Performing the SVD of K_{12} yields the expression:

$$K_{12} = \Phi\,\Omega\,\Psi^T\,, \tag{10}$$

where as before Ω is the diagonal matrix of singular values, and Φ and Ψ are both unitary in the unit sphere of dimension R_2. This in turn leads to the definition:

$$\Gamma = \Phi\Psi^T\,, \tag{11}$$

which can be shown (cf. (Bellegarda et al., 1994)) to represent the least squares rotation that must be applied (in that unit sphere) to $\bar{\lambda}_{2,k}$ to obtain an estimate of $P\bar{\lambda}_{1,k}P^T$.

Now what is needed is to apply this transformation to the centroids $z_{2,\ell}$ $(1 \leq \ell \leq L)$ of the affective categories in the affective space, so as to map them to the domain space. We first project each vector into the unit sphere, resulting in:

$$\bar{z}_{2,\ell} = \Sigma_2^{-1/2}\,(z_{2,\ell} - \mu_2)\,, \tag{12}$$

as prescribed in (7). We then synthesize from $\bar{z}_{2,\ell}$ a unit sphere vector corresponding to the estimate in the projected domain space. From the foregoing, this estimate is given by:

$$\hat{\bar{z}}_{1,\ell} = \Gamma\,\bar{z}_{2,\ell}\,. \tag{13}$$

Finally, we restore the resulting contribution at the appropriate place in the domain space, by reversing the transformation (6):

$$\hat{z}_{1,\ell} = \Sigma_1^{1/2}\,\hat{\bar{z}}_{1,\ell} + \mu_1\,. \tag{14}$$

Combining the three steps (12)–(14) together, the overall mapping can be written as:

$$\hat{z}_{1,\ell} = (\Sigma_1^{1/2}\Gamma\Sigma_2^{-1/2})\,z_{2,\ell} + (\mu_1 - \Sigma_1^{1/2}\Gamma\Sigma_2^{-1/2}\mu_2)\,. \tag{15}$$

This expression stipulates how to leverage the *observed* affective anchors $z_{2,\ell}$ in the affective space to obtain an estimate of the *unobserved* affective anchors $\hat{z}_{1,\ell}$ in the domain space, for $1 \leq \ell \leq L$. The overall procedure is illustrated in Fig. 5 (in the simple case of two dimensions).

Once the affective anchors are suitably embedded into the domain space, we proceed as before to compare the representation of a given input text to each of these anchors, which leads to the desired quantitative assessment for the overall emotional affinity of the text.

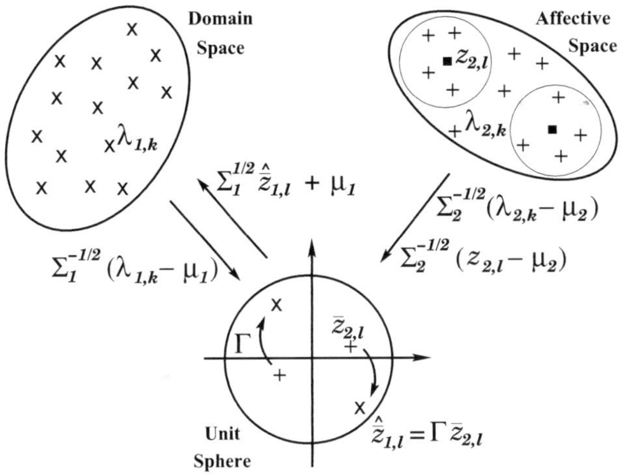

Figure 5: *Affective Anchor Embedding (2-D Case).*

5 Emotion Classification

To summarize, using either latent affective folding or latent affective embedding, we end up with an estimate $\hat{z}_{1,\ell}$ of the affective anchor for each emotion ℓ in the domain space $\mathcal{L}_1$. What remains to be described is how to perform emotion classification in that space.

To proceed, we first need to specify how to represent in that space an input text not seen in the training corpus, say t_p (where $p > N_1$). For each entry in $\mathcal{T}_1$, we compute for the new text the weighted counts (1) with $j = p$. The resulting feature vector, a column vector of dimension N_1, can be thought of as an additional column of the matrix W_1. Assuming the matrices U_1 and S_1 do not change appreciably, the SVD expansion (2) therefore implies:

$$t_p = U_1\, S_1\, v_{1,p}^T\,, \tag{16}$$

where the R_1-dimensional vector $v_{1,p}^T$ acts as an additional column of the matrix V_1^T. Thus, the representation of the new text in the domain space can be obtained from $z_{1,p} = v_{1,p} S_1$.

All is needed now is a suitable closeness measure to compare this representation to each affective anchor $\hat{z}_{1,\ell}$ ($1 \leq \ell \leq L$). From (Bellegarda, 2008), a natural metric to consider is the cosine of the angle between them. This yields:

$$\mathcal{C}(z_{1,p}, \hat{z}_{1,\ell}) = \frac{z_{1,p}\, \hat{z}_{1,\ell}^T}{\|z_{1,p}\|\, \|\hat{z}_{1,\ell}\|}\,, \tag{17}$$

for any $1 \leq \ell \leq L$. Using (17), it is a simple matter to directly compute the relevance of the input text to each emotional category. It is important to note that word weighting is now implicitly taken into account by the LSM formalism.

6 Experimental Evaluation

In order to evaluate the latent affective framework described above, we used the data set that was developed for the SemEval 2007 task on "Affective Text" (Strapparava and Mihalcea, 2007). This task was focused on the emotion classification of news headlines. Headlines typically consist of a few words and are often written by creative people with the intention to "provoke" emotions, and consequently attract the readers' attention. These characteristics make this kind of data particularly suitable for use in an automatic emotion recognition setting, as the affective/emotional features (if present) are guaranteed to appear in these short sentences. The test data accordingly consisted of 1,250 short news headlines[2] extracted from news web sites (such as Google news, CNN) and/or newspapers, and annotated along $L = 6$ emotions (ANGER, DISGUST, FEAR, JOY, SADNESS, and SURPRISE) by different evaluators.

For baseline purposes, we considered the following approaches: (i) a simple word accumulation system, which annotates the emotions in a text based on the presence of words from the WordNet-Affect lexicon; and (ii) three LSA-based systems implemented as in Fig. 1, which only differ in the way each emotion is represented in the LSA space: either based on a specific word only (e.g., JOY), or the word plus its WordNet synset, or the word plus all WordNet synsets labelled with that emotion in WordNet-Affect (cf. (Strapparava and Mihalcea, 2007)). In all three cases, the large corpus used for LSA processing was the Wall Street Journal text collection (Graff et al., 1995), comprising about 86,000 articles.

For the latent affective framework, we needed to select two separate training corpora. For the "domain" corpus, we selected a collection of about $N_1 = 8,500$ relatively short English sentences (with a vocabulary of roughly $M_1 = 12,000$ words) originally compiled for the purpose of a building a concatenative text-to-speech voice. Though not

[2]Development data was merged into the original SemEval 2007 test set to produce a larger test set.

Table I: Results on SemEval-2007 Test Corpus.

Approach Considered	Precision	Recall	F-Measure
Baseline Word Accumulation	44.7	2.4	4.6
LSA (Specific Word Only)	11.5	65.8	19.6
LSA (With WordNet Synset)	12.2	77.5	21.1
LSA (With All WordNet Synsets)	11.4	89.6	20.3
Latent Affective Folding	18.8	90.1	31.1
Latent Affective Embedding	20.9	91.7	34.0

completely congruent with news headlines, we felt that the type and range of topics covered was close enough to serve as a good proxy for the domain. For the "affective" corpus, we relied on about $N_2 = 5,000$ mood-annotated blog entries from LiveJournal.com, with a filtered[3] vocabulary of about $M_2 = 20,000$ words. The indication of mood being explicitly specified when posting on LiveJournal, without particular coercion from the interface, mood-annotated posts are likely to reflect the true mood of the blog authors (Strapparava and Mihalcea, 2008). The moods were then mapped to the $L = 6$ emotions considered in the classification.

Next, we formed the domain and affective matrices W_1 and W_2 and processed them as in (2) and (5). We used $R_1 = 100$ for the dimension of the domain space $\mathcal{L}_1$ and $R_2 = L = 6$ for the dimension of the affective space $\mathcal{L}_2$. We then compared latent affective folding and embedding to the above systems. The results are summarized in Table I.

Consistent with the observations in (Strapparava and Mihalcea, 2008), word accumulation secures the highest precision at the cost of the lowest recall, while LSA-based systems achieve high recall but significantly lower precision. Encouragingly, the F-measure obtained with both latent affective mapping techniques is substantially higher than with all four baseline approaches. Of the two techniques, latent embedding performs better, presumably because the embedded affective anchors are less sensitive than the folded affective anchors to the distribution of words within the affective corpus. Both techniques seem to exhibit an improved ability to resolve distinctions between emotional connotations.

[3]Extensive text pre-processing is usually required on blog entries, to address typos and assorted creative license.

7 Conclusion

We have proposed a data-driven strategy for emotion analysis which focuses on two coupled phases: (i) separately encapsulate both the foundations of the domain considered and the overall affective fabric of the language, and (ii) exploit the emergent relationship between these two semantic levels of description in order to inform the emotion classification process. We address (i) by leveraging the latent topicality of two distinct corpora, as uncovered by a global LSM analysis of domain-oriented and emotion-oriented training documents. The two descriptions are then superimposed to produce the desired connection between all terms and emotional categories. Because this connection automatically takes into account the influence of the entire training corpora, it is more encompassing than that based on the relatively few affective terms typically considered in conventional processing.

Empirical evidence gathered on the "Affective Text" portion of the SemEval-2007 corpus (Strapparava and Mihalcea, 2007) shows the effectiveness of the proposed strategy. Classification performance with latent affective embedding is slightly better than with latent affective folding, presumably because of its ability to more richly describe the affective space. Both techniques outperform standard LSA-based approaches, as well as affectively weighted word accumulation. This bodes well for the general deployability of latent affective processing across a wide range of applications.

Future efforts will concentrate on characterizing the influence of the parameters R_1 and R_2 on the vector spaces $\mathcal{L}_1$ and $\mathcal{L}_2$, and the corresponding trade-off between modeling power and generalization properties. It is also of interest to investigate how incorporating higher level units (such as common lexical compounds) into the LSM procedure might further increase performance.

References

A. Abbasi (2007), "Affect Intensity Analysis of Dark Web Forums," in *Proc. IEEE Int. Conf. Intelligence and Security Informatics (ISI)*, New Brunswick, NJ, 282–288.

C. Ovesdotter Alm, D. Roth, and R. Sproat (2005), "Emotions from Text: Machine Learning for Text–Based Emotion Prediction," in *Proc. Conf. Human Language Technology and Empirical Methods in NLP*, Vancouver, BC, 579–586.

J.R. Bellegarda (2005), "Latent Semantic Mapping: A Data–Driven Framework for Modeling Global Relationships Implicit in Large Volumes of Data," *IEEE Signal Processing Magazine*, 22(5):70–80.

J.R. Bellegarda (2008), *Latent Semantic Mapping: Principles & Applications*, Synthesis Lectures on Speech and Audio Processing Series, Fort Collins, CO: Morgan & Claypool.

J.R. Bellegarda, P.V. de Souza, A. Nadas, D. Nahamoo, M.A. Picheny and L.R. Bahl (1994), "The Metamorphic Algorithm: A Speaker Mapping Approach to Data Augmentation," *IEEE Trans. Speech and Audio Processing*, 2(3):413–420.

E. Cosatto, J. Ostermann, H.P. Graf, and J. Schroeter (2003), "Lifelike talking faces for interactive services," in *Proc. IEEE*, 91(9), 1406–1429.

S. Deerwester, S.T. Dumais, G.W. Furnas, T.K. Landauer, and R. Harshman (1990), "Indexing by Latent Semantic Analysis," *J. Amer. Soc. Information Science*, 41:391–407.

P. Ekman (1993), "Facial Expression and Emotion", *American Psychologist*, 48(4), 384–392.

C. Fellbaum, Ed., (1998), *WordNet: An Electronic Lexical Database*, Cambridge, MA: MIT Press.

D. Graff, R. Rosenfeld, and D. Paul (1995), "CSR-III Text," Linguistic Data Consortium, #LDC95T6.

P. Johnson–Laird and K. Oatley (1989), "The Language of Emotions: An Analysis of a Semantic Field," *Cognition and Emotion*, 3:81–123.

J. Liscombe, G. Riccardi, and D. Hakkani-Tür (2005), "Using Context to Improve Emotion Detection in Spoken Dialog Systems," *Proc. Interspeech*, Lisbon, Portugal, 1845–1848.

H. Liu, H. Lieberman, and T. Selker (2003), "A Model of Textual Affect Sensing Using Real-World Knowledge," in *Proc. Intelligent User Interfaces (IUI)*, Miami, FL, 125–132.

A. Mehrabian (1995), "Framework for a Comprehensive Description and Measurement of Emotional States," *Genetic, Social, and General Psychology Monographs*, 121(3):339–361.

R. Mihalcea and C. Strapparava (2006), "Learning to Laugh (Automatically): Computational Models for Humor Recognition," *J. Computational Intelligence*, 22(2):126–142.

M. Mohler and R. Mihalcea (2009), "Text-to-text Semantic Similarity for Automatic Short Answer Grading," in *Proc. 12th Conf. European Chap. ACL*, Athens, Greece, 567–575.

B. Pang and L. Lee (2008), "Opinion Mining and Sentiment Analysis," in *Foundations and Trends in Information Retrieval*, 2(1-2):1–135.

R.W. Picard (1997), *Affective Computing*, Cambridge, MA: MIT Press.

M. Pivec and P. Kearney (2007), "Games for Learning and Learning from Games," *Informatica*, 31:419–423.

J.A. Russell (1980), "A Circumplex Model of Affect," *J. Personality and Social Psychology*, 39:1161–1178.

S. Ryan, B. Scott, H. Freeman, and D. Patel (2000), *The Virtual University: The Internet and Resource-based Learning*, London, UK: Kogan Page.

M. Schröder (2006), "Expressing Degree of Activation in Synthetic Speech," *IEEE Trans. Audio, Speech, and Language Processing*, 14(4):1128–1136.

P.J. Stone (1997), "Thematic Text Analysis: New agendas for Analyzing Text Content," in *Text Analysis for the Social Sciences: Methods for Drawing Statistical Inferences from Texts and Transcripts*, C.W. Roberts, Ed., Mahwah, NJ: Lawrence Erlbaum Assoc. Publishers, 35–54.

C. Strapparava and R. Mihalcea (2007), "SemEval-2007 Task 14: Affective Text," in *Proc. 4th Int. Workshop on Semantic Evaluations (SemEval 2007)*, Prague, Czech Republic.

C. Strapparava and R. Mihalcea (2008), "Learning to Identify Emotions in Text," in *Proc. 2008 ACM Symposium on Applied Computing*, New York, NY, 1556–1560.

C. Strapparava, A. Valitutti, and O. Stock (2006), "The Affective Weight of Lexicon," in *Proc. 5th Int. Conf. Language Resources and Evaluation (LREC)*, Lisbon, Portugal.

P. Subasic and A. Huettner (2001), "Affect Analysis of Text Using Fuzzy Semantic Typing," *IEEE Trans. Fuzzy Systems*, 9(4):483–496.

C.M. Whissell (1989), "The Dictionary of Affect in Language," in *Emotion: Theory, Research, and Experience*, R. Plutchik and H. Kellerman, Eds., New York, NY: Academic Press, 13–131.

Emotion Detection in Email Customer Care

Narendra Gupta, Mazin Gilbert, and Giuseppe Di Fabbrizio
AT&T Labs - Research, Inc.
Florham Park, NJ 07932 - USA
{ngupta,mazin,pino}@research.att.com

Abstract

Prompt and knowledgeable responses to customers' emails are critical in maximizing customer satisfaction. Such emails often contain complaints about unfair treatment due to negligence, incompetence, rigid protocols, unfriendly systems, and unresponsive personnel. In this paper, we refer to these emails as *emotional emails*. They provide valuable feedback to improve contact center processes and customer care, as well as, to enhance customer retention. This paper describes a method for extracting *salient features* and identifying emotional emails in customer care. Salient features reflect customer frustration, dissatisfaction with the business, and threats to either leave, take legal action and/or report to authorities. Compared to a baseline system using word ngrams, our proposed approach with salient features resulted in a 20% absolute F-measure improvement.

1 Introduction

Emails are becoming the preferred communication channel for customer service. For customers, it is a way to avoid long hold times on call centers phone calls and to keep a record of the information exchanges with the business. For businesses, it offers an opportunity to best utilize customer service representatives by evenly distributing the work load over time, and for representatives, it allows time to research the issue and respond to the customers in a manner consistent with business policies. Businesses can further exploit the offline nature of this channel by automatically routing the emails involving critical issues to specialized representatives. Besides concerns related to products and services, businesses ensure that emails complaining about unfair treatment due to negligence, incompetence, rigid protocols and unfriendly systems, are always handled with care. Such emails, referred to as *emotional emails*, are critical to *reduce the churn* i.e., retaining customers who otherwise would have taken their business elsewhere, and, at the same time, they are a valuable source of information for improving business processes.

In recurring service oriented businesses, a large number of customer emails may contain routine complaints. While such complaints are important and are addressed by customer service representatives, our purpose here is to identify emotional emails where severity of the complaints and customer dissatisfaction are relatively high. Emotional emails may contain abusive and probably emotionally charged language, but we are mainly interested in identifying messages where, in addition to the *flames*, the customer includes a concrete description of the problem experienced with the company providing the service. In the context of customer service, customers express their concerns in many ways. Sometimes they convey a negative emotional component articulated by phrases like `disgusted` and `you suck`. In other cases, there is a minimum emotional involvement by enumerating factual sentences such as `you overcharged`, or `take my business elsewhere`. In many cases, both the emotional and factual components are actually present. In this work, we have identified eight dif-

Proceedings of the NAACL HLT 2010 Workshop on Computational Approaches to Analysis and Generation of Emotion in Text, pages 10–16,
Los Angeles, California, June 2010.

ferent ways that customers use to express their emotions in emails. Throughout this paper, these ways will be referred to as *Salient Features*. We cast the identification of emotional email as a text classification problem, and show that using salient features we can significantly improve the identification accuracy. Compared to a baseline system which uses Boosting (Schapire, 1999) withnword n-grams features, our proposed system using salient features resulted in improvement in f-measure from 0.52 to 0.72.

In section 2, we provide a summary of previous work and its relationship with our contribution. In section 3, we describe our method for emotion detection and extraction of salient features. A series of experiments demonstrating improvement in classification performance is presented in section 4. We conclude the paper by highlighting the main contribution of this work in section 5.

2 Previous Work

Extensive work has been done on emotion detection. In the context of human-computer dialogs, although richer features including acoustic and intonation are available, there is a general consensus (Litman and Forbes-Riley, 2004b; Lee and Narayanan, 2005) about the use of lexical features to significantly improve the accuracy of emotion detection.

Research has also been done in predicting basic emotions (also referred to as *affects*) within text (Alm et al., 2005; Liu et al., 2003). To render speech with prosodic contour conveying the emotional content of the text, one of 6 types of human emotions (e.g., angry, disgusted, fearful, happy, sad, and surprised) are identified for each sentence in the running text. Deducing such emotions from lexical constructs is a hard problem evidenced by little agreement among humans. A $Kappa$ value of 0.24-0.51 was shown in Alm et al. (2005). Liu et al. (2003) have argued that the absence of affect laden surface features i.e., key words, from the text does not imply absence of emotions, therefore they have relied more on common-sense knowledge. Instead of deducing types emotions in each sentence, we are interested in knowing if the entire email is emotional or not. Additionally we are also interested in the intensity and the cause of those emotions.

There is also a body of work in areas of creating Semantic Orientation (SO) dictionaries (Hatzivassiloglou and McKeown, 1997; Turney and Littman, 2003; Esuli and Sebastiani, 2005) and their use in identifying emotions laden sentences and polarity (Yu and Hatzivassiloglou, 2003; Kim and Hovy, 2004; Hu and Liu, 2004) of those emotions. While such dictionaries provide a useful starting point, their use alone does not yield satisfactory results. In Wilson et al. (2005), classification of phrases containing positive, negative or neutral emotions is discussed. For this problem they show high agreement among human annotators (Kappa of 0.84). They also show that labeling phrases as positive, negative or neutral only on the basis of presence of key word from such dictionaries yields a classification accuracy of 48%. An obvious reason for this poor performance is that semantic orientations of words are context dependent.

Works reported in Wilson et al. (2005); Pang et al. (2002) and Dave et al. (2003) have attempted to mitigate this problem by using supervised methods. They report classification results using a number of different sets of features, including unigram word features. Wilson et al. (2005) reports an improvement (63% to 65.7% accuracy) in performance by using a host of features extracted from syntactic dependencies. Similarly, Gamon (2004) shows that the use of deep semantic features along with word unigrams improve performances. Pang et al. (2002) and Dave et al. (2003) on the other hand confirmed that word unigrams provide the best classification results. This is in line with our experience as well and could be due to sparseness of the data. We also used supervised methods to predict emotional emails. To train predictive models we used word ngrams (uni-, bi- and tri-grams) and a number of binary features indicating the presence of words/phrases from specific dictionaries.

Spertus (1997) discusses a system called Smoky which recognizes hostile messages and is quite similar to our work. While Smoky is interested in identifying messages that contain *flames*, our research on emotional emails looks deeper to discover the reasons for such flames. Besides word unigrams, Smoky uses rules to derive additional features for classification. These features are intended to capture different manifestations of the flames. Similarly, in our work we also use rules (in our case implemented as table look-up) to derive additional features of emotional emails.

3 Emotion detection in emails

We use supervised machine learning techniques to detect emotional emails. In particular, our emotion detector is a statistical classifier model trained using hand labeled training examples. For each example, a set of salient features is extracted. The major components of our system are described below.

3.1 Classifier

For detecting emotional emails we used Boostexter as text classification. Our choice of machine learning algorithm was not strategic and we have no reason to believe that SVMs or maximum entropy–based classifiers will not perform equally well. Boostexter, which is based on the boosting family of algorithms, was first proposed by Schapire (1999). It has been applied successfully to numerous text classification applications (Gupta et al., 2005) at AT&T. Boosting builds a highly accurate classifier by combining many "weak" base classifiers, each one of which may only be moderately accurate. Boosting constructs the collection of base classifiers iteratively. On each iteration t, the boosting algorithm supplies the base learner weighted training data and the base learner generates a base classifier h_t. Set of nonnegative weights w_t encode how important it is that h_t correctly classifies each email. Generally, emails that were most often misclassified by the preceding base classifiers will be given the most weight so as to force the base learner to focus on the "hardest" examples. As described in Schapire and Singer (1999), Boostexter uses *confidence rated* base classifiers h that for every example x (in our case it is the customer emails) output a real number $h(x)$ whose sign (-1 or +1) is interpreted as a prediction(+1 indicates emotional email), and whose magnitude $|h(x)|$ is a measure of "confidence." The output of the final classifier f is $f(x) = \sum_{t=1}^{T} h_t(x)$, i.e., the sum of confidence of all classifiers h_t. The real-valued predictions of the final classifier f can be mapped onto a confidence value between 0 and 1 by a logistic function;

$$conf(x = \text{emotional email}) = \frac{1}{1 + e^{-f(x)}}.$$

The learning procedure in boosting minimizes the negative conditional log likelihood of the training data under this model, namely:

$$\sum_i \ln(1 + e^{-y_i f(x_i)}).$$

Here i iterates over all training examples and y_i is the label of ith example.

3.2 Feature extraction

Emotional emails are a reaction to perceived excessive loss of time and/or money by customers. Expressions of such reactions in emails are salient features of emotional emails. For our data we have identified the eight features listed below. While many of these features are of general nature and can be present in most customer service related emotional emails, in this paper we make no claims about their completeness.

1. Expression of negative emotions: Explicitly expressing customers affective states by phrases like `it upsets me`, `I am frustrated`;

2. Expression of negative opinions about the company: by evaluative expressions like `dishonest dealings`, `disrespectful`. These could also be insulting expressions like `stink`, `suck`, `idiots`;

3. Threats to take their business elsewhere: by expression like `business elsewhere`, `look for another provider`. These expressions are neither emotional or evaluative;

4. Threats to report to authorities: `federal agencies`, `consumer protection`. These are domain dependent names of agencies. The mere presence of such names implies customer threat;

5. Threats to take legal action: `seek retribution`, `lawsuit`. These expressions may also not be emotional or evaluative in nature;

6. Justification about why they should have been treated better. A common way to do this is

to say things like long time customer, loyal customer, etc. Semantic orientations of most phrases used to express this feature are positive;

7. Disassociate themselves from the company, by using phrases like you people, your service representative, etc. These are analogous to rule class "Noun Phrases used as Appositions" in Spertus (1997).

8. State what was done wrong to them: grossly overcharged, on hold for hours, etc. These phrases may have negative or neutral semantic orientations.

In addition to the word unigrams, salient features of emotional emails are also used for training/testing the emotional email classifier. While labeling the training data, labelers look for salient features within the email and also the severity of the loss perceived by the customer. For example, email 1 in Fig. 1 is labeled as emotional because customer perception of loss is severe to the point that the customer may cancel the service. On the other hand, email 2 is not emotional because customer perceived loss is not severe to the point of service cancellation. This customer would be satisfied in this instant if he/she receives the requested information in a timely fashion.

To extract salient features from an email, eight separate lists of phrases customers use to express each of the salient features were manually created. These lists were extracted from the training data and can be considered as basic rules that identify emotional emails. In the labeling guide for critical emails labelers were instructed to look for salient features in the email and keep a list of encountered phrases. We further enriched these lists by: a) using general knowledge of English, we added variations to existing phrases and b) searching a large body of email text (different from testing) for different phrases in which key words from known phrases participated. For example from the known phrase lied to we used the word lied and found a phrase blatantly lied. Using these lists we extracted eight binary salient features for each email, indicating presence/absence of phrases from the corresponding list in the email.

1. You are making this very difficult for me. I was assured that my <SERVICE> would remain at <CURRENCY> per month. But you raised it to <CURRENCY> per month. If I had known you were going to go back on your word, I would have looked for another Internet provider. Present bill is <CURRENCY>, including <CURRENCY> for <SERVICE>.

2. I cannot figure out my current charges. I have called several times to straighten out a problem with my service for <PHONENO1> and <PHONENO2>. I am tired of being put on hold. I cannot get the information from the automated phone service.

Figure 1: Email samples: 1) emotional; 2) neutral

4 Experiments and evaluation

We performed several experiments to compare the performance of our emotional email classifier with that using a ngram based text classifier. For these experiments we labeled 620 emails as training examples and 457 emails as test examples. Training examples were labeled independently by two different labelers[1] with relatively high degree of agreement among them. Kappa (Cohen, 1960) value of 0.814 was observed versus 0.5-0.7 reported for emotion labeling tasks (Alm and Sproat, 2005; Litman and Forbes-Riley, 2004a). Because of the relatively high agreement among these labelers, with different back ground, we did not feel the need to check the agreement among more than 2 labelers. Table 1 shows that emotional emails are about 12-13% of the total population.

Set	Number of examples	Critical Emails
Training	620	12%
Test	457	13%

Table 1: Distribution of emotional emails

[1]One of the labeler was one of the authors of this paper and other had linguistic back ground.

Due to the limited size of the training data we used cross validation (leave-one-out) technique on the test set to evaluate outcomes of different experiments. In this round robin approach, each example from the test set is tested using a model trained on all remaining 1076 (620 plus 456) examples. Test results on all 457 test examples are averaged.

Throughout all of our experiments, we computed the classification accuracy of detecting emotional emails using precision, recall and F-measure. Notice for our test data a classifier with majority vote has a classification accuracy of 87%, but since none of the emotional emails are identified, recall and F-measure are both zero. On the other hand, a classifier which generates many more false positives for each true positive, will have a lower classification accuracy but a higher (non-zero) F-measure than the majority vote classifier. Fig. 2 shows precision/recall curves for different experiments. The black circles represent the operating point corresponding to the best F-measure for each curve. Actual values of these points are provided in Table 2.

As a baseline experiment we used word ngram features to train a classifier model. The graph labeled as "ngram features" in Fig. 2 shows the performance of this classifier. The best F-measure in this case is only 0.52. Obviously this low performance can be attributed to the small training set and the large feature space formed by word ngrams.

	Recall	Prec.	F-Mes.
Ngram Features	0.45	0.61	0.52
Rule based: Threshholding on Salient Features counts			
≥ 4	0.41	0.93	0.57
≥ 3	0.63	0.74	0.68
≥ 2	0.81	0.53	0.63
Salient Features	0.77	0.65	0.70
ngram & Salient Features	0.65	0.81	0.72
Ngram & Random Features	0.57	0.67	0.61

Table 2: Recall and precision corresponding to best F-measure for different classifier models

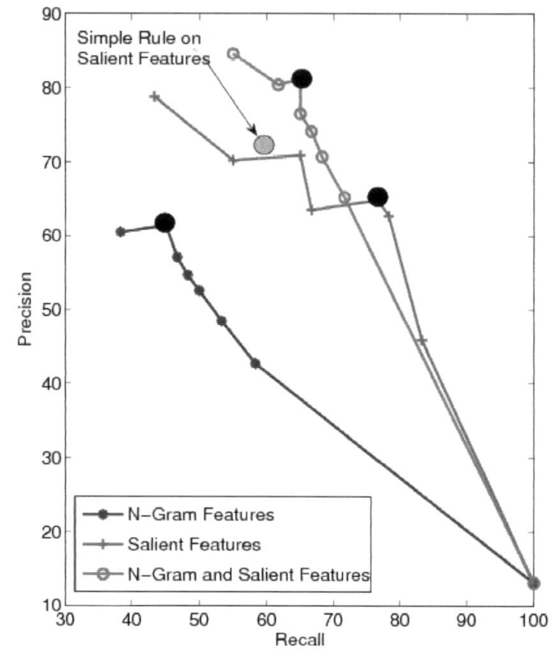

Figure 2: Precision/Recall curves for different experiments. Large black circles indicate the operating point with best F-Measure

4.1 Salient features

The baseline system was compared with a similar system using salient features. First, we used a simple classification rule that we formulated by looking at the training data. According to this rule, if an email contained three or more salient features it was classified as an emotional email. We classified the test data using this rule and obtained and an F-measure of 0.68 (see row labeled as ≥ 3 in Table 2). Since no confidence thresholding can be used with the deterministic rule, its performance is indicated by a single point marked by the gray circle in Fig. 2. This result clearly demonstrates high utility of our salient features. To verify that the salient features threshold count of 3 used in our simple classification rule is the best, we also evaluated the performance of the rule for the salient features with threshold count of 2 and 4 (row labeled as ≥ 2 and ≥ 4 in Table 2).

In our next set experiments, we trained a classifier model using salient features alone and with word ngrams. Corresponding cross validation results on the test data are annotated in Table 2 and in

Fig. 2 as "Salient Features" and "N-grams & Salient Features", respectively. Incremental improvement in best F-measure clearly shows: a) BoosTexter is able to learn better rules than the simple rule of identifying three or more salient features. b) Even though salient features provide a significant improvement in performance, there is still discriminative information in ngram features. A direct consequence of the second observation is that the detection accuracy can be further improved by extending/refining the phrase lists and/or by using more labeled data so that to exploit the discriminative information in the word ngram features.

Salient Features of emotional emails are the consequence of our knowledge of how customers react to their excessive loss. To empirically demonstrate that eight different salient features used in identification of emotional emails do provide complementary evidence, we randomly distributed the phrases in eight lists. We then used them to extract eight binary features in the same manner as before. Best F-measure for this experiment is shown in the last row of Table 2, and labeled as "N-gram & Random Features". Degradation in performance of this experiment clearly demonstrates that salient features used by us provide complimentary and not redundant information.

5 Conclusions

Customer emails complaining about unfair treatment are often emotional and are critical for businesses. They provide valuable feedback for improving business processes and coaching agents. Furthermore careful handling of such emails helps to improve customer retention. In this paper, we presented a method for emotional email identification. We introduced the notion of salient features for emotional emails, and demonstrated high agreement among two labelers in detecting emotional emails. We also demonstrated that extracting salient features from the email text and using them to train a classifier model can significantly improve identification accuracy. Compared to a baseline classifier which uses only the word ngrams features, the addition of the salient features improved the F-measure from 0.52 to 0.72. Our current research is focused on improving the salient feature extraction process. More specifically by leveraging publically available Semantic orientation dictionaries, and by enriching our dictionaries using phrases extracted from a large corpus by matching syntactic patterns of some seed phrases.

References

Alm, Cecilia and Richard Sproat. 2005. Emotional sequencing and development in fairy tales. In *Proceedings of the First International Conference on Affective Computing and Intelligent Interaction*.

Alm, Cecilia Ovesdotter, Dan Roth, and Richard Sproat. 2005. Emotions from text: machine learning for text-based emotion prediction. In *HLT '05: Proceedings of the conference on Human Language Technology and Empirical Methods in Natural Language Processing*. Association for Computational Linguistics, Morristown, NJ, USA, pages 579–586.

Cohen, J. 1960. A coefficient of agreement for nominal scales. *Educational and Psychological Measurement* 20(1):37–46.

Dave, Kushal, Steve Lawrence, and David M. Pennock. 2003. Mining the peanut gallery: Opinion extraction and semantic classification of product reviews. In *Proceedings of WWW*. pages 519–528.

Esuli, A. and F. Sebastiani. 2005. Determining the semantic orientation of terms through gloss classificaion. In *Proceedings of CIKM-05, 14th ACM International Conference on Information and Knowledge Management*. Bremen, DE., pages 617–624.

Gamon, M. 2004. Sentiment classification on customer feedback data: Noisy data large feature vectors and the role of linguistic analysis. In *Proceedings of COLING 2004*. Geneva, Switzerland, pages 841–847.

Gupta, Narendra, Gokhan Tur, Dilek Hakkani-Tür, Srinivas Banglore, Giuseppe Riccardi, and Mazin Rahim. 2005. The AT&T Spoken Language Understanding System. *IEEE Transactions on Speech and Audio Processing* 14(1):213–222.

Hatzivassiloglou, Vasileios and Kathleen McKeown. 1997. Predicting the semantic orientation of adjectives. In *Proceedings of the Joint ACL/EACL Conference*. pages 174–181.

Hu, Minqing and Bing Liu. 2004. Mining and summarizing customer reviews. In *Proceedings of the ACM SIGKDD Conference on Knowledge Discovery and Data Mining (KDD)*. pages 168–177.

Kim, Soo-Min and Eduard Hovy. 2004. Determining the sentiment of opinions. In *Proceedings of the International Conference on Computational Linguistics (COLING)*.

Lee, Chul Min and Shrikanth S. Narayanan. 2005. Toward detecting emotions in spoken dialogs. *IEEE Transactions on Speech and Audio Processing* 13(2):293–303.

Litman, D. and K. Forbes-Riley. 2004a. Annotating student emotional states in spoken tutoring dialogues. In *Proceedings of the 5th SIGdial Workshop on Discourse and Dialogue (SIGdial)*. Boston, MA.

Litman, D. and K. Forbes-Riley. 2004b. Predicting student emotions in computer-human tutoring dialogues. In *Proceedings of the 42nd Annual Meeting of the Association for Compuational Linguistics (ACL)*. Barcelone, Spain.

Liu, Hugo, Henry Lieberman, and Ted Selker. 2003. A model of textual affect sensing using real-world knowledge. In *IUI '03: Proceedings of the 8th international conference on Intelligent user interfaces*. ACM Press, Miami, Florida, USA, pages 125–132.

Pang, Bo, Lillian Lee, and Shivakumar Vaithyanathan. 2002. Thumbs up? Sentiment classification using machine learning techniques. In *Proceedings of the 2002 Conference on Empirical Methods in Natural Language Processing (EMNLP)*. Philadelphia, Pennsylvania, pages 79–86.

Schapire, R.E. 1999. A brief introduction to boosting. In *Proceedings of IJCAI*.

Schapire, R.E. and Y. Singer. 1999. Improved boosting algorithms using confidence-rated predictions. *Machine Learning* 37(3):297–336.

Spertus, Ellen. 1997. Smokey: Automatic recognition of hostile messages. In *In Proc. of Innovative Applications of Artificial Intelligence*. pages 1058–1065.

Turney, P. and M. Littman. 2003. Measuring praise and criticism: Inference of semantic orientation from association. *ACM Transactions on Information Systems* 21(4):315–346.

Wilson, Theresa, Janyce Wiebe, and Paul Hoffmann. 2005. Recognizing contextual polarity in phrase-level sentiment analysis. In *HLT '05: Proceedings of the conference on Human Language Technology and Empirical Methods in Natural Language Processing*. Association for Computational Linguistics, Morristown, NJ, USA, pages 347–354.

Yu, Hong and Vasileios Hatzivassiloglou. 2003. Towards answering opinion questions: Separating facts from opinions and identifying the polarity of opinion sentences. In *Proceedings of the Conference on Empirical Methods in Natural Language Processing (EMNLP)*.

Toward Plot Units: Automatic Affect State Analysis

Amit Goyal and **Ellen Riloff** and **Hal Daume III** and **Nathan Gilbert**
School of Computing
University of Utah
Salt Lake City, UT 84112
{amitg,riloff,hal,ngilbert}@cs.utah.edu

Abstract

We present a system called AESOP that automatically produces affect states associated with characters in a story. This research represents a first step toward the automatic generation of plot unit structures from text. AESOP incorporates several existing sentiment analysis tools and lexicons to evaluate the effectiveness of current sentiment technology on this task. AESOP also includes two novel components: a method for acquiring *patient polarity verbs*, which impart negative affect on their patients, and *affect projection rules* to propagate affect tags from surrounding words onto the characters in the story. We evaluate AESOP on a small collection of fables.

1 Introduction

In the 1980s, plot units (Lehnert, 1981) were proposed as a knowledge structure for representing narrative stories and generating summaries. Plot units are fundamentally different from the story representations that preceded them because they focus on the emotional states and tensions between characters as the driving force behind interesting plots and cohesive stories. Plot units were used in narrative summarization studies, both in computer science and psychology (Lehnert et al., 1981), but the computational models of plot units relied on tremendous amounts of manual knowledge engineering.

Given the recent swell of activity in automated methods for sentiment analysis, we embarked on a project to see whether current techniques could automatically detect the affect states needed for plot unit analysis. Plot units are complex structures that include affect states, causal links, and cross-character links, and generating complete plot unit structures is beyond the scope of this work. As an initial step toward the long-term goal of automatically generating plot units, we began by creating a system to automatically identify the affect states associated with characters. An *affect state* represents the emotional state of a character, based on their perspective of events in the story. Plots units include three types of affect states: positive (+) states, negative (-) states, and mental (M) states that have neutral emotion (these are often associated with plans and goals).

Our system, called AESOP, pulls together a variety of existing technologies in sentiment analysis to automatically identify words and phrases that have positive/negative polarity or that correspond to speech acts (for mental states). However, we needed to develop a method to automatically map these affect tags onto characters in the story.[1] To address this issue, we created *affect projection rules* that propagate affect tags from words and phrases to characters in the story via syntactic relations.

During the course of our research, we came to appreciate that affect states, of the type required for plot units, can represent much more than just direct expressions of emotion. A common phenomena are affect states that result from a character being acted upon in a positive or negative way. For example, *"the cat ate the mouse"* produces a positive affect state for the cat and a negative affect

[1]This is somewhat analogous to, but not exactly the same as, associating opinion words with their targets or topics (Kim and Hovy, 2006; Stoyanov and Cardie, 2008).

Proceedings of the NAACL HLT 2010 Workshop on Computational Approaches to Analysis and Generation of Emotion in Text, pages 17–25,
Los Angeles, California, June 2010.

The Father and His Sons
(s1) A father had a family of sons who were perpetually quarreling among themselves. (s2) When he failed to heal their disputes by his exhortations, he determined to give them a practical illustration of the evils of disunion; and for this purpose he one day told them to bring him a bundle of sticks. (s3) When they had done so, he placed the faggot into the hands of each of them in succession, and ordered them to break it in pieces. (s4) They tried with all their strength, and were not able to do it. (s5) He next opened the faggot, took the sticks separately, one by one, and again put them into his sons' hands, upon which they broke them easily. (s6) He then addressed them in these words: "My sons, if you are of one mind, and unite to assist each other, you will be as this faggot, uninjured by all the attempts of your enemies; but if you are divided among yourselves, you will be broken as easily as these sticks."

(a) "Father and Sons" Fable

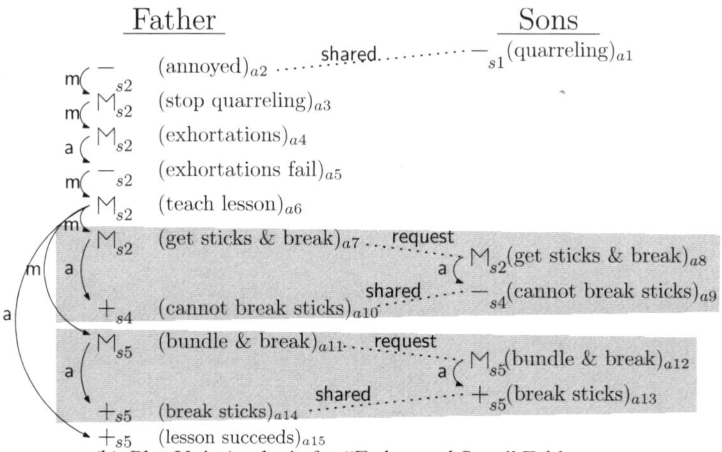

(b) Plot Unit Analysis for "Father and Sons" Fable

state for the mouse because obtaining food is good but being eaten is bad. This type of world knowledge is difficult to obtain, yet essential for plot unit analysis. In AESOP, we use corpus statistics to automatically learn a set of *negative patient polarity verbs* which impart a negative polarity on their patient (e.g., *eaten, killed, injured, fired*). To acquire these verbs, we queried a large corpus with patterns to identify verbs that frequently occur with agents who stereotypically have evil intent.

We evaulate our complete system on a set of AESOP's fables. In this paper, we also explain and categorize different types of situations that can produce affect states, several of which cannot be automatically recognized by existing sentiment analysis technology. We hope that one contribution of our work will be to create a better awareness of, and appreciation for, the different types of language understanding mechanisms that will ultimately be necessary for comprehensive affect state analysis.

2 Overview of Plot Units

Narratives can often be understood in terms of the emotional reactions and affect states of the characters therein. The plot unit formalism (Lehnert, 1981) provides a representational mechanism for affect states and the relationships between them. Plot unit structures can be used for tasks such as narrative summarization and question answering.

Plot unit structures consist of *affect states* for each character in a narrative, and links explaining the relationships between these affect states. The affect states themselves each have a type: (+) for positive states, (-) for negative states, and (M) for mental states (with neutral affect). Although affect states are *not* events per se, events often trigger affect states. If an event affects multiple characters, it can trigger multiple affect states, one for each character.

Affect states are further connected by causal links, which explain how the narrative hangs together. These include motivations (m), actualizations (a), terminations (t) and equivalences (e). Causal links exist between affect states for the same character. Cross-character links explain how single events affect two characters. For instance, if one character *requests* something of the other, this is an M-to-M link, since it spans a shared mental affect for both characters. Other speech acts can be represented as M to + (promise) or M to - (threat).

To get a better feeling of the plot unit representation, a short fable, "The Father and His Sons," is shown in Figure 1(a) and our annotation of its plot unit structure is shown in Figure 1(b). In this fable, there are two characters (the "Father" and the "Sons") who go through a series of affect states, depicted chronologically in the two columns.

In this example, the first affect state is a negative state for the sons, who are quarreling ($a1$). This state is *shared* by the father (via a cross-character link) who has a negative annoyance state ($a2$). The father then decides that he wants to stop the sons from quarreling, which is a mental event ($a3$). The causal link from $a2$ to $a3$ with an m label indicates a "motivation." His first attempt is by exhortations ($a4$).

This produces an M ($a3$) linked to an M ($a4$) with a m (motivation) link, which represents subgoaling. The father's overall goal is to stop the quarreling ($a3$) and in order to do so, he creates a subgoal of exhorting the sons to stop ($a4$). The exhortations fail, which produces a negative state ($a5$) for the father. The a causal link indicates an "actualization", representing the failure of the plan ($a4$).

The failure of the father's exhortations leads to a new subgoal: to teach the sons a lesson ($a6$). The m link from $a5$ to $a6$ is an example of "enablement." At a high level, this subgoal has two parts, indicated by the two gray regions ($a7 - a10$ and $a11 - a14$). The first gray region begins with a cross-character link (M to M), which indicates a request (in this case, to break a bundle of sticks). The sons fail at this, which upsets them ($a9$) but pleases the father ($a10$). The second gray region depicts the second part of the father's subgoal; he makes a second request ($a11$ to $a12$) to separate the bundle and break the sticks, which the sons successfully do, making them happy ($a13$) and the father happy ($a14$). This latter structure (the second gray region) is an HONORED REQUEST plot unit. At the end, the father's plan succeeds ($a15$) which is an actualization (a link) of his goal to teach the sons a lesson ($a6$).

In this example, as well as the others that we annotated in our gold standard, (see Section 5.1), we annotated *conservatively*. In particular, in reading the story, we may *assume* that the father's original plan of stopping the son's quarrelling also succeeded. However, this is not mentioned in the story and therefore we chose not to represent it. It is also important to note that plot unit representations can have t (termination) and e (equivalence) links that point backwards in time, but they do not occur in the Father and Sons fable.

3 Where Do Affect States Come From?

We began this research with the hope that recent research in sentiment analysis would supply us with effective tools to recognize affect states. However, we soon realized that affect states, as required for plot unit analysis, go well beyond the notions of positive/negative polarity and private states that have been studied in recent sentiment analysis work. In this section, we explain the wide variety of situations that can produce an affect state, based on our observations in working with fables. Most likely, an even wider variety of situations could produce affect states in other text genres.

3.1 Direct Expressions of Emotion

Plot units can include affect states that correspond to explicit expressions of positive/negative emotional states, as has been studied in the realm of sentiment analysis. For example, *"Max was disappointed"* produces a negative affect state for Max, and *"Max was pleased"* produces a positive affect state for Max. However, the affect must relate to an event that occurs in the story's plot. For example, a hypothetical expression of emotion would not yield an affect state (e.g., *"if the rain stops, she will be pleased"*).

3.2 Situational Affect States

Positive and negative affect states also frequently represent good and bad situational states that characters find themselves in. These states do not represent emotion, but indicate whether a situation is good or bad for a character based on world knowledge. For example, *"Wolf, who had a bone stuck in his throat, ..."* produces a negative affect state for the wolf. Similarly, *"The Old Woman recovered her sight..."* produces a positive affect state. Sentiment analysis is not sufficient to generate these affect states. Sometimes, however, a direct expression of emotion will also be present (e.g., *"Wolf was unhappy because he had a bone stuck..."*), providing redundancy and multiple opportunities to recognize the correct affect state for a character.

Situational affect states are common and often motivate plans and goals that are central to the plot.

3.3 Plans and Goals

Plans and goals are another common reason for affect states. The existence of a plan or goal is usually represented as a mental state (M). Plans and goals can be difficult to detect automatically. A story may reveal that a character has a plan or goal in a variety of ways, such as:

Direct expressions of plans/goals: a plan or goal may be explicitly stated (e.g., *"the lion wanted to find food"*). In this case, a mental state (M) should be generated.

Speech acts: a plan or goal may be revealed through a speech act between characters. For example, *"the wolf asked an eagle to extract the bone"* is a directive speech act that indicates the wolf's plan to resolve its negative state (having a bone stuck). This example illustrates how a negative state (bone stuck) can motivate a mental state (plan). When a speech act involves multiple characters, it produces multiple mental states. For example, a mental state should also be produced for the eagle, because it now has a plan to help the wolf (by virtue of being asked).

Inferred plans/goals: plans and goals sometimes must be inferred from actions. For example, *"the lion hunted deer"* reveals the lion's plan to obtain food. Similarly, *the serpent spat poison into the man's water"* implies that the serpent had a plan to kill the man.

Plans and goals also produce positive/negative affect states when they succeed/fail. For example, if the eagle successfully extracts the bone from the wolf's throat, then both the wolf and the eagle will have positive affect states, because both were successful in their respective goals. A directive speech act between two characters coupled with positive affect states for both characters is a common plot unit structure called an HONORED REQUEST, depicted by the second gray block shown in Fig.1(b).

The affect state for a character is always with respect to *its* view of the situation. For example, consider: *"The owl besought a grasshopper to stop chirping. The grasshopper refused to desist, and chirped louder and louder."* Both the owl and the grasshopper have M affect states representing the request from the owl to the grasshopper (i.e., the owl's plan to stop the chirping is to ask the grasshopper to knock it off). The grasshopper refuses the request, so a negative affect state is produced for the owl, indicating that its plan failed. However, a positive affect state is produced for the grasshopper, because its goal was to continue chirping which was accomplished by refusing the request. This scenario is also a common plot unit structure called a DENIED REQUEST.

3.4 Patient Role Affect States

Many affect states come directly from events. In particular, when a character is acted upon (the *theme* or *patient* of an event), a positive or negative affect state often results for the character. These affect states reflect world knowledge about what situations are good and bad. For example:

Negative patient roles: *killed X, ate X, chased X, captured X, fired X, tortured X*

Positive patient roles: *rescued X, fed X, adopted X, housed X, protected X, rewarded X*

For example, *"a man captured a bear"* indicates a negative state for the bear. Overall, this sentence would generate a SUCCESS plot unit consisting of an M state and a + state for the man (with an actualization a causal link between them representing the plan's success) and a - state for the bear (as a cross-character link indicating that what was good for the man was bad for the bear). A tremendous amount of world knowledge is needed to generate these states from such a seemingly simple sentence. Similarly, if a character is rescued, fed, or adopted, then a + affect state should be produced for the character based on knowledge that these events are desirable. We are not aware of existing resources that can automatically identify affect polarity with respect to event roles. In Section 4.1.2, we explain how we automatically acquire *Patient Polarity Verbs* from a corpus to identify some of these affect states.

4 AESOP: Automatic Affect State Analysis

We created a system, called AESOP, to try to automatically identify the types of affect states that are required for plot unit analysis. AESOP incorporates existing resources for sentiment analysis and speech act recognition, and includes two novel components: *patient polarity verbs*, which we automatically generate using corpus statistics, and *affect projection rules*, which automatically project and infer affect labels via syntactic relations.

AESOP produces affect states in a 3-step process. First, AESOP labels individual words and phrases with an M, +, or - affect tag. Second, it identifies all references to the two main characters of the story. Third, AESOP applies affect projection rules to propagate affect states onto the characters, and in some cases, to infer new affect states.

4.1 Step 1: Assigning Affect Tags to Words

4.1.1 Sentiment Analysis Resources

AESOP incorporates several existing sentiment analysis resources to recognize affect states associated with emotions and speech acts.

• OpinionFinder[2] (Wilson et al., 2005) (Version 1.4) is used to identify all three types of states. We use the +/- labels assigned by its contextual polarity classifier (Wilson, 2005) to create +/- affect tags. The MPQASD tags produced by its Direct Subjective and Speech Event Identifier (Choi et al., 2006) are used as M affect tags.

• Subjectivity Lexicon[3] (Wilson, 2005): The positive/negative words in this list are assigned +/- affect tags, when they occur with the designated part-of-speech (POS).

• Semantic Orientation Lexicon[4] (Takamura et al., 2005): The positive/negative words in this list are assigned +/- affect tags, when they occur with the designated part-of-speech.

• A list of 228 speech act verbs compiled from (Wierzbicka, 1987)[5], which are used for M states.

4.1.2 Patient Polarity Verbs

As we discussed in Section 3.4, existing resources are not sufficient to identify affect states that arise from a character being acted upon. Sentiment lexicons, for example, assign polarity to verbs irrespective of their agents or patients. To fill this gap, we tried to automatically acquire verbs that have a strong patient polarity (i.e., the patient will be in a good or bad state by virtue of being acted upon).

We used corpus statistics to identify verbs that frequently occur with agents who typically have evil (negative) or charitable (positive) intent. First, we identified 40 words that are stereotypically evil agents, such as *monster*, *villain*, *terrorist*, and *murderer*, and 40 words that are stereotypically charitable agents, such as *hero*, *angel*, *benefactor*, and *rescuer*. Next, we searched the google Web 1T 5-gram corpus[6] using patterns designed to identify verbs that co-occur with these words as agents. For each agent term, we applied the pattern "*ed by [a,an,the] AGENT" and extracted the list of matching verbs.[7]

Next, we rank the extracted verbs by computing the ratio between the frequency of the verb with a negative agent versus a positive agent. If this ratio is > 1, then we save the verb as a *negative patient polarity verb* (i.e., it imparts negative polarity to its patient). This process produced 408 negative patient polarity verbs, most of which seemed clearly negative for the patient. Table 1 shows the top 20 extracted verbs. We also tried to identify positive patient polarity verbs using a positive-to-negative ratio, but the extracted verbs were often neutral for the patient, so we did not use them.

scammed	damaged	disrupted	ripped
raided	corrupted	hindered	crippled
slammed	chased	undermined	possesed
dogged	tainted	grounded	levied
patched	victimized	posesed	bothered

Table 1: Top 20 negative patient polarity verbs

4.2 Step 2: Identifying the Characters

The problem of coreference resolution in fables is somewhat different than for other genres, primarily because characters are often animals (e.g., *"he"="owl"*). So we hand-crafted a simple rule-based coreference system. For the sake of this task, we made two assumptions: (1) There are only two characters per fable, and (2) Both characters are mentioned in the fable's title.

We then apply heuristics to determine number and gender for the characters based on word lists, WordNet (Miller, 1990) and POS tags. If no determination of a character's gender or number can be made from these resources, a process of elimination is employed. Given the two character assumption, if one character is known to be male, but there are female pronouns in the fable, then the other character is assumed to be female. The same is done for number agreement. Finally, if there is only one character between a pronoun and the beginning of a document,

[2]http://www.cs.pitt.edu/mpqa/opinionfinderrelease/

[3]http://www.cs.pitt.edu/mpqa/lexiconrelease/collectinfo1.html

[4]http://www.lr.pi.titech.ac.jp/~takamura/pndic_en.html

[5]http://openlibrary.org/b/OL2413134M/English speech act_verbs

[6]http://www.ldc.upenn.edu/Catalog/CatalogEntry.jsp?catalogId=LDC2006T13

[7]The corpus is not POS tagged so there is no guarantee these will be verbs, but they usually are in this construction.

the pronoun is assumed to corefer with that character. The character then assumes the gender and number of that pronoun. Lastly, WordNet is used to obtain a small set of non-pronominal, non-string-match resolutions by exploiting hypernym relations, for instance, linking *Peasant* with *the man*.

4.3 Step 3: Affect Projection

Our goal is to produce affect states for each character in the story. Therefore every affect tag needs to be attributed to a character, or discarded. Since plots typically revolve around actions, we used the verbs as the basis for projecting affect tags onto the characters. In some cases, we also spawn new affect tags associated with mental states to indicate that an action is likely the manifestation of a plan.

We developed 6 types of *affect projection rules* that orchestrate how affect tags are assigned to the characters based on verb argument structure. We use the Sundance shallow parsing toolkit (Riloff and Phillips, 2004) to generate a syntactic analysis of each sentence, including syntactic chunking, clause segmentation, and active/passive voice recognition. We normalize the verb phrases (VPs) with respect to voice (i.e., we transform the passive voice constructions into an active voice equivalent) to simplify our rules. We then make the assumption that the Subject of the VP is its AGENT and the Direct Object of the VP is its PATIENT.[8] The affect projection rules only project affect states onto AGENTS and PATIENTS that correspond to a character in the story. The five types of rules are described below.

1. AGENT **VP** : This case applies when the VP has no PATIENT, or a PATIENT that is not a character in the story, or the PATIENT corefers with the AGENT. All affect tags associated with the VP are projected onto the AGENT. For example, *"Mary **laughed** (+)"* projects a positive affect state onto Mary.

2. **VP** PATIENT[9]: All affect tags associated with the VP are projected onto the PATIENT, unless both M and +/- tags exist, in which case only the +/- tags are projected. For example, *"**loved** (+) the cat"*, projects a positive affect state onto the cat.

3. AGENT **VP** PATIENT: This case applies when the AGENT and PATIENT refer to different characters. All affect tags associated with the VP are projected onto the PATIENT, unless both M and +/- tags exist, in which case only the +/- tags are projected (as in Rule #2). If the VP has an M tag, then we also project an M tag onto the AGENT (representing a shared, cross-character mental state). If the VP has a +/- tag, then we project a + tag onto the agent (as an inference that the AGENT accomplished some action).

4. AGENT **VERB1** to **VERB2** PATIENT. We divide this into two cases: (a) If the agent and patient refer to the same character, then Rule #1 is applied (e.g., *"Bo decided to teach himself..."*). (b) If the agent and patient are different, we apply Rule #1 to **VERB1** to agent and Rule #2 to **VERB2**. If no affect tags are assigned to either verb, then we create an M affect state for the agent (assuming that the VP represents some sort of plan).

5. If a noun phrase refers to a character and includes a modifying adjective with an affect tag, then the affect is mapped onto the character. For example, *"the **happy** (+) fox"*.

Finally, if an adverb or adjectival phrase (e.g., predicate adjective) has an affect tag, then that affect tag is mapped onto the preceding VP and the projection rules above are applied. For all of the rules, if a clause contains a negation word, then we flip the polarity of all words in that clause. Our negation list contains: *no, not, never, fail, failed, fails, don't, and didn't.*

5 Evaluation

5.1 Data Set

Plot unit analysis of ordinary text is enormously complex – even the idea of *manually* creating gold standard annotations seemed like a monumental task. So we began our exploration with simpler and more constrained texts that seemed particularly appropriate for plot unit analysis: fables. Fables have two desirable attributes: (1) they have a small cast of characters, and (2) they typically revolve around a moral, which is exemplified by a short and concise plot. Even so, fables are challenging for NLP due to anthropomorphic characters, flowery language, and sometimes archaic vocabulary.

[8] We are not actually doing thematic role recognition, so this will not always be correct, but it is a reasonable approximation.

[9] Agent is missing or not a character.

State	M (66)			+ (52)			- (39)			All (157)		
System	*R*	*P*	*F*	*R*	*P*	*F*	*R*	*P*	*F*	*R*	*P*	*F*
Bsent baseline	.65	.10	.17	.52	.08	.14	.74	.06	.11	.63	.08	.14
Bclause baseline	.48	.28	.35	.44	.22	.29	.69	.17	.27	.52	.22	.31
All 4 resources (w/proj. rules)	.48	.43	.45	.23	.39	.29	.23	.41	.29	.34	.41	.37
OpinionFinder	.36	.42	.39	.00	.00	.00	.00	.00	.00	.15	.35	.21
Subjectivity Lexicon	.45	.43	.44	.23	.35	.28	.21	.44	.28	.32	.41	.36
Semantic Dictionary	.42	.45	.43	.00	.00	.00	.00	.00	.00	.18	.45	.26
Semantic Orientation Lexicon	.41	.43	.42	.17	.53	.26	.08	.43	.13	.25	.45	.32
PPV Lexicon	.41	.42	.41	.02	.17	.04	.21	.73	.33	.23	.44	.30
AESOP (All 4 + PPV)	.48	.40	.44	.25	.36	.30	.33	.46	.38	.37	.40	.38

Table 2: Evaluation results for 2 baselines, 4 sentiment analysis resources with projection rules, and our PPV lexicon with projection rules. (The # in parentheses is the number of occurrences of that state in the gold standard).

We collected 34 fables from an Aesop's Fables web site[10], choosing fables that have a true plot (some only contain quotes) and exactly two characters. We divided them into a development set of 11 stories, a tuning set of 8 stories, and a test set of 15 stories. The Father and Sons story from Figure 1(a) is an example from our set.

Creating a gold standard was itself a substantial undertaking. Plot units are complex structures, and training non-experts to produce them did not seem feasible in the short term. So three of the authors discussed and iteratively refined manual annotations for the development and tuning set stories until we became comfortable that we had a common understanding for the annotation task. Then to create our gold standard test set, two authors independently created annotations for the test set, and a third author adjudicated the differences. The gold standard contains complete plot unit annotations, including affect states, causal links, and cross-character links. For the experiments in this paper, however, only the affect state annotations were used.

5.2 Baselines

We created two baselines to measure what would happen if we use all 4 sentiment analysis resources *without* any projection rules. The first one (Bsent) operates at the sentence level. It naively projects every affect tag that occurs in a sentence onto every character in the same sentence. The second baseline (Bclause) operates identically, but at the clause level.

[10]http://www.pacificnet.net/~johnr/aesop/

5.3 Evaluation

As our evaluation metrics we used recall (R), precision (P), and F-measure (F). We evaluate each system on individual affect states (+, - and M) as well as across all affect states. The evaluation is done at the sentence level. Meaning, if a system produces the same affect state as present in the gold standard for a sentence, we count it as a correct affect state. Our main evaluation also requires each affect state to be associated with the correct character.

Table 2 shows the coverage of our two baseline systems as well as the four Sentiment Analysis Resources used with our projection rules. We can make several observations:

- As expected, the baselines achieve relatively high recall, but low precision.
- Each of the sentiment analysis resources alone is useful, and using them with the projection rules leads to improved performance over the baselines (10 points in F score for M and 6 points overall). This shows that the projection rules are helpful in identifying the characters associated with each affect state.
- The PPV Lexicon, alone, is quite good at capturing negative affect states. Together with the projection rules, this leads to good performance on identifying mental states as well.

To better assess our projection rules, we evaluated the systems both with respect to characters and without respect to characters. In this evaluation, system-produced states are correct even if they are assigned to the wrong character. Table 3 reveals several results: (1) For the baseline: there is a large drop when

State	M (66)			+ (52)			- (39)			All (157)		
System	*R*	*P*	*F*	*R*	*P*	*F*	*R*	*P*	*F*	*R*	*P*	*F*
Bclause w/o char	.65	.37	.47	.50	.25	.33	.77	.19	.30	.63	.26	.37
AESOP w/o char	.55	.44	.49	.33	.47	.39	.36	.50	.42	.43	.46	.44
Bclause w/ char	.48	.28	.35	.44	.22	.29	.69	.17	.27	.52	.22	.31
AESOP w/ char	.48	.40	.44	.25	.36	.30	.33	.46	.38	.37	.40	.38

Table 3: Evaluating affect states with and without respect to character.

State	M (66)			+ (52)			- (39)			All (157)		
System	*R*	*P*	*F*	*R*	*P*	*F*	*R*	*P*	*F*	*R*	*P*	*F*
Bclause PCoref	.48	.28	.35	.44	.22	.29	.69	.17	.27	.52	.22	.31
AESOP PCoref	.48	.40	.44	.25	.36	.30	.33	.46	.38	.37	.40	.38
Bclause ACoref	.42	.45	.43	.25	.34	.29	.54	.24	.33	.39	.33	.36
AESOP ACoref	.41	.54	.47	.12	.40	.18	.26	.45	.33	.27	.49	.35

Table 4: Final results of Bclause and AESOP systems with perfect and automated coreference

evaluated with respect to the correct character. (2) For AESOP: there is a smaller drop in both precision and recall for M and -, suggesting that our projection rules are doing well for these affect states. (3) For AESOP: there is a large drop in both precision and recall for +, suggesting that there is room for improvement of our projection rules for positive affect.

Finally, we wish to understand the role that coreference plays. Table 4 summarizes the results with perfect coreference and with automated coreference. AESOP is better than both baselines when we use perfect coreference (PCoref), which indicates that the affect projection rules are useful. However, when we use automated coreference (ACoref), recall goes down and precision goes up. Recall goes down because our automated coreference system is precision oriented: it only says "coreferent" if it is sure.

The increase in precision when moving to automated coreference is bizarre. We suspect it is primarily due to the handling of quotations. Our perfect coreference system resolves first and second person pronouns in quotations, but the automated system does not. Thus, with automated coreference, we almost never produce affect states from quotations. This is a double-edged sword: sometimes quotes contain important affect states, sometimes they do not. For example, from the Father and Sons fable, "if you are **divided** among yourselves, you will be **broken** as easily as these sticks." Automated coreference does not produce any character resolutions and therefore AESOP produces no affect states. In this case this is the right thing to do. However, in another well-known fable, a tortoise says to a hare: "although you be as **swift** as the wind, I have **beaten** you in the race." Here, perfect coreference produces multiple affect states, which *are* related to the plot: the hare recieves a negative affect state for having been beaten in the race.

6 Conclusions

AESOP demonstrates that sentiment analysis tools can successfully recognize many affect states when coupled with syntax-based projection rules to map the affect states onto characters. We also showed that *negative patient polarity verbs* can be harvested from a corpus to identify characters that are in a negative state due to an action. However, performance is still modest, revealing that much work remains to be done. In future work, new methods will be needed to represent affect states associated with plans/goals, events, and inferences.

7 Acknowledgments

The authors thank the anonymous reviewers for many helpful comments. This work was supported in part by the Department of Homeland Security Grant N0014-07-1-0152, the DARPA Machine Reading program under contract FA8750-09-C-0172, and the NSF grant IIS-0712764.

References

Yejin Choi, Eric Breck, and Claire Cardie. 2006. Joint extraction of entities and relations for opinion recognition. In *EMNLP '06: Proceedings of the 2006 Conference on Empirical Methods in Natural Language Processing*, pages 431–439, Morristown, NJ, USA. Association for Computational Linguistics.

S. Kim and E. Hovy. 2006. Extracting Opinions, Opinion Holders, and Topics Expressed in Online News Media Text. In *Proceedings of ACL/COLING Workshop on Sentiment and Subjectivity in Text.*

W. Lehnert, J. Black, and B. Reiser. 1981. Summarizing Narratives. In *Proceedings of the Seventh International Joint Conference on Artificial Intelligence.*

W. G. Lehnert. 1981. Plot Units and Narrative Summarization. *Cognitive Science*, 5(4):293–331.

G. Miller. 1990. Wordnet: An On-line Lexical Database. *International Journal of Lexicography*, 3(4).

E. Riloff and W. Phillips. 2004. An Introduction to the Sundance and AutoSlog Systems. Technical Report UUCS-04-015, School of Computing, University of Utah.

V. Stoyanov and C. Cardie. 2008. Topic Identification for Fine-Grained Opinion Analysis. In *Conference on Computational Linguistics (COLING 2008).*

Hiroya Takamura, Takashi Inui, and Manabu Okumura. 2005. Extracting semantic orientations of words using spin model. In *ACL '05: Proceedings of the 43rd Annual Meeting on Association for Computational Linguistics.*

A. Wierzbicka. 1987. *English speech act verbs: a semantic dictionary.* Academic Press, Sydney, Orlando.

T. Wilson, P. Hoffmann, S. Somasundaran, J. Kessler, J. Wiebe, Y. Choi, C. Cardie, E. Riloff, and S. Patwardhan. 2005. OpinionFinder: A system for subjectivity analysis. In *Proceedings of HLT/EMNLP 2005 Interactive Demonstrations.*

Theresa Wilson. 2005. Recognizing contextual polarity in phrase-level sentiment analysis. In *In Proceedings of HLT-EMNLP.*

Emotions Evoked by Common Words and Phrases: Using Mechanical Turk to Create an Emotion Lexicon

Saif M. Mohammad and Peter D. Turney
Institute for Information Technology,
National Research Council Canada.
Ottawa, Ontario, Canada, K1A 0R6
{saif.mohammad,peter.turney}@nrc-cnrc.gc.ca

Abstract

Even though considerable attention has been given to semantic orientation of words and the creation of large polarity lexicons, research in emotion analysis has had to rely on limited and small emotion lexicons. In this paper, we show how we create a high-quality, moderate-sized emotion lexicon using Mechanical Turk. In addition to questions about emotions evoked by terms, we show how the inclusion of a word choice question can discourage malicious data entry, help identify instances where the annotator may not be familiar with the target term (allowing us to reject such annotations), and help obtain annotations at sense level (rather than at word level). We perform an extensive analysis of the annotations to better understand the distribution of emotions evoked by terms of different parts of speech. We identify which emotions tend to be evoked simultaneously by the same term and show that certain emotions indeed go hand in hand.

1 Introduction

When analyzing text, automatically detecting emotions such as joy, sadness, fear, anger, and surprise is useful for a number of purposes, including identifying blogs that express specific emotions towards the topic of interest, identifying what emotion a newspaper headline is trying to evoke, and devising automatic dialogue systems that respond appropriately to different emotional states of the user. Often different emotions are expressed through different words. For example, *delightful* and *yummy* indicate the emotion of joy, *gloomy* and *cry* are indicative of sadness, *shout* and *boiling* are indicative of anger, and so on. Therefore an **emotion lexicon**—a list of emotions and words that are indicative of each emotion—is likely to be useful in identifying emotions in text.

Words may evoke different emotions in different contexts, and the emotion evoked by a phrase or a sentence is not simply the sum of emotions conveyed by the words in it, but the emotion lexicon will be a useful component for any sophisticated emotion detecting algorithm. The lexicon will also be useful for evaluating automatic methods that identify the emotions evoked by a word. Such algorithms may then be used to automatically generate emotion lexicons in languages where no such lexicons exist. As of now, high-quality high-coverage emotion lexicons do not exist for any language, although there are a few limited-coverage lexicons for a handful of languages, for example, the WordNet Affect Lexicon (WAL) (Strapparava and Valitutti, 2004) for six basic emotions and the General Inquirer (GI) (Stone et al., 1966), which categorizes words into a number of categories, including positive and negative semantic orientation.

Amazon has an online service called Mechanical Turk that can be used to obtain a large amount of human annotation in an efficient and inexpensive manner (Snow et al., 2008; Callison-Burch, 2009).[1] However, one must define the task carefully to obtain annotations of high quality. Several checks must be placed to ensure that random and erroneous annotations are discouraged, rejected, and re-annotated.

In this paper, we show how we compiled a moderate-sized English emotion lexicon by manual

[1] https://www.mturk.com/mturk/welcome

Proceedings of the NAACL HLT 2010 Workshop on Computational Approaches to Analysis and Generation of Emotion in Text, pages 26–34,
Los Angeles, California, June 2010.

annotation through Amazon's Mechanical Turk service. This dataset, which we will call **EmoLex**, is many times as large as the only other known emotion lexicon, WordNet Affect Lexicon. More importantly, the terms in this lexicon are carefully chosen to include some of the most frequent nouns, verbs, adjectives, and adverbs. Beyond unigrams, it has a large number of commonly used bigrams. We also include some words from the General Inquirer and some from WordNet Affect Lexicon, to allow comparison of annotations between the various resources.

We perform an extensive analysis of the annotations to answer several questions that have not been properly addressed so far. For instance, how hard is it for humans to annotate words with the emotions they evoke? What percentage of commonly used terms, in each part of speech, evoke an emotion? Are emotions more commonly evoked by nouns, verbs, adjectives, or adverbs? Is there a correlation between the semantic orientation of a word and the emotion it evokes? Which emotions tend to go together; that is, which emotions are evoked simultaneously by the same term? This work is intended to be a pilot study before we create a much larger emotion lexicon with tens of thousands of terms.

We focus on the emotions of joy, sadness, anger, fear, trust, disgust, surprise, and anticipation—argued by many to be the basic and prototypical emotions (Plutchik, 1980). Complex emotions can be viewed as combinations of these basic emotions.

2 Related work

WordNet Affect Lexicon (Strapparava and Valitutti, 2004) has a few hundred words annotated with the emotions they evoke.[2] It was created by manually identifying the emotions of a few seed words and then marking all their WordNet synonyms as having the same emotion. The General Inquirer (Stone et al., 1966) has 11,788 words labeled with 182 categories of word tags, including positive and negative semantic orientation.[3] It also has certain other affect categories, such as pleasure, arousal, feeling, and pain but these have not been exploited to a significant degree by the natural language processing community.

Work in emotion detection can be roughly classified into that which looks for specific emotion denoting words (Elliott, 1992), that which determines tendency of terms to co-occur with seed words whose emotions are known (Read, 2004), that which uses hand-coded rules (Neviarouskaya et al., 2009), and that which uses machine learning and a number of emotion features, including emotion denoting words (Alm et al., 2005).

Much of this recent work focuses on six emotions studied by Ekman (1992). These emotions—joy, sadness, anger, fear, disgust, and surprise— are a subset of the eight proposed in Plutchik (1980). We focus on the Plutchik emotions because the emotions can be naturally paired into opposites—joy–sadness, anger–fear, trust–disgust, and anticipation–surprise. Natural symmetry apart, we believe that prior work on automatically computing word–pair antonymy (Lin et al., 2003; Mohammad et al., 2008; Lobanova et al., 2010) can now be leveraged in automatic emotion detection.

3 Emotion annotation

In the subsections below we present the challenges in obtaining high-quality emotion annotation, how we address those challenges, how we select the target terms, and the questionnaire we created for the annotators.

3.1 Key challenges

Words used in different senses can evoke different emotions. For example, the word *shout* evokes a different emotion when used in the context of admonishment, than when used in "*Give me a shout if you need any help.*" Getting human annotations on word senses is made complicated by decisions about which sense-inventory to use and what level of granularity the senses must have. On the one hand, we do not want to choose a fine-grained sense-inventory because then the number of word–sense combinations will become too large and difficult to easily distinguish, and on the other hand we do not want to work only at the word level because when used in different senses a word may evoke different emotions.

Yet another challenge is how best to convey a

[2] http://wndomains.fbk.eu/wnaffect.html

[3] http://www.wjh.harvard.edu/~inquirer

word sense to the annotator. Long definitions will take time to read and limit the number of annotations we can obtain for the same amount of resources. Further, we do not want to bias the annotator towards an emotion through the definition. We want the users to annotate a word only if they are already familiar with it and know its meanings. And lastly, we must ensure that malicious and erroneous annotations are rejected.

3.2 Our solution

In order to overcome the challenges described above, before asking the annotators questions about what emotions are evoked by a target term, we first present them with a word choice problem pertaining to the target. They are provided with four different words and asked which word is closest in meaning to the target. This single question serves many purposes. Through this question we convey the word sense for which annotations are to be provided, without actually providing annotators with long definitions. If an annotator is not familiar with the target word and still attempts to answer questions pertaining to the target, or is randomly clicking options in our questionnaire, then there is a 75% chance that they will get the answer to this question wrong, and we can discard all responses pertaining to this target term by the annotator (that is, we discard answers to the emotion questions provided by the annotator for this target term).

We generated these word choice problems automatically using the *Macquarie Thesaurus* (Bernard, 1986). Published thesauri, such as *Roget's* and *Macquarie*, divide the vocabulary into about a thousand categories, which may be interpreted as coarse senses. If a word has more than one sense, then it can be found in more than one thesaurus category. Each category also has a head word which best captures the meaning of the category.

Most of the target terms chosen for annotation are restricted to those that are listed in exactly one thesaurus category. The word choice question for a target term is automatically generated by selecting the following four alternatives (choices): the head word of the thesaurus category pertaining to the target term (the correct answer); and three other head words of randomly selected categories (the distractors). The four alternatives are presented to the annotator in random order.

Only a small number of the words in the WordNet Affect Lexicon are listed in exactly one thesaurus category (have one sense), and so we included target terms that occurred in two thesaurus categories as well. For these questions, we listed head words from both the senses (categories) as two of the alternatives (probability of a random choice being correct is 50%). Depending on the alternative chosen, we can thus determine the sense for which the subsequent emotion responses are provided by the annotator.

3.3 Target terms

In order to generate an emotion lexicon, we first identify a list of words and phrases for which we want human annotations. We chose the *Macquarie Thesaurus* as our source pool for unigrams and bigrams. Any other published dictionary would have worked well too. However, apart from over 57,000 commonly used English word types, the *Macquarie Thesaurus* also has entries for more than 40,000 commonly used phrases. From this list of unigrams and bigrams we chose those that occur frequently in the Google n-gram corpus (Brants and Franz, 2006). Specifically we chose the 200 most frequent n-grams in the following categories: noun unigrams, noun bigrams, verb unigrams, verb bigrams, adverb unigrams, adverb bigrams, adjective unigrams, adjective bigrams, words in the General Inquirer that are marked as having a negative semantic orientation, words in General Inquirer that are marked as having a positive semantic orientation. When selecting these sets, we ignored terms that occurred in more than one *Macquarie Thesaurus* category. Lastly, we chose all words from each of the six emotion categories in the WordNet Affect Lexicon that had at most two senses in the thesaurus (occurred in at most two thesaurus categories). The first and second column of Table 1 list the various sets of target terms as well as the number of terms in each set for which annotations were requested. $\textbf{EmoLex}_{\textbf{Uni}}$ stands for all the unigrams taken from the thesaurus. $\textbf{EmoLex}_{\textbf{Bi}}$ refers to all the bigrams. $\textbf{EmoLex}_{\textbf{GI}}$ are all the words taken from the General Inquirer. $\textbf{EmoLex}_{\textbf{WAL}}$ are all the words taken from the WordNet Affect Lexicon.

3.4 Mechanical Turk HITs

An entity submitting a task to Mechanical Turk is called the **requester**. A requester first breaks the task into small independently solvable units called **HITs (Human Intelligence Tasks)** and uploads them on the Mechanical Turk website. The requester specifies the compensation that will be paid for solving each HIT. The people who provide responses to these HITs are called **Turkers**. The requester also specifies the number of different Turkers that are to annotate each HIT. The annotation provided by a Turker for a HIT is called an **assignment**.

We created Mechanical Turk HITs for each of the terms specified in Table 1. Each HIT has a set of questions, all of which are to be answered by the same person. We requested five different assignments for each HIT (each HIT is to be annotated by five different Turkers). Different HITS may be attempted by different Turkers, and a Turker may attempt as many HITs as they wish. Below is an example HIT for the target word "startle".

> **Title:** Emotions evoked by words
> **Reward per HIT:** $0.04
> **Directions:** Return HIT if you are not familiar with the prompt word.
>
> Prompt word: **startle**
>
> 1. Which word is closest in meaning (most related) to *startle*?
>
> - automobile
> - shake
> - honesty
> - entertain
>
> 2. How positive (good, praising) is the word startle?
>
> - startle is not positive
> - startle is weakly positive
> - startle is moderately positive
> - startle is strongly positive
>
> 3. How negative (bad, criticizing) is the word startle?
>
> - startle is not negative
> - startle is weakly negative
> - startle is moderately negative
> - startle is strongly negative
>
> 4. How much does the word *startle* evoke or produce the emotion joy (for example, *happy* and *fun* may strongly evoke joy)?
>
> - *startle* does not evoke joy
> - *startle* weakly evokes joy
> - *startle* moderately evokes joy
> - *startle* strongly evokes joy
>
> [Questions 5 to 11 are similar to 4, except that joy is replaced with one of the other seven emotions: sadness (*failure* and *heart-break*); fear (*horror* and *scary*); anger (*rage* and *shouting*); trust (*faith* and *integrity*); disgust (*gross* and *cruelty*); surprise (*startle* and *sudden*); anticipation (*expect* and *eager*).]

EmoLex	# of terms Initial	# of terms Master	Annotns. per word
EmoLex$_{Uni}$:			
adjectives	200	196	4.7
adverbs	200	192	4.7
nouns	200	187	4.6
verbs	200	197	4.7
EmoLex$_{Bi}$:			
adjectives	200	182	4.7
adverbs	187	171	4.7
nouns	200	193	4.7
verbs	200	186	4.7
EmoLex$_{GI}$:			
negatives in GI	200	196	4.7
positives in GI	200	194	4.8
EmoLex$_{WAL}$:			
anger terms in WAL	107	84	4.8
disgust terms in WAL	25	25	4.8
fear terms in WAL	58	58	4.8
joy terms in WAL	109	92	4.8
sadness terms in WAL	86	73	4.7
surprise terms in WAL	39	38	4.7
Union	**2176**	**2081**	**4.75**

Table 1: Break down of target terms into various categories. Initial refers to terms chosen for annotation. Master refers to terms for which three or more valid assignments were obtained using Mechanical Turk.

Before going live, the survey was approved by the ethics committee at the National Research Council Canada.

4 Annotation analysis

The first set of emotion annotations on Mechanical Turk were completed in about nine days. The Turkers spent a minute on average to answer the questions in a HIT. This resulted in an hourly pay of slightly more than $2.

Once the assignments were collected, we used automatic scripts to validate the annotations. Some assignments were discarded because they failed certain tests (described below). A subset of the discarded assignments were officially rejected (the Turkers were not paid for these assignments) because instructions were not followed. About 500 of the 10,880 assignments (2,176 × 5) included at least one unanswered question. These assignments were discarded and rejected. More than 85% of the remaining assignments had the correct answer for the word choice question. This was a welcome result showing that, largely, the annotations were done in a responsible manner. We discarded all assignments that had the wrong answer for the word choice question. If an annotator obtained an overall score that is less than 66.67% on the word choice questions (that is, got more than one out of three wrong), then we assumed that, contrary to instructions, HITs for words not familiar to the annotator were attempted. We discarded and rejected *all* assignments by such annotators (not just the assignments for which they got the word choice question wrong).

HITs pertaining to all the discarded assignments were uploaded for a second time on Mechanical Turk and the validation process was repeated. After the second round, we had three or more valid assignments for 2081 of the 2176 target terms. We will refer to this set of assignments as the **master set**. We create the emotion lexicon from this master set containing 9892 assignments from about 1000 Turkers who attempted 1 to 450 assignments each. About 100 of them provided 20 or more assignments each (more than 7000 assignments in all). The master set has, on average, about 4.75 assignments for each of the 2081 target terms. (See Table 1 for more details.)

4.1 Emotions evoked by words

The different emotion annotations for a target term were consolidated by determining the **majority class** of emotion intensities. For a given term–emotion pair, the majority class is that intensity level that is chosen most often by the Turkers to represent the degree of emotion evoked by the word. Ties are broken by choosing the stronger intensity level. Table 2 lists the percent of 2081 target terms assigned a majority class of no, weak, moderate, and strong emotion. For example, it tells us that 7.6% of the target terms strongly evoke joy. The table also presents an average of the numbers in each column (micro average). Observe that the percentages for individual emotions do not vary greatly from the average. The last row lists the percent of target terms that evoke some emotion (any of the eight) at the various intensity levels. We calculated this using the intensity level of the strongest emotion expressed by each target. Observe that 30.1% of the target terms strongly evoke at least one of the eight basic emotions.

	Intensity			
Emotion	no	weak	moderate	strong
anger	78.8	9.4	6.2	5.4
anticipation	71.4	13.6	9.4	5.3
disgust	82.6	8.8	4.9	3.5
fear	76.5	11.3	7.3	4.7
joy	72.6	9.6	10.0	7.6
sadness	76.0	12.4	5.8	5.6
surprise	84.8	7.9	4.1	3.0
trust	73.3	12.0	9.8	4.7
micro average	**77.0**	**10.6**	**7.2**	**5.0**
any emotion	**17.9**	**23.4**	**28.3**	**30.1**

Table 2: Percent of 2081 terms assigned a majority class of no, weak, moderate, and strong emotion.

Emotion	**% of terms**
anger	15.4
anticipation	20.9
disgust	11.0
fear	14.5
joy	21.9
sadness	14.4
surprise	9.8
trust	20.6
micro average	**16.1**
any emotion	**67.9**

Table 3: Percent of 2081 target terms that are evocative.

Even though we asked Turkers to annotate emotions at four levels of intensity, practical NLP applications often require only two levels—evoking particular emotion (**evocative**) or not (**non-evocative**). For each target term–emotion pair, we convert the four-level annotations into two-level annotations by placing all no- and weak-intensity assignments in the non-evocative bin, all moderate- and strong-intensity assignments in the evocative bin, and then choosing the bin with the majority assignments. Table 3 gives percent of target terms considered to be

EmoLex	anger	anticipation	disgust	fear	joy	sadness	surprise	trust	any
EmoLex$_{Uni}$:									
adjectives	12	21	8	11	30	13	10	19	72
adverbs	12	16	7	8	21	6	11	25	65
nouns	4	21	2	9	16	3	3	21	47
verbs	12	21	7	11	15	12	11	17	56
EmoLex$_{Bi}$:									
adjectives	12	24	8	10	26	14	7	18	64
adverbs	3	26	1	5	15	4	8	25	54
nouns	9	30	6	12	15	6	2	24	56
verbs	8	34	2	5	29	6	9	28	67
EmoLex$_{GI}$:									
negatives in GI	45	5	34	35	1	37	11	2	78
positives in GI	0	23	0	0	48	0	6	47	77
EmoLex$_{WAL}$:									
anger terms in WAL	**90**	2	54	41	0	32	2	0	91
disgust terms in WAL	40	4	**92**	36	0	20	8	0	96
fear terms in WAL	25	17	31	**79**	0	36	34	0	87
joy terms in WAL	3	32	3	1	**89**	1	18	38	95
sadness terms in WAL	17	0	9	15	0	**93**	1	1	94
surprise terms in WAL	7	23	0	21	52	10	**76**	7	86

Table 4: Percent of terms, in each target set, that are evocative. Highest individual emotion scores for EmoLex$_{WAL}$ are shown bold. Observe that WAL fear terms are marked most as fear evocative, joy terms as joy evocative, and so on.

evocative. The last row in the table gives the percentage of terms evocative of some emotion (any of the eight). Table 4 shows how many terms in each category are evocative of the different emotions.

4.1.1 Analysis and discussion

Table 4 shows that a sizable percent of nouns, verbs, adjectives, and adverbs are evocative. Adverbs and adjectives are some of the most emotion inspiring terms and this is not surprising considering that they are used to qualify a noun or a verb. Anticipation, trust, and joy come through as the most common emotions evoked by terms of all four parts of speech.

The **EmoLex$_{WAL}$** rows are particularly interesting because they serve to determine how much the Turker annotations match annotations in the Wordnet Affect Lexicon (WAL). The most common Turker-determined emotion for each of these rows is marked in bold. Observe that WAL anger terms are mostly marked as anger evocative, joy terms as joy evocative, and so on. The **EmoLex$_{WAL}$** rows also indicate which emotions get confused for which, or which emotions tend to be evoked simultaneously by a term. Observe that anger terms tend also to be evocative of disgust. Similarly, fear and sadness go together, as do joy, trust, and anticipation.

The **EmoLex$_{GI}$** rows rightly show that words marked as negative in the General Inquirer, mostly evoke negative emotions (anger, fear, disgust, and sadness). Observe that the percentages for trust and joy are much lower. On the other hand, positive words evoke anticipation, joy, and trust.

4.1.2 Agreement

In order to analyze how often the annotators agreed with each other, for each term–emotion pair, we calculated the percentage of times the majority class has size 5 (all Turkers agree), size 4 (all but one agree), size 3, and size 2. Observe that for more than 50% of the terms, at least four annotators agree with each other. Table 5 presents these agreement values. Since many NLP systems may rely only on two intensity values (evocative or non-evocative), we also calculate agreement at that level (Table 6). Observe that for more than 50% of the terms, all five annotators agree with each other, and for more than 80% of the terms, at least four annotators agree. This shows a high degree of agreement on emotion annotations despite no real control over the educational background and qualifications of the annotators.

	Majority class size			
Emotion	two	three	four	five
anger	13.1	25.6	27.4	33.7
anticipation	31.6	35.2	20.7	12.3
disgust	14.0	21.6	29.0	35.1
fear	15.0	29.9	28.6	26.2
joy	17.6	26.4	23.0	32.7
sadness	14.2	24.6	28.1	32.8
surprise	17.0	29.3	32.3	21.2
trust	22.4	27.8	22.4	27.2
micro average	**18.1**	**27.6**	**26.4**	**27.7**

Table 5: Agreement at four intensity levels for emotion (no, weak, moderate, and strong): Percent of 2081 terms for which the majority class size was 2, 3, 4, and 5.

	Majority class size		
Emotion	three	four	five
anger	15.0	25.9	58.9
anticipation	32.3	33.7	33.8
disgust	12.8	24.6	62.4
fear	14.9	25.6	59.4
joy	18.4	27.0	54.5
sadness	13.6	22.0	64.2
surprise	17.5	31.4	50.9
trust	23.9	29.3	46.6
micro average	**18.6**	**27.4**	**53.8**

Table 6: Agreement at two intensity levels for emotion (evocative and non-evocative): Percent of 2081 terms for which the majority class size was 3, 4, and 5.

4.2 Semantic orientation of words

We consolidate the semantic orientation (polarity) annotations in a manner identical to the process for emotion annotations. Table 7 lists the percent of 2081 target terms assigned a majority class of no, weak, moderate, and strong semantic orientation. For example, it tells us that 16% of the target terms are strongly negative. The last row in the table lists the percent of target terms that have some semantic orientation (positive or negative) at the various intensity levels. Observe that 35% of the target terms are strongly evaluative (positively or negatively).

Just as in the case for emotions, practical NLP applications often require only two levels of semantic orientation—having particular semantic orientation or not (**evaluative**) or not (**non-evaluative**). For each target term–emotion pair, we convert the four-level semantic orientation annotations into two-level ones, just as we did for the emotions. Table 8 gives

	Intensity			
Polarity	no	weak	moderate	strong
negative	60.8	10.8	12.3	16.0
positive	48.3	11.7	20.7	19.0
micro average	**54.6**	**11.3**	**16.5**	**17.5**
any polarity	**14.7**	**17.4**	**32.7**	**35.0**

Table 7: Percent of 2081 terms assigned a majority class of no, weak, moderate, and strong polarity.

Polarity	**% of terms**
negative	31.3
positive	45.5
micro average	**38.4**
any polarity	**76.1**

Table 8: Percent of 2081 target terms that are evaluative.

percent of target terms considered to be evaluative. The last row in the table gives the percentage of terms evaluative with respect to some semantic orientation (positive or negative). Table 9 shows how many terms in each category are positively and negatively evaluative.

4.2.1 Analysis and discussion

Observe in Table 9 that, across the board, a sizable number of terms are evaluative with respect to some semantic orientation. Interestingly unigram nouns have a markedly lower proportion of negative terms, and a much higher proportion of positive terms. It may be argued that the default semantic orientation of noun concepts is positive, and that usually it takes a negative adjective to make the phrase negative.

The **EmoLex$_{\mathbf{GI}}$** rows in the two tables show that words marked as having a negative semantic orientation in the General Inquirer are mostly marked as negative by the Turkers. And similarly, the positives in GI are annotated as positive. Again, this is confirmation that the quality of annotation obtained is high. The **EmoLex$_{\mathbf{WAL}}$** rows show that anger, disgust, fear, and sadness terms tend not to have a positive semantic orientation and are mostly negative. In contrast, and expectedly, the joy terms are positive. The surprise terms are more than twice as likely to be positive than negative.

4.2.2 Agreement

In order to analyze how often the annotators agreed with each other, for each term–emotion pair, we cal-

EmoLex	negative	positive	any
EmoLex$_{Uni}$:			
adjectives	33	55	87
adverbs	29	54	82
nouns	6	44	51
verbs	22	41	62
EmoLex$_{Bi}$:			
adjectives	30	48	78
adverbs	10	52	61
nouns	13	49	61
verbs	12	57	68
EmoLex$_{GI}$:			
negatives in GI	**90**	2	92
positives in GI	2	**91**	91
EmoLex$_{WAL}$:			
anger terms in WAL	96	0	96
disgust terms in WAL	96	0	96
fear terms in WAL	87	3	89
joy terms in WAL	4	92	96
sadness terms in WAL	90	1	91
surprise terms in WAL	23	57	81

Table 9: Percent of terms, in each target set, that are evaluative. The highest individual polarity EmoLex$_{GI}$ row scores are shown bold. Observe that the positive GI terms are marked mostly as positively evaluative and the negative terms are marked mostly as negatively evaluative.

culated the percentage of times the majority class has size 5 (all Turkers agree), size 4 (all but one agree), size 3, and size 2. Table 10 presents these agreement values. Observe that for more than 50% of the terms, at least four annotators agree with each other. Table 11 gives agreement values at the two-intensity level. Observe that for more than 50% of the terms, all five annotators agree with each other, and for more than 80% of the terms, at least four annotators agree.

5 Conclusions

We showed how Mechanical Turk can be used to create a high-quality, moderate-sized, emotion lexicon for a very small cost (less than US$500). Notably, we used automatically generated word choice questions to detect and reject erroneous annotations and to reject all annotations by unqualified Turkers and those who indulge in malicious data entry. We compared a subset of our lexicon with existing gold standard data to show that the annotations obtained are indeed of high quality. A detailed analysis of the lexicon revealed insights into how prevalent emotion bearing terms are among common unigrams and bigrams. We also identified which emotions tend to be evoked simultaneously by the same term. The lexicon is available for free download.[4]

	Majority class size			
Polarity	two	three	four	five
negative	11.8	28.7	29.4	29.8
positive	21.2	30.7	19.0	28.8
micro average	**16.5**	**29.7**	**24.2**	**29.3**

Table 10: Agreement at four intensity levels for polarity (no, weak, moderate, and strong): Percent of 2081 terms for which the majority class size was 2, 3, 4, and 5.

	Majority class size		
Polarity	three	four	five
negative	11.8	21.2	66.9
positive	23.1	26.3	50.5
micro average	**17.5**	**23.8**	**58.7**

Table 11: Agreement at two intensity levels for polarity (evaluative and non-evaluative): Percent of 2081 terms for which the majority class size was 3, 4, and 5.

Since this pilot experiment with about 2000 target terms was successful, we will now obtain emotion annotations for tens of thousands of English terms. We will use the emotion lexicon to identify emotional tone of larger units of text, such as newspaper headlines and blog posts. We will also use it to evaluate automatically generated lexicons, such as the polarity lexicons by Turney and Littman (2003) and Mohammad et al. (2009). We will explore the variance in emotion evoked by near-synonyms, and also how common it is for words with many meanings to evoke different emotions in different senses.

Acknowledgments

This research was funded by the National research Council Canada (NRC). Thanks to Diana Inkpen and Diman Ghazi for early discussions on emotion. Thanks to Joel Martin for encouragement and support. Thanks to Norm Vinson and the Ethics Committee at NRC for examining, guiding, and approving the survey. And last but not least, thanks to the more than 1000 anonymous people who answered the emotion survey with diligence and care.

[4]http://www.purl.org/net/emolex

References

Cecilia Ovesdotter Alm, Dan Roth, and Richard Sproat. 2005. Emotions from text: Machine learning for text-based emotion prediction. In *Proceedings of the Joint Conference on Human Language Technology / Empirical Methods in Natural Language Processing (HLT/EMNLP-2005)*, pages 579–586, Vancouver, Canada.

J.R.L. Bernard, editor. 1986. *The Macquarie Thesaurus*. Macquarie Library, Sydney, Australia.

Thorsten Brants and Alex Franz. 2006. Web 1t 5-gram version 1. *Linguistic Data Consortium*.

Chris Callison-Burch. 2009. Fast, cheap and creative: Evaluating translation quality using amazon's mechanical turk. In *Proceedings of the Conference on Empirical Methods in Natural Language Processing (EMNLP-2009)*, pages 286–295, Singapore.

Paul Ekman. 1992. An argument for basic emotions. *Cognition and Emotion*, 6(3):169–200.

Clark Elliott. 1992. *The affective reasoner: A process model of emotions in a multi-agent system*. Ph.D. thesis, Institute for the Learning Sciences, Northwestern University.

Dekang Lin, Shaojun Zhao, Lijuan Qin, and Ming Zhou. 2003. Identifying synonyms among distributionally similar words. In *Proceedings of the 18th International Joint Conference on Artificial Intelligence (IJCAI-03)*, pages 1492–1493, Acapulco, Mexico.

A. Lobanova, T. van der Kleij, and J. Spenader. 2010. Defining antonymy: A corpus-based study of opposites by lexico-syntactic patterns. *International Journal of Lexicography (in press)*, 23:19–53.

Saif Mohammad, Bonnie Dorr, and Codie Dunn. 2008. Computing word-pair antonymy. In *Proceedings of the Conference on Empirical Methods in Natural Language Processing (EMNLP-2008)*, pages 982–991, Waikiki, Hawaii.

Saif Mohammad, Cody Dunne, and Bonnie Dorr. 2009. Generating high-coverage semantic orientation lexicons from overtly marked words and a thesaurus. In *Proceedings of Empirical Methods in Natural Language Processing (EMNLP-2009)*, pages 599–608, Singapore.

Alena Neviarouskaya, Helmut Prendinger, and Mitsuru Ishizuka. 2009. Compositionality principle in recognition of fine-grained emotions from text. In *Proceedings of the Proceedings of the Third International Conference on Weblogs and Social Media (ICWSM-09)*, pages 278–281, San Jose, California.

R Plutchik. 1980. A general psychoevolutionary theory of emotion. *Emotion: Theory, research, and experience*, 1(3):3–33.

Jonathon Read. 2004. *Recognising affect in text using pointwise-mutual information*. Ph.D. thesis, Department of Informatics, University of Sussex.

Rion Snow, Brendan O'Connor, Daniel Jurafsky, and Andrew Ng. 2008. Cheap and fast - but is it good? Evaluating nonexpert annotations for natural language tasks. In *Proceedings of the Conference on Empirical Methods in Natural Language Processing (EMNLP-2008)*, pages 254–263, Waikiki, Hawaii.

Philip Stone, Dexter C. Dunphy, Marshall S. Smith, Daniel M. Ogilvie, and associates. 1966. *The General Inquirer: A Computer Approach to Content Analysis*. The MIT Press.

Carlo Strapparava and Alessandro Valitutti. 2004. Wordnet-Affect: An affective extension of WordNet. In *Proceedings of the 4th International Conference on Language Resources and Evaluation (LREC-2004)*, pages 1083–1086, Lisbon, Portugal.

Peter Turney and Michael Littman. 2003. Measuring praise and criticism: Inference of semantic orientation from association. *ACM Transactions on Information Systems (TOIS)*, 21(4):315–346.

A Corpus-based Method for Extracting Paraphrases of Emotion Terms

Fazel Keshtkar
University of Ottawa
Ottawa, ON, K1N 6N5, Canada
akeshtka@site.uOttawa.ca

Diana Inkpen
University of Ottawa
Ottawa, ON, K1N 6N5, Canada
diana@site.uOttawa.ca

Abstract

Since paraphrasing is one of the crucial tasks in natural language understanding and generation, this paper introduces a novel technique to extract paraphrases for emotion terms, from non-parallel corpora. We present a bootstrapping technique for identifying paraphrases, starting with a small number of seeds. WordNet Affect emotion words are used as seeds. The bootstrapping approach learns extraction patterns for six classes of emotions. We use annotated blogs and other datasets as texts from which to extract paraphrases, based on the highest-scoring extraction patterns. The results include lexical and morpho-syntactic paraphrases, that we evaluate with human judges.

1 Introduction

Paraphrases are different ways to express the same information. Algorithms to extract and automatically identify paraphrases are of interest from both linguistic and practical points of view. Many major challenges in Natural Language Processing applications, for example multi-document summarization, need to avoid repetitive information from the input documents. In Natural Language Generation, paraphrasing is employed to create more varied and natural text. In our research, we extract paraphrases for emotions, with the goal of using them to automatically-generate emotional texts (such as friendly or hostile texts) for conversations between intelligent agents and characters in educational games. Paraphrasing is applied to generate text with more variety. To our knowledge, most current applications manually collect paraphrases for specific applications, or they use lexical resources such as WordNet (Miller et al., 1993) to identify paraphrases.

This paper introduces a novel method for extracting paraphrases for emotions from texts. We focus on the six basic emotions proposed by Ekman (1992): *happiness*, *sadness*, *anger*, *disgust*, *surprise*, and *fear*.

We describe the construction of the paraphrases extractor. We also propose a k-window algorithm for selecting contexts that are used in the paraphrase extraction method. We automatically learn patterns that are able to extract the emotion paraphrases from corpora, starting with a set of seed words. We use data sets such as blogs and other annotated corpora, in which the emotions are marked. We use a large collection of non-parallel corpora which are described in Section 3. These corpora contain many instances of paraphrases different words to express the same emotion.

An example of sentence fragments for one emotion class, *happiness*, is shown in Table 1. From them, the paraphrase pair that our method will extract is:

```
"so happy to see"
"very glad to visit".
```

In the following sections, we give an overview of related work on paraphrasing in Section 2. In Section 3 we describe the datasets used in this work. We explain the details of our paraphrase extraction method in Section 4. We present results of our evaluation and discuss our results in Section 5, and finally in Section 6 we present the conclusions and future work.

Proceedings of the NAACL HLT 2010 Workshop on Computational Approaches to Analysis and Generation of Emotion in Text, pages 35–44,
Los Angeles, California, June 2010.

his little boy was so happy to see him	
princess and she were very glad to visit him	

Table 1: Two sentence fragments (candidate contexts) from the emotion class *happy*, from the blog corpus.

2 Related Work

Three main approaches for collecting paraphrases were proposed in the literature: manual collection, utilization of existing lexical resources, and corpus-based extraction of expressions that occur in similar contexts (Barzilay and McKeown, 2001). Manually-collected paraphrases were used in natural language generation (NLG) (Iordanskaja et al., 1991). Langkilde et al. (1998) used lexical resources in statistical sentence generation, summarization, and question-answering. Barzilay and McKeown (2001) used a corpus-based method to identify paraphrases from a corpus of multiple English translations of the same source text. Our method is similar to this method, but it extracts paraphrases only for a particular emotion, and it needs only a regular corpus, not a parallel corpus of multiple translations.

Some research has been done in paraphrase extraction for natural language processing and generation for different applications. Das and Smith (2009) presented a approach to decide whether two sentences hold a paraphrase relationship. They applied a generative model that generates a paraphrase of a given sentence, then used probabilistic inference to reason about whether two sentences share the paraphrase relationship. In another research, Wang et. al (2009) studied the problem of extracting technical paraphrases from a parallel software corpus. Their aim was to report duplicate bugs. In their method for paraphrase extraction, they used: sentence selection, global context-based and co-occurrence-based scoring. Also, some studies have been done in paraphrase generation in NLG (Zhao et al., 2009), (Chevelu et al., 2009). Bootstrapping methods have been applied to various natural language applications, for example to word sense disambiguation (Yarowsky, 1995), lexicon construction for information extraction (Riloff and Jones, 1999), and named entity classification (Collins and Singer, 1999). In our research, we use the bootstrapping approach to learn paraphrases for emotions.

3 Data

The text data from which we will extract paraphrases is composed of four concatenated datasets. They contain sentences annotated with the six basic emotions. The number of sentences in each dataset is presented in Table 2. We briefly describe the datasets, as follows.

3.1 LiveJournal blog dataset

We used the blog corpus that Mishne collected for his research (Mishne, 2005). The corpus contains 815,494 blog posts from Livejournal [1], a free weblog service used by millions of people to create weblogs. In Livejournal, users are able to optionally specify their current emotion or mood. To select their emotion/mood users can choose from a list of 132 provided moods. So, the data is annotated by the user who created the blog. We selected only the texts corresponding to the six emotions that we mentioned.

3.2 Text Affect Dataset

This dataset (Strapparava and Mihalcea, 2007) consists of newspaper headlines that were used in the SemEval 2007-Task 14. It includes a development dataset of 250 annotated headlines, and a test dataset of 1000 news headlines. We use all of them. The annotations were made with the six basic emotions on intensity scales of [-100, 100], therefore a threshold is used to choose the main emotion of each sentence.

3.3 Fairy Tales Dataset

This dataset consists in 1580 annotated sentences (Alm et al., 2005), from tales by the Grimm brothers, H.C. Andersen, and B. Potter. The annotations used the extended set of nine basic emotions of Izard (1971). We selected only those marked with the six emotions that we focus on.

3.4 Annotated Blog Dataset

We also used the dataset provided by Aman and Szpakowicz (2007). Emotion-rich sentences were selected from personal blogs, and annotated with the six emotions (as well as a non-emotion class, that we ignore here). They worked with blog posts and collected directly from the Web. First, they prepared

[1] http://www.livejournalinc.com

Dataset	Happiness	Sadness	Anger	Disgust	Surprise	Fear
LiveJournal	7705	1698	4758	1191	1191	3996
TextAffect	334	214	175	28	131	166
Fairy tales	445	264	216	217	113	165
Annotated blog dataset	536	173	115	115	172	179

Table 2: The number of emotion-annotated sentences in each dataset.

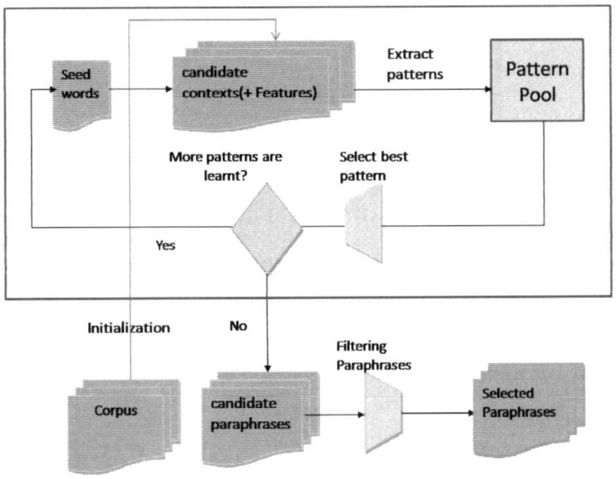

Figure 1: High-level view of the paraphrase extraction method.

a list of seed words for six basic emotion categories proposed by Ekman (1992). Then, they took words commonly used in the context of a particular emotion. Finally, they used the seed words for each category, and retrieved blog posts containing one or more of those words for the annotation process.

4 Method for Paraphrase Extraction

For each of the six emotions, we run our method on the set of sentences marked with the corresponding emotion from the concatenated corpus. We start with a set of seed words form WordNet Affect (Strapparava and Valitutti, 2004), for each emotion of interest. The number of seed words is the following: for happiness 395, for surprise 68, for fear 140, for disgust 50, for anger 250, and for sadness 200. Table 3 shows some of seeds for each category of emotion.

Since sentences are different in our datasets and they are not aligned as parallel sentences as in (Barzilay and McKeown, 2001), our algorithm constructs pairs of similar sentences, based on the local context. On the other hand, we assume that, if the contexts surrounding two seeds look similar, then these contexts are likely to help in extracting new paraphrases.

Figure 1 illustrates the high-level architecture of our paraphrase extraction method. The input to the method is a text corpus for a emotion category and a manually defined list of seed words. Before bootstrapping starts, we run the k-window algorithm on every sentence in the corpus, in order to construct *candidate contexts*. In Section 4.5 we explain how the bootstrapping algorithm processes and selects the paraphrases based on strong surrounding contexts. As it is shown in Figure 1, our method has several stages: extracting candidate contexts, using them to extract patterns, selecting the best patterns, extracting potential paraphrases, and filtering them to obtain the final paraphrases.

4.1 Preprocessing

During preprocessing, HTML and XML tags are eliminated from the blogs data and other datasets, then the text is tokenized and annotated with part of speech tags. We use the Stanford part-of-speech tagger and chunker (Toutanova et al., 2003) to identify noun and verb phrases in the sentences. In the next step, we use a sliding window based on the k-window approach, to identify candidate contexts that contain the target seeds.

4.2 The k-window Algorithm

We use the k-window algorithm introduced by Bostad (2003) in order to identify all the tokens surrounding a specific term in a window with size of $\pm k$. Here, we use this approach to extract candidate patterns for each seed, from the sentences. We start with one seed and truncate all contexts around the seed within a window of $\pm k$ words before and $\pm k$ words after the seed, until all the seeds are processed. For these experiments, we set the value of k to ± 5. Therefore

Happiness: avidness, glad, warmheartedness, exalt, enjoy, comforting, joviality, amorous, joyful, like, cheer, adoring, fascinating, happy, impress, great, satisfaction, cheerful, charmed, romantic, joy, pleased, inspire, good, fulfill, gladness, merry
Sadness: poor, sorry, woeful, guilty, miserable, glooming, bad, grim, tearful, glum, mourning, joyless, sadness, blue, rueful, hamed, regret, hapless, regretful, dismay, dismal, misery, godforsaken, oppression, harass, dark, sadly, attrition
Anger: belligerence, envious, aggravate, resentful, abominate, murderously, greedy, hatred, disdain, envy, annoy, mad, jealousy, huffiness, sore, anger, harass, bother, enraged, hateful, irritating, hostile, outrage, devil, irritate, angry
Disgust: nauseous, sicken, foul, disgust, nausea, revolt, hideous, horror, detestable, wicked, repel, offensive, repulse, yucky, repulsive, queasy, obscene, noisome
Surprise: wondrous, amaze, gravel, marvel, fantastic, wonderful, surprising, marvelous, wonderment, astonish, wonder, admiration, terrific, dumfounded, trounce
Fear: fearful, apprehensively, anxiously, presage, horrified, hysterical, timidity, horrible, timid, fright, hesitance, affright, trepid, horrific, unassertive, apprehensiveness, hideous, scarey, cruel, panic, scared, terror, awful, dire, fear, dread, crawl, anxious, distrust, diffidence

Table 3: Some of the seeds from WordNet Affect for each category of emotion.

the longest candidate contexts will have the form $w_1, w_2, w_3, w_4, w_5, seed, w_6, w_7, w_8, w_9, w_{10}, w_{11}$. In the next subsection, we explain what features we extract from each candidate context, to allow us to determine similar contexts.

4.3 Feature Extraction

Previous research on word sense disambiguation on contextual analysis has acknowledged several local and topical features as good indicators of word properties. These include surrounding words and their part of speech tags, collocations, keywords in contexts (Mihalcea, 2004). Also recently, other features have been proposed: bigrams, named entities, syntactic features, and semantic relations with other words in the context.

We transfer the candidate phrases extracted by the sliding *k*-window into the vector space of features. We consider features that include both lexical and syntactic descriptions of the paraphrases for all pairs of two candidates. The lexical features include the sequence of tokens for each phrase in the paraphrase pair; the syntactic feature consists of a sequence of part-of-speech (PoS) tags where equal words and words with the same root and PoS are marked. For example, the value of the syntactic feature for the pair `''so glad to see''` and `''very happy to visit''` is "$RB_1\ JJ_1\ TO\ VB_1$" and "$RB_1\ JJ_2\ TO\ VB_2$", where indices indicate word equalities. However, based on the above evidences and our previous research, we also investigate other features that are well suited for our goal. Table 5 lists the features that we used for paraphrase extraction. They include some term frequency features. As an example, in Table 4 we show extracted features from a relevant context.

Candidate context: He was further annoyed by the jay bird
'PRP VBD RB VBN IN DT NN NN',65,8,'VBD RB',?,was, ?,?,?,He/PRP,was/VBD,further/RB,annoyed,by/IN,the/DT, jay/NN,bird/NN,?,?,jay,?,'IN DT NN',2,2,0,1

Table 4: An example of extracted features.

4.4 Extracting Patterns

From each candidate context, we extracted the features as described above. Then we learn extraction patterns, in which some words might be substituted by their part-of-speech. We use the seeds to build initial patterns. Two candidate contexts that contain the same seed create one positive example. By using each initial seed, we can extract all contexts surrounding these positive examples. Then we select the stronger ones. We used Collins and Singer method (Collins and Singer, 1999) to compute the strength of each example. If we consider x as a context, the strength as a positive example of x is de-

Features	Description
F1	Sequence of part-of-speech
F2	Length of sequence in bytes
F3	Number of tokens
F4	Sequence of PoS between the seed and the first verb before the seed
F5	Sequence of PoS between the seed and the first noun before the seed
F6	First verb before the seed
F7	First noun before the seed
F8	Token before the seed
F9	Seed
F10	Token after the seed
F11	First verb after the seed
F12	First noun after the seed
F13	Sequence of PoS between the seed and the first verb after the seed
F14	Sequence of PoS between the seed and the first noun after the seed
F15	Number of verbs in the candidate context
F16	Number of nouns in the candidate context
F17	Number of adjective in the candidate context
F18	Number of adverbs in the candidate context

Table 5: The features that we used for paraphrase extraction.

fined as:

$$Strength(x) = count(x+)/count(x) \quad (1)$$

In Equation 1, $count(x+)$ is the number of times context x surrounded a seed in a positive example and $count(x)$ is frequency of the context x. This allows us to score the potential pattern.

4.5 Bootstrapping Algorithm for Paraphrase Extraction

Our bootstrapping algorithm is summarized in Figure 2. It starts with a set of seeds, which are considered initial paraphrases. A set of extraction patterns is initially empty. The algorithm generates candidate contexts, from the aligned similar contexts. The candidate patterns are scored by how many paraphrases they can extract. Those with the highest scores are added to the set of extraction patterns. Using the extended set of extraction patterns, more paraphrase pairs are extracted and added to the set of paraphrases. Using the enlarged set of paraphrases, more extraction patterns are extracted. The process keeps iterating until no new patterns or no new paraphrases are learned.

Our method is able to accumulate a large lexicon of emotion phrases by bootstrapping from the manually initialized list of seed words. In each iteration, the paraphrase set is expanded with related phrases found in the corpus, which are filtered by using a measure of strong surrounding context similarity. The bootstrapping process starts by selecting a subset of the extraction patterns that aim to extract the paraphrases. We call this set the pattern pool. The phrases extracted by these patterns become candidate paraphrases. They are filtered based on how many patterns select them, in order to produce the final paraphrases from the set of candidate paraphrases.

5 Results and Evaluation

The result of our algorithm is a set of extraction patterns and a set of pairs of paraphrases. Some of the paraphrases extracted by our system are shown in Table 6. The paraphrases that are considered correct are shown under *Correct paraphrases*. As explained in the next section, two human judges agreed that these are acceptable paraphrases. The results considered incorrect by the two judges are shown un-

Algorithm 1: Bootstrapping Algorithm.

```
For each seed for an emotion
  Loop until no more paraphrases or no more contexts are learned.
    1- Locate the seeds in each sentence
    2- Find similar contexts surrounding a pair of two seeds
    3- Analyze all contexts surrounding the two seeds to extract
       the strongest patterns
    4- Use the new patterns to learn more paraphrases
```

Figure 2: Our bootstrapping algorithm for extracting paraphrases.

der *Incorrect paraphrases*. Our algorithm learnt 196 extraction patterns and produced 5926 pairs of paraphrases. Table 7 shows the number of extraction patterns and the number of paraphrase pairs that were produced by our algorithm for each class of emotions. For evaluation of our algorithm, we use two techniques. One uses human judges to judge if a sample of paraphrases extracted by our method are correct; we also measures the agreement between the judges (See Section 5.1). The second estimates the recall and the precision of our method (See Section 5.2. In the following subsections we describe these evaluations.

5.1 Evaluating Correctness with Human Judges

We evaluate the correctness of the extracted paraphrase pairs, using the same method as Brazilay and McKeown (2001). We randomly selected 600 paraphrase pairs from the lexical paraphrases produced by our algorithm: for each class of emotion we selected 100 paraphrase pairs. We evaluated their correctness with two human judges. They judged whether the two expressions are good paraphrases or not.

We provided a page of guidelines for the judges. We defined paraphrase as "approximate conceptual equivalence", the same definition used in (Barzilay and McKeown, 2001). Each human judge had to choose a "Yes" or "No" answer for each pair of paraphrases under test. We did not include example sentences containing these paraphrases. A similar Machine Translation evaluation task for word-to-word translation was done in (Melamed, 2001).

Figure 3 presents the results of the evaluation: the correctness for each class of emotion according to judge A, and according to judge B. The judges were graduate students in computational linguistics, native speakers of English.

We also measured the agreement between the two judges and the Kappa coefficient (Siegel and Castellan, 1988). If there is complete agreement between two judges $Kappa$ is 1, and if there is no agreement between the judges then $Kappa = 0$. The $Kappa$ values and the agreement values for our judges are presented in Figure 4.

The inter-judge agreement over all the paraphrases for the six classes of emotions is 81.72%, which is 490 out of the 600 paraphrases pairs in our sample. Note that they agreed that some pairs are good paraphrases, or they agreed that some pairs are not good paraphrases, that is why the numbers in Figure 4 are higher than the correctness numbers from Figure 3. The $Kappa$ coefficient compensates for the chance agreement. The $Kappa$ value over all the paraphrase pairs is 74.41% which shows a significant agreement.

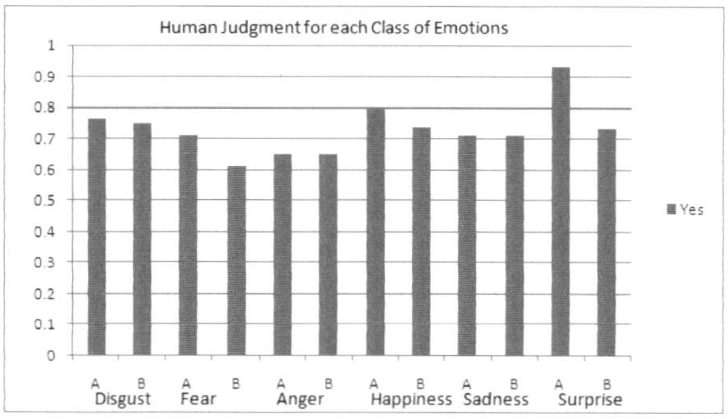

Figure 3: The correctness results according the judge A and judge B, for each class of emotion.

5.2 Estimating Recall

Evaluating the *Recall* of our algorithm is difficult due to following reasons. Our algorithm is not able to cover all the English words; it can only detect

Disgust
Correct paraphrases: being a wicked::getting of evil; been rather sick::feeling rather nauseated; feels somewhat queasy::felt kind of sick; damn being sick::am getting sick *Incorrect paraphrases*: disgusting and vile::appealing and nauseated; get so sick::some truly disgusting
Fear
Correct paraphrases: was freaking scared::was quite frightened; just very afraid::just so scared; tears of fright::full of terror; freaking scary::intense fear; *Incorrect paraphrases*: serious panic attack::easily scared; not necessarily fear::despite your fear
Anger
Correct paraphrases: upset and angry::angry and pissed; am royally pissed::feeling pretty angry; made me mad::see me angry; do to torment::just to spite *Incorrect paraphrases*: very pretty annoying::very very angry; bitter and spite::tired and angry
Happiness
Correct paraphrases: the love of::the joy of; in great mood::in good condition; the joy of::the glad of; good feeling::good mood *Incorrect paraphrases*: as much eagerness::as many gladness; feeling smart::feel happy
Sadness
Correct paraphrases: too depressing::so sad; quite miserable::quite sorrowful; strangely unhappy::so misery; been really down::feel really sad *Incorrect paraphrases*: out of pity::out of misery; akward and depressing::terrible and gloomy
Surprise
Correct paraphrases: amazement at::surprised by; always wonder::always surprised; still astounded::still amazed; unexpected surprise::got shocked *Incorrect paraphrases*: passion and tremendous::serious and amazing; tremendous stress::huge shock

Table 6: Examples of paraphrases extracted by our algorithm (correctly and incorrectly).

Class of Emotion	# Paraphrases Pairs	# Extraction Patterns
Disgust	1125	12
Fear	1004	31
Anger	670	47
Happiness	1095	68
Sadness	1308	25
Surprise	724	13
Total	5926	196

Table 7: The number of lexical and extraction patterns produced by the algorithm.

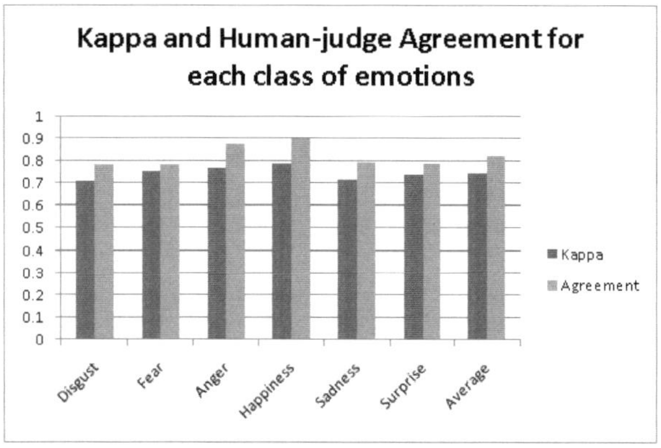

Figure 4: The *Kappa* coefficients and the agreement between the two human judges.

Category of Emotions	Precision	Recall
Disgust	82.33%	92.91%
Fear	82.64%	88.20%
Anger	93.67%	80.57%
Happiness	82.00%	90.89%
Sadness	82.00%	89.88%
Surprise	79.78%	89.50%
Average	84.23%	88.66%

Table 8: Precision and Recall for a sample of texts, for each category of emotion, and their average.

paraphrasing relations with words which appeared in our corpus. Moreover, to compare directly with an electronic thesaurus such as WordNet is not feasible, because WordNet contains mostly synonym sets between words, and only a few multi-word expressions. We decided to estimate recall manually, by asking a human judge to extract paraphrases by hand from a sample of text. We randomly selected 60 texts (10 for each emotion class) and asked the judge to extract paraphrases from these sentences. For each emotion class, the judge extracted expressions that reflect the emotion, and then made pairs that were conceptually equivalent. It was not feasible to ask a second judge to do the same task, because the process is time-consuming and tedious.

In Information Retrieval, *Precision* and *Recall* are defined in terms of a set of retrieved documents and a set of relevant documents [2]. In the following sections we describe how we compute the *Precision* and *Recall* for our algorithm compared to the manually extracted paraphrases.

From the paraphrases that were extracted by the algorithm from the same texts, we counted how many of them were also extracted by the human judge. Equation 2 defines the Precision. On average, from 89 paraphrases extracted by the algorithm, 74 were identified as paraphrases by the human judge (84.23%). See Table 8 for the values for all the classes.

$$P = \frac{\#\ Correctly\ Retrieved\ Paraphrases\ by\ the\ Algorithm}{All\ Paraphrases\ Retrieved\ by\ the\ Algorithm} \qquad (2)$$

For computing the *Recall* we count how many of the paraphrases extracted by the human judge were correctly extracted by the algorithm (Equation 3).

$$R = \frac{\#\ Correctly\ Retrieved\ Paraphrases\ by\ the\ Algorithm}{All\ Paraphrases\ Retrieved\ by\ the\ Human\ Judge} \qquad (3)$$

5.3 Discussion and Comparison to Related Work

To the best of our knowledge, no similar research has been done in extracting paraphrases for emotion terms from corpora. However, Barzilay and McKeown (2001) did similar work to corpus-based iden-

[2] http://en.wikipedia.org/wiki/

tification of general paraphrases from multiple English translations of the same source text. We can compare the pros and cons of our method compared to their method. The advantages are:

- In our method, there is no requirement for the corpus to be parallel. Our algorithm uses the entire corpus together to construct its bootstrapping method, while in (Barzilay and McKeown, 2001) the parallel corpus is needed in order detect positive contexts.

- Since we construct the candidate contexts based on the k-window approach, there is no need for sentences to be aligned in our method. In (Barzilay and McKeown, 2001) sentence alignment is essential in order to recognize identical words and positive contexts.

- The algorithm in (Barzilay and McKeown, 2001) has to find positive contexts first, then it looks for appropriate patterns to extract paraphrases. Therefore, if identical words do not occur in the aligned sentences, the algorithm fails to find positive contexts. But, our algorithm starts with given seeds that allow us to detect positive context with the k-window method.

A limitation of our method is the need for the initial seed words. However, obtaining these seed words is not a problem nowadays. They can be found in on line dictionaries, WordNet, and other lexical recourses.

6 Conclusion and Future Work

In this paper, we introduced a method for corpus-based extraction of paraphrases for emotion terms. We showed a method that used a bootstrapping technique based on contextual and lexical features and is able to successfully extract paraphrases using a non-parallel corpus. We showed that a bootstrapping algorithm based on contextual surrounding context features of paraphrases achieves significant performance on our data set.

In future work, we will extend this techniques to extract paraphrases from more corpora and for more types of emotions. In terms of evaluation, we will use the extracted paraphrases as features in machine learning classifiers that classify candidate sentences into classes of emotions. If the results of the classification are good, this mean the extracted paraphrases are of good quality.

References

Cecilia Ovesdotter Alm, Dan Roth, and Richard Sproat. 2005. Emotions from text: machine learning for text-based emotion prediction. In *Proceedings of the Human Language Technology Conference Conference on Empirical Methods in Natural Language Processing (HLT/EMNLP 2005)*.

Saima Aman and Stan Szpakowicz. 2007. Identifying expressions of emotion in text. In *TSD*, pages 196–205.

Regina Barzilay and Kathleen McKeown. 2001. Extracting paraphrases from a parallel corpus. In *Proceeding of ACL/EACL, 2001, Toulouse*.

Thorstein Bostad. 2003. *Sentence Based Automatic Sentiment Classification*. Ph.D. thesis, University of Cambridge, Computer Speech Text and Internet Technologies (CSTIT), Computer Laboratory, Jan.

Jonathan Chevelu, Thomas Lavergne, Yves Lepage, and Thierry Moudenc. 2009. Introduction of a new paraphrase generation tool based on Monte-Carlo sampling. In *Proceedings of ACL-IJCNLP 2009, Singapore*, pages 249–25.

Michael Collins and Yoram Singer. 1999. Unsupervised models for named entity classification. In *proceedings of the Joint SIGDAT Conference on Empirical Methods in Natural Language Processing and Very Large Corpora*.

Dipanjan Das and Noah A. Smith. 2009. Paraphrase identification as probabilistic quasi-synchronous recognition. In *Proceedings of ACL-IJCNLP 2009, Singapore*, pages 468–476.

Paul Ekman. 1992. An argument for basic emotions. *Cognition and Emotion*, 6:169–200.

L. Iordanskaja, Richard Kittredget, and Alain Polguere, 1991. *Natural Language Generation in Artificial Intelligence and Computational Linguistics*. Kluwer Academic.

Carroll E. Izard. 1971. *The Face of Emotion*. Appleton-Century-Crofts., New York.

Irene Langkilde and Kevin Knight. 1998. Generation that exploits corpus-based statistical knowledge. In *COLING-ACL*.

Ilya Dan Melamed. 2001. *Empirical Methods for Exploiting Parallel Texts*. MIT Press.

Rada Mihalcea. 2004. Co-training and self-training for word sense disambiguation. In *Natural Language Learning (CoNLL 2004)*, Boston, May.

George Miller, Richard Beckwith, Christiane Fellbaum, Derek Gross, and Katherine Miller, 1993. *Introduction to Wordnet: An On-Line Lexical Database*. Cognitive Science Laboratory, Princeton University, August.

Gilad Mishne. 2005. Experiments with mood classification in blog posts. *ACM SIGIR*.

Ellen Riloff and Rosie Jones. 1999. Learning dictionaries for information extraction by multi-level bootstrapping. In *Proceedings of the Sixteenth National Conference on Artificial Intelligence*, page 10441049. The AAAI Press/MIT Press.

Sidney Siegel and John Castellan, 1988. *Non Parametric Statistics for Behavioral Sciences.* . McGraw-Hill.

Carlo Strapparava and Rada Mihalcea. 2007. Semeval-2007 task 14: Affective text. In *Proceedings of the 4th International Workshop on the Semantic Evaluations (SemEval 2007), Prague, Czech Republic, June 2007.*

Carlo Strapparava and Alessandro Valitutti. 2004. Wordnet-affect: an affective extension of wordnet. In *Proceedings of the 4th International Conference on Language Resources and Evaluation (LREC 2004), Lisbon, May 2004*, pages 1083–1086.

Kristina Toutanova, Dan Klein, Christopher Manning, and Yoram Singer. 2003. Feature-rich part-of-speech tagging with a cyclic dependency network. In *Proceedings of HLT-NAACL*, pages 252–259.

Xiaoyin Wang, David Lo, Jing Jiang, Lu Zhang, and Hong Mei. 2009. Extracting paraphrases of technical terms from noisy parallel software corpora. In *Proceedings of ACL-IJCNLP 2009, Singapore*, pages 197–200.

David Yarowsky. 1995. Unsupervised word sense disambiguation rivaling supervised methods. In *Proceedings of the 33rd Annual Meeting of the Association for Computational Linguistics*, pages 189–196.

Shiqi Zhao, Xiang Lan, Ting Liu, , and Sheng Li. 2009. Application-driven statistical paraphrase generation. In *Proceedings of ACL-IJCNLP 2009, Singapore*, pages 834–842.

A Text-driven Rule-based System for Emotion Cause Detection

Sophia Yat Mei Lee[†]
[†]Department of Chinese and Bilingual Studies
The Hong Kong Polytechnic University

Ying Chen[†*]
[*]Department of Computer Engineering
China Agriculture University

Chu-Ren Huang[†‡]
[‡]Institute of Linguistics
Academia Sinica

{sophiaym, chenying3176, churenhuang}@gmail.com

Abstract

Emotion cause detection is a new research area in emotion processing even though most theories of emotion treat recognition of a triggering cause event as an integral part of emotion. As a first step towards fully automatic inference of cause-emotion correlation, we propose a text-driven, rule-based approach to emotion cause detection in this paper. First of all, a Chinese emotion cause annotated corpus is constructed based on our proposed annotation scheme. By analyzing the corpus data, we identify seven groups of linguistic cues and generalize two sets of linguistic rules for detection of emotion causes. With the linguistic rules, we then develop a rule-based system for emotion cause detection. In addition, we propose an evaluation scheme with two phases for performance assessment. Experiments show that our system achieves a promising performance for cause occurrence detection as well as cause event detection. The current study should lay the ground for future research on the inferences of implicit information and the discovery of new information based on cause-event relation.

1 Introduction

Text-based emotion processing has attracted plenty of attention in NLP. Most research has focused on the emotion detection and classification by identifying the emotion types, for instances *happiness* and *sadness*, for a given sentence or document (Alm 2005, Mihalcea and Liu 2006, Tokuhisa et al. 2008). However, on top of this surface level information, deeper level information regarding emotions, such as the experiencer, cause, and result of an emotion, needs to be extracted and analyzed for real world applications (Alm 2009). In this paper, we aim at mining one of the crucial deep level types of information, i.e. emotion cause, which provides useful information for applications ranging from economic forecasting, public opinion mining, to product design. Emotion cause detection is a new research area in emotion processing. In emotion processing, the cause event and emotion correlation is a fertile ground for extraction and entailment of new information. As a first step towards fully automatic inference of cause-emotion correlation, we propose a text-driven, rule-based approach to emotion cause detection in this paper.

Most theories of emotion treat recognition of a triggering cause event as an integral part of emotional experience (Descartes 1649, James 1884, Plutchik 1962, Wierzbicka 1999). In this study, cause events refer to the explicitly expressed arguments or events that evoke the presence of the corresponding emotions. They are usually expressed by means of propositions, nominalizations, and nominals. For example, "*they like it*" is the cause event of the emotion *happiness* in the sentence "*I was very happy that they like it*". Note that we only take into account emotions that are explicitly expressed, which are usually presented by emotion keywords, e.g. "*This surprises me*". Implicit emotions that require inference or connotation are not processed in this first study. In this study, we first build a Chinese emotion cause annotated corpus with five primary emotions, i.e. *happiness*, *sadness*, *anger*, *fear*, and *surprise*. We then examine various linguistic cues which help detect emotion cause events: the position of cause event and experiencer relative to the emotion keyword, causative verbs (e.g. *rang4* "to cause"), action verbs (e.g. *xiang3dao4* "to think about"), epistemic markers (e.g. *kan4jian4* "to see"), conjunctions (e.g. *yin1wei4* "because"), and prepositions (e.g. *dui4yu2* "for"). With the help of

Proceedings of the NAACL HLT 2010 Workshop on Computational Approaches to Analysis and Generation of Emotion in Text, pages 45–53,
Los Angeles, California, June 2010.

these cues, a list of linguistic rules is generalized. Based on the linguistic rules, we develop a rule-based system for emotion cause detection. Experiments show that such a rule-based system performs promisingly well. We believe that the current study should lay the ground for future research on inferences and discovery of new information based on cause-event relation, such as detection of implicit emotion or cause, as well as prediction of public opinion based on cause events, etc.

The paper is organized as follows. Section 2 discusses the related work on various aspects of emotion analysis. Section 3 describes the construction of the emotion cause corpus. Section 4 presents our rule-based system for emotion cause detection. Section 5 describes its evaluation and performance. Section 6 highlights our main contributions.

2 Previous Work

We discuss previous studies on emotion analysis in this section, and underline fundamental yet unresolved issues. We survey the previous attempts on textual emotion processing and how the present study differs.

2.1 Emotion Classes

Various approaches to emotion classification were proposed in different fields, such as philosophy (Spinoza 1675, James 1884), biology (Darwin 1859, linguistics (Wierzbicka 1999, Kövecses 2000), neuropsychology (Plutchik 1962, Turner 1996), and computer science (Ortony et al. 1988, Picard 1995), as well as varying from language to language. Although there is lack of agreement among different theories on emotion classification, a small number of primary emotions are commonly assumed. Other emotions are secondary emotions which are the mixtures of the primary emotions.

Researchers have attempted to propose the list of primary emotions, varying from two to ten basic emotions (Ekman 1984, Plutchik 1980, Turner 2000). *Fear* and *anger* appear on every list, whereas *happiness* and *sadness* appear on most of the lists. These four emotions, i.e. *fear*, *anger*, *happiness*, and *sadness*, are the most common primary emotions. Other less common primary emotions are *surprise*, *disgust*, *shame*, *distress*, *guilt*, *interest*, *pain*, and *acceptance*.

In this study, we adopt Turner's emotion classification (2000), which identifies five primary emotions, namely *happiness*, *sadness*, *fear*, *anger*, and *surprise*. Turner's list consists of primary emotions agreed upon by most previous work.

2.2 Emotion Processing in Text

Textual emotion processing is still in its early stages in NLP. Most of the previous works focus on emotion classification given a known emotion context such as a sentence or a document using either rule-based (Masum et al. 2007, Chaumartin 2007) or statistical approaches (Mihalcea and Liu 2005, Kozareva et al. 2007). However, the performance is far from satisfactory. What is more, many basic issues remain unresolved, for instances, the relationships among emotions, emotion type selection, etc. Tokuhisa et al. (2008) was the first to explore both the issues of emotion detection and classification. It created a Japanese emotion-provoking event corpus for an emotion classification task using an unsupervised approach. However, only 49.4% of cases were correctly labeled. Chen et al. (2009) developed two cognitive-based Chinese emotion corpora using a semi-unsupervised approach, i.e. an emotion-sentence (sentences containing emotions) corpus and a neutral-sentence (sentences containing no emotion) corpus. They showed that studies based on the emotion-sentence corpus (~70%) outperform previous corpora.

Little research, if not none, has been done to examine the interactions between emotions and the corresponding cause events, which may make a great step towards an effective emotion classification model. The lack of research on cause events restricted current emotion analysis to simple classificatory work without exploring the potentials of the rich applications of putting emotion 'in context'. In fact, emotions can be invoked by perceptions of external events and in turn trigger reactions. The ability to detect implicit invoking causes as well as predict actual reactions will add rich dimensions to emotion analysis and lead to further research on event computing.

3 Emotion Cause Corpus

This section briefly describes how the emotion cause corpus is constructed. We first explain what an emotion cause is and discuss how emotion cause is linguistically expressed in Chinese. We then describe the corpus data and the annotation scheme. For more detailed discussion on the construction of the emotion cause corpus, please refer to Lee et al. (2010).

3.1 Cause Events

Following Talmy (2000), the cause of an emotion should be an event itself. In this work, it is called a cause event. By cause event, we do not necessarily mean the actual trigger of the emotion or what leads to the emotion. Rather, it refers to the immediate cause of the emotion, which can be the actual trigger event or the perception of the trigger event. Adapting TimeML annotation scheme (Saurí et al. 2004), events refer to situations that happen or occur. In this study, cause events specifically refer to the explicitly expressed arguments or events that are highly linked with the presence of the corresponding emotions. In Lee et al.'s (2010) corpus, cause events are categorized into two types: verbal events and nominal events. Verbal events refer to events that involve verbs (i.e. propositions and nominalizations), whereas nominal events are simply nouns (i.e. nominals). Some examples of cause event types are given in bold face in (1)-(6).

(1) *Zhe4*-DET *tou2*-CL *niu2*-cattle *de*-POSS *zhu3ren2*-owner, ***yan3kan4*-see *zi4ji3*-oneself *de*-POSS *niu2*-cattle *re3chu1*-cause *huo4*-trouble *lai2*-come *le*-ASP**, *fei1chang2-very* *hai4pa4*-frighten, *jiu4*-then *ba3*-PREP *zhe4*-DET *tou2*-CL *niu2*-cattle *di1jia4*-low price *mai4chu1*-sell.
"The owner was frightened to see that **his cattle caused troubles**, so he sold it at a low price."

(2) *Mei2*-not *xiang3dao4*-think ***ta1*-3.SG.F *shuo1*-say *de*-POSS *dou1*-all *shi4*-is *zhen1*-true *hua4*-word**, *rang4*-lead *ta1*-3.SG.M *zhen4jing1*-shocked *bu4yi3*-very.
"He was shocked that **what she said was the truth.**"

(3) *Ta1*-3.SG.M *dui4*-for *zhe4*-DET *ge4*-CL ***chong1man3*-full of *nong2hou4*-dense *ai4yi4*-love *de*-DE *xiang3fa3*-idea** *gao1xing4*-happy *de*-DE *shou3wu3zu2dao3*-flourish.
"He was very happy about **this loving idea**."

(4) ***Zhe4*-DET *ci4*-CL *yan3chu1*-performance *de*-POSS *jing1zhi4*-exquisite** *dao4shi4*-is *ling4*-cause *wo3*-1.SG *shi2fen1*-very *jing1ya4*-surprise.
"I was very surprised by **this exquisite performance**."

(5) ***Ni2ao4*-Leo *de*-POSS *hua4*-word** *hen3*-very *ling4*-make *kai3luo4lin2*-Caroline *shang1xin1*-sad.
"Caroline was very saddened by **Leo's words**."

(6) *Dui4yu2*-for ***wei4lai2-future***, *lao3shi2shuo1*-frankly *wo3*-1.SG *hen3*-very *hai4pa4*-scared.
"Frankly, I am very scared about **the future**."

The causes in (1) and (2) are propositional causes, which indicate the actual events involved in causing the emotions. The ones in (3) and (4) are nominalized causes, whereas (5) and (6) involve nominal causes

3.2 Corpus Data and Annotation Scheme

Based on the list of 91 Chinese primary emotion keywords identified in Chen et al. (2009), we extract 6,058 instances of sentences by keyword matching from the Sinica Corpus[1], which is a tagged balanced corpus of Mandarin Chinese containing a total of ten million words. Each instance contains the focus sentence with the emotion keyword "<FocusSentence>" plus the sentence before "<PrefixSentence>" and after "<SuffixSentence>" it. The extracted instances include all primary emotion keywords occurring in the Sinica Corpus except for the emotion class *happiness*, as the keywords of *happiness* exceptionally outnumber other emotion classes. In order to balance the number of each emotion class, we set the upper limit at about 1,600 instances for each primary emotion.

Note that the presence of emotion keywords does not necessarily convey emotional information due to different possible reasons such as negative polarity and sense ambiguity. Hence, by manual inspection, we remove instances that 1) are non-emotional; 2) contain highly ambiguous emotion keywords, such as *ru2yi4* "wish-fulfilled", *hai4xiu1* "to be shy", *wei2nan2* "to feel awkward", from the corpus. After the removal, the remaining instances in the emotion cause corpus is 5,629. Among the remaining instances, we also remove the emotion keywords in which the instances do not express that particular emotion and yet are emotional. The total emotion keywords in the corpus is 5,958.

For each emotional instance, two annotators manually annotate cause events of each keyword. Since more than one emotion can be present in an

[1] http://dbo.sinica.edu.tw/SinicaCorpus/

instance, the emotion keywords are tagged as <emotionword id=0>, <emotionword id=1>, and so on.

573 Y 0/shang1 xin1/Sadness
<PrefixSentence> ma1ma ye3 wen4 le ling2 ju1, dan4 shi4 mei2 you3 ren4 jian4 dao4 xiao3 bai2. </PrefixSentence> <FocusSentence>wei4 le [*01n] zhe4 jian4 shi4 [*02n] , wo3 ceng2 <emotionword id=0>shang1 xin1</emotionword> le hou2 jiu3,dan4 ye3 wu2 ji3 yu4 shi4. </FocusSentence> <SuffixSentence>mei3 dang1 zai4 kan4 dao4 bai2 se4 de qi4 gou3, bu4 jin4 hui4 xiang3 qi3 xiao3 bai2 </SuffixSentence>

573 Y 0/to be sad/Sadness
<PrefixSentence> Mom also asked the neighbors, but no one ever saw Little White. </PrefixSentence> <FocusSentence> Because of [*01n] this [*02n] , I have been feeling very <emotionword id=0> sad </emotionword> for a long time, but this did not help. </FocusSentence> <SuffixSentence> Whenever [I] see a white stray dog, [I] cannot help thinking of Little White. </SuffixSentence>

Figure 1: An Example of Cause Event Annotation

Figure 1 shows an example of annotated emotional sentences in corpus, presented as pinyin with tones, followed by an English translation. For an emotion keyword tagged as <id=0>, [*01n] marks the beginning of its cause event while [*02n] marks the end. The "0" shows which index of emotion keyword it refers to, "1" marks the beginning of the cause event, "2" marks the end, and "n" indicates that the cause is a nominal event. For an emotion keyword tagged as <id=1>, [*11e] marks the beginning of the cause event while [*12e] marks the end, in which "e" refers to a verbal event, i.e. either a proposition or a nominalization. An emotion keyword can sometimes be associated with more than one cause, in which case both causes are marked. The emotional sentences containing no explicitly expressed cause event remain as they are.

The actual number of extracted instances of each emotion class to be analyzed, the positive emotional instances, and the instances with cause events are presented in Table 1.

Table 1: Summary of Corpus Data

Emotions	No. of Instances		
	Extracted	Emotional	With Causes
Happiness	1,644	1,327	1,132 (85%)
Sadness	901	616	468 (76%)
Fear	897	689	567 (82%)
Anger	1,175	847	629 (74%)
Surprise	1,341	781	664 (85%)
Total	5,958	4,260 (72%)	3,460 (81%)

We can see that 72% of the extracted instances express emotions, and 81% of the emotional instances have a cause. The corpus contains *happiness* (1,327) instances the most and *sadness* (616) the least. For each emotion type, about 81% of the emotional sentences, on average, are considered as containing a cause event, with *surprise* the highest (85%) and *anger* the lowest (73%). This indicates that an emotion mostly occurs with the cause event explicitly expressed in the text, which confirms the prominent role of cause events in expressing an emotion.

4 A Rule-based System for Cause Detection

4.1 Linguistic Analysis of Emotion Causes

By analyzing the corpus data, we examine the correlations between emotions and cause events in terms of various linguistic cues: the position of cause event, verbs, epistemic markers, conjunctions, and prepositions. We hypothesize that these cues will facilitate the detection of emotion cause events.

First, we calculate the distribution of cause event types of each emotion as well as the position of cause events relative to emotion keywords and experiencers. The total number of emotional instances regarding each emotion is given in Table 2.

Table 2: Cause Event Position of Each Emotion

Emotions	Cause Type (%)		Cause Position (%)	
	Event	Nominal	Left	Right
Happiness	76	6	74	29
Sadness	67	8	80	20
Fear	68	13	52	48
Anger	55	18	71	26
Surprise	73	12	59	41

Table 2 suggests that emotion cause events tend to be expressed by verbal events than nominal events and that cause events tend to occur at the position to the left of the emotion keyword, with *fear* (52%) being no preference. This may be attributed to the fact that *fear* can be triggered by either factive or potential causes, which is rare for other primary emotions. For *fear*, factive causes tend to take the left position whereas potential causes tend to take the right position.

Second, we identify seven groups of linguistic cues that are highly collocated with cause events (Lee et al. 2010), as shown in Table 3.

Table 3: Seven Groups of Linguistic Cues

Group	Cue Words
I	'to cause': *rang4, ling4, shi3*
II	'to think about': e.g. *xiang3 dao4, xiang3 qi3, yi1 xiang3* 'to talk about': e.g. *shuo1dao4, jiang3dao4, tan2dao4*
III	'to say': e.g. *shuo1, dao4*
IV	'to see': e.g. *kan4dao4, kan4jian4, jian4dao4* 'to hear': e.g. *ting1dao4, ting1 shuo1* 'to know': e.g. *zhi1dao4, de2zhi1, fa1xian4* 'to exist': *you3*
V	'for' as in 'I will do this for you': *wei4, wei4le* 'for' as in 'He is too old for the job': *dui4, dui4yu2*
VI	'because': *yin1, yin1wei4, you2yu2*
VII	'is': *deshi4* 'at': *yu2* 'can': *neng2*

Group I includes three common causative verbs, and Group II a list of verbs of thinking and talking. Group III is a list of say verbs. Group IV includes four types of epistemic markers which are usually verbs marking the cognitive awareness of emotion in the complement position (Lee and Huang 2009). The epistemic markers include verbs of seeing, hearing, knowing, and existing. Group V covers some prepositions which all roughly mean 'for'. Group VI contains the conjunctions that explicitly mark the emotion cause. Group VII includes other linguistic cues that do not fall into any of the six groups. Each group of linguistic cues serves as an indicator marking the cause events in different structures of emotional constructions, in which Group I specifically marks the end of the cause events while the other six groups marks the beginning of the cause events.

4.2 Linguistic Rules for Cause Detection

We examine 100 emotional sentences of each emotion keyword randomly extracted from the development data, and generalize some rules for identifying the cause of the corresponding emotion verb (Lee 2010). The cause is considered as a proposition. It is generally assumed that a proposition has a verb which optionally takes a noun occurring before it as the subject and a noun after it as the object. However, a cause can also be expressed as a nominal. In other words, both the predicate and the two arguments are optional provided that at least one of them is present.

We also manually identify the position of the experiencer as well as the linguistic cues discussed in Section 4.1. All these components may occur in the clause containing the emotion verb (focus clause), the clause before the focus clause, or the clause after the focus clause. The abbreviations used in the rules are given as follows:

C = Cause event
E = Experiencer
K = Keyword/emotion verb
B = Clause before the focus clause
F = Focus clause/the clause containing the emotion verb
A = Clause after the focus clause

For illustration, an example of the rule description is given in Rule 1.

Rule 1:
i) C(B/F) + I(F) + E(F) + K(F)
ii) E = the nearest Na/Nb/Nc/Nh after I in F
iii) C = the nearest (N)+(V)+(N) before I in F/B

Rule 1 indicates that the experiencer (E) appears to be the nearest Na (common noun)/ Nb (proper noun)/ Nc (place noun)/ Nh (pronoun) after Group I cue words in the focus clause (F), while, at the same time, it comes before the keyword (K). Besides, the cause (C) comes before Group I cue words. We simplify the proposition as a structure of (N)+(V)+(N), which is very likely to contain the cause event. Theoretically, in identifying C, we should first look for the nearest verb occurring before Group I cue words in the focus sentence (F) or the clause before the focus clause (B), and consider this verb as an anchor. From this verb, we search to the left for the nearest noun, and consider it as the subject; we then search to the right for the nearest noun until the presence of the cue words, and consider it as the object. The detected subject, verb, and object form the cause event. In most cases, the experiencer is covertly expressed. It is, however, difficult to detect such causes in practice as causes may contain no verbs, and the two arguments are optional. Therefore, we take the clause instead of the structure of (N)+(V)+(N) as the actual cause. Examples are given in (7) and (8). For both sentences, the clause that comes before the cue word is taken as the cause event of the emotion in question.

(7) [C *yi1 la1 ke4 xi4 jun1 wu3 qi4 de bao4 guang1*], [I *shi3*] [E *lian2 he2 guo2 da4 wei2*][K ***zhen4 jing1***] .
"[C The revealing of Iraq's secret bacteriological weapons] [K shocked] [E the United Nations]."

(8) [C *heng2 shan1 jin1 tian1 ti2 chu1 ci2 cheng2*], [I *ling4*] [E *da4 ban3*] *zhi4 wei2* [K ***fen4 nu4***] 。
"[C Yokoyama submitted his resignation today], [K angered] [E the people of Osaka]."

Table 4 summarizes the generalized rules for detecting the cause events of the five primary emotions in Chinese. We identify two sets of rules: 1) the specific rules that apply to all emotional instances (i.e. rules 1-13); 2) the general rules that apply to the emotional instances in which causes are not found after applying the specific set of rules (i.e. rules 14 and 15).

Table 4: Linguistic Rules for Cause Detection

No.	Rules
1	i) C(B/F) + I(F) + E(F) + K(F) ii) E = the nearest Na/Nb/Nc/Nh after I in F iii) C = the nearest (N)+(V)+(N) before I in F/B
2	i) E(B/F) + II/IV/V/VI(B/F) + C(B/F) + K(F) ii) E=the nearest Na/Nb/Nc/Nh before II/IV/V/VI in B/F iii) C = the nearest (N)+(V)+(N) before K in F
3	i) II/IV/V/VI (B) + C(B) + E(F) + K(F) ii) E = the nearest Na/Nb/Nc/Nh before K in F iii) C = the nearest (N)+(V)+(N) after II/IV/V/VI in B
4	i) E(B/F) + K(F) + IV/VII(F) + C(F/A) ii) E = a: the nearest Na/Nb/Nc/Nh before K in F; b: the first Na/Nb/Nc/Nh in B iii) C = the nearest (N)+(V)+(N) after IV/VII in F/A
5	i) E(F)+K(F)+VI(A)+C(A) ii) E = the nearest Na/Nb/Nc/Nh before K in F iii) C = the nearest (N)+(V)+(N) after VI in A
6	i) I(F) + E(F) + K(F) + C(F/A) ii) E = the nearest Na/Nb/Nc/Nh after I in F iii) C = the nearest (N)+(V)+(N) after K in F or A
7	i) E(B/F) + *yue4* C *yue4* K "the more C the more K" (F) ii) E = the nearest Na/Nb/Nc/Nh before the first *yue4* in B/F iii) C = the V in between the two *yue4*'s in F
8	i) E(F) + K(F) + C(F) ii) E = the nearest Na/Nb/Nc/Nh before K in F iii) C = the nearest (N)+(V)+(N) after K in F
9	i) E(F) + IV(F) + K(F) ii) E = the nearest Na/Nb/Nc/Nh before IV in F iii) C = IV+(an aspectual marker) in F
10	i) K(F) + E(F) + *de* "possession"(F) + C(F) ii) E = the nearest Na/Nb/Nc/Nh after K in F iii) C = the nearest (N)+V+(N)+的+N after *de* in F
11	i) C(F) + K(F) + E(F) ii) E = the nearest Na/Nb/Nc/Nh after K in F iii) C = the nearest (N)+(V)+(N) before K in F
12	i) E(B) + K(B) + III (B) + C(F) ii) E = the nearest Na/Nb/Nc/Nh before K in F iii) C = the nearest (N)+(V)+(N) after III in F
13	i) III(B) + C(B) + E(F) + K(F) ii) E = the nearest Na/Nb/Nc/Nh before K in F iii) C = the nearest (N)+(V)+(N) after III in B
14	i) C(B) + E(F) + K(F) ii) E = the nearest Na/Nb/Nc/Nh before K in F iii) C = the nearest (N)+(V)+(N) before K in B
15	i) E(B) +C(B) + K(F) ii) E = the first Na/Nb/Nc/Nh in B iii) C = the nearest (N)+(V)+(N) before K in B

Constraints are set to each rule to filter out incorrect causes. For instances, in Rule 1, the emotion keyword cannot be followed by the words *de* "possession"/ *deshi4* "is that"/ *shi4* "is" since it is very likely to have the cause event occurring after such words; in Rule 2, the cue word in III *yuo3* "to exist" is excluded as it causes noises; whereas for Rule 4, it only applies to instances containing keywords of *happiness*, *fear*, and *surprise*.

5 Experiment

5.1 Evaluation Metrics

An evaluation scheme is designed to assess the ability to extract the cause of an emotion in context. We specifically look into two phases of the performance of such a cause recognition system. Phase 1 assesses the detection of an emotion co-occurrence with a cause; Phrase 2 evaluates the recognition of the cause texts for an emotion.

Overall Evaluation:
The definitions of related metrics are presented in Figure 2. For each emotion in a sentence, if neither the gold-standard file nor the system file has a cause, both precision and recall score 1; otherwise, precision and recall are calculated by the scoring method *ScoreForTwoListOfCauses*. As an emotion may have more than one cause, *ScoreForTwoListOfCauses* calculates the overlap scores between two lists of cause texts. Since emotion cause recognition is rather complicated, two relaxed string match scoring methods are selected to compare two cause texts, *ScoreForTwoStrings*: Relaxed Match 1 uses the minimal overlap between the gold-standard cause and the system cause. The system cause is considered as correct provided that there is at least one overlapping Chinese character; Relaxed Match 2 is more rigid which takes into account the overlap text length during scoring.

Phase 1: The Detection of Cause Occurrence

The detection of cause occurrence is considered a preliminary task for emotion cause recognition and is compounded by the fact that neutral sentences are difficult to detect, as observed in Tokuhisa et al. (2008). For Phase 1, each emotion keyword in a sentence has a binary tag: Y (i.e. with a cause) or N (without a cause). Similar to other NLP tasks, we adopt the common evaluation metrics, i.e. accuracy, precision, recall, and F score.

Phase 2: The Detection of Causes

The evaluation in Phase 2 is limited to the emotion keywords with a cause either in the gold-standard file or in the system file. The performance is calculated as in Overall Evaluation scheme.

Overall evaluation formula:

$$\text{Precision (GF, SF)} = \frac{\sum_{Si \in GF} \sum_{emj \in Si} \text{ScoreForTwoListOfCauses}\ (SList_j, GCList_j)}{\sum_{Si \in SF} \sum_{emj \in Si} 1}$$

$$\text{Recall (GF, SF)} = \frac{\sum_{Si \in GF} \sum_{emj \in Si} \text{ScoreForTwoListOfCauses}\ (SCList_j, GCList_j)}{\sum_{Si \in GF} \sum_{emj \in Si} 1}$$

Where GF and SF are the gold-standard cause file and system cause file respectively, and both files include the same sentences. S_i is a sentence, and em_j is an emotion keyword in S_i. $GCList_j$ and $SCList_j$ are the lists of the gold-standard causes and system causes respectively for the emotion keyword em_j.

ScoreForTwoListOfCauses (GCList, SCList):

If there is no cause in either GCList or SCList: Precision = 1; Recall = 1

Else:

$$\text{Precision} = \frac{\sum_{SCj \in SCList} \max_{GCi \in GCList} ScoreTwoStrings(GC_i, SC_j)}{|\, SCList \,|}$$

$$\text{Recall} = \frac{\sum_{GCi \in GCList} \max_{SCj \in SCList} ScoreTwoStrings(GC_i, SC_j)}{|\, GCList \,|}$$

ScoreForTwoStrings(GC, SC): GC is a gold-standard cause text, and SC is a system cause text.

Relaxed Match 1: If overlap existing, both precision and recall are 1; Else, both are 0.

Relaxed Match 2:

$$\text{Precision (GC, SC)} = \frac{Len(overlapText)}{Len(SC)}$$

$$\text{Recall (GC, SC)} = \frac{Len(overlapText)}{Len(GC)}$$

Figure 2: The Definitions of Metrics for Cause Detection

5.2 Results and Discussion

We use 80% sentences as the development data, and 20% as the test data. The baseline is designed as follows: find a verb to the left of the keyword in question, and consider the clause containing the verb as a cause.

Table 5 shows the performances of the overall evaluation. We find that the overall performances of our system have significantly improved using Relaxed Match 1 and Relaxed Match 2 by 19% and 19% respectively. Although the overall performance of our system (47.95% F-score for Relaxed Match 1 and 41.67% for Relaxed Match 2) is not yet very high, it marks a good start for emotion

	Relaxed Match 1			Relaxed Match 2		
	Precision	Recall	F-score	Precision	Recall	F-score
Baseline	25.94	31.99	28.65	17.77	29.62	22.21
Our System	45.06	51.24	47.95	39.89	43.63	41.67

Table 5: The Overall Performances

	Baseline			Rule-based System		
Emotions	Precision	Recall	F-score	Precision	Recall	F-score
With causes	99.42	79.74	88.50	96.871	80.851	88.139
Without causes	4.39	66.67	8.23	13.158	52.632	21.053

Table 7: The Detailed Performances in Phase 1

	Relaxed Match 1			Relaxed Match 2		
	Precision	Recall	F-score	Precision	Recall	F-score
Baseline	25.37	39.28	30.83	17.09	36.29	23.24
Our System	44.64	61.30	51.66	39.18	51.68	44.57

Table 8: The Detailed Performances in Phase 2

	Baseline	Rule-based System
Accuracy	79.56	79.38

Table 6: The Overall Accuracy in Phase 1

cause detection and extraction.

Table 6 and 7 show the performances of the baseline and our rule-based system in Phase 1. Table 6 shows the overall accuracy, and Table 7 shows the detailed performances. In Table 6, we find that our system and the baseline have similar high accuracy scores. Yet Table 7 shows that both systems achieve a high performance for emotions with a cause, but much worse for emotions without a cause. It is important to note that even though the naive baseline system has comparably high performance with our rule-based system in judging whether there is a cause in context, this result is biased by two facts. First, as the corpus contains more than 80% of sentences with emotion, a system which is biased toward detecting a cause, such as the baseline system, naturally performs well. In addition, once the actual cause is examined, we can see that the baseline actually detects a lot of false positives in the sense that the cause it identifies is only correct in 4.39%. Our rule-based system shows great promise in being able to deal with neutral sentences effectively and being able to detect the correct cause at least three times more often than the baseline.

Table 8 shows the performances in Phase 2. Comparing to the baseline, we find that our rules improve the performance of cause recognition using Relaxed Match 1 and 2 scoring by 21% and 21% respectively. On the one hand, the 7% gap in F-score between Relaxed Match 1 and 2 also indicates that our rules can effectively locate the clause of a cause. On the other hand, the rather low performances of the baseline show that most causes recognized by the baseline are wrong although the baseline effectively detects the cause occurrence, as indicated in Table 7. In addition, we check the accuracy (precision) and contribution (recall) of each rule. In descending order, the top four accurate rules are: Rules 7, 10, 11, and 1; and the top four contributive rules are: Rules 2, 15, 14, and 3.

6 Conclusion

Emotion processing has been a great challenge in NLP. Given the fact that an emotion is often triggered by cause events and that cause events are integral parts of emotion, we propose a linguistic-driven rule-based system for emotion cause detection, which is proven to be effective. In particular, we construct a Chinese emotion cause corpus annotated with emotions and the corresponding cause events. Since manual detection of cause events is labor-intensive and time-consuming, we intend to use the emotion cause corpus to produce automatic extraction system for emotion cause events with machine learning methods. We believe that our rule-based system is useful for many real world applications. For instance, the information regarding causal relations of emotions is important for product design, political evaluation, etc. Such a system also shed light on emotion processing as the detected emotion cause events can serve as clues for the identification of implicit emotions.

References

Alm, C. O., D. Roth and R. Sproat. 2005. Emotions from Text: Machine Learning for Text-based Emotion Prediction. In *Proceedings of the Human Language Technology Conference and the 2005 Conference on Empirical Methods in Natural Language Processing,* Vancouver, Canada, 6-8 October, pp. 579-586.

Alm, C. O. 2009. *Affect in Text and Speech.* VDM Verlag: Saarbrücken.

Chen, Y., S. Y. M. Lee and C.-R. Huang. 2009. A Cognitive-based Annotation System for Emotion Computing. In *Proceedings of the Third Linguistic Annotation Workshop (The LAW III), ACL 2009.*

Chaumartin, F.-R. 2007. A Knowledgebased System for Headline Sentiment Tagging. In *Proceedings of the 4th International Workshop on Semantic Evaluations.*

Darwin, C. 1859. *On the Origin of Species by Means of Natural Selection.* London: John Murray.

Descartes, R. 1649. The Passions of the Soul. In J. Cottingham et al. (Eds), *The Philosophical Writings of Descartes.* Vol. 1, 325-404.

Ekman, P. 1984. Expression and the Nature of Emotion. In Scherer, K. and P. Ekman (Eds.), *Approaches to Emotion.* Hillsdale, N.J.: Lawrence Erlbaum. 319-343.

James, W. 1884. What is an Emotion? *Mind*, 9(34):188–205.

Kozareva, Z., B. Navarro, S. Vazquez, and A. Nibtoyo. 2007. UA-ZBSA: A Headline Emotion Classification through Web Information. In *Proceedings of the 4th International Workshop on Semantic Evaluations.*

Kövecses, Z. 2000. *Metaphor and Emotion: Language, Culture and Body in Human Feeling.* Cambridge: Cambridge University Press.

Lee, S. Y. M. 2010. *A Linguistic Approach towards Emotion Detection and Classification.* Ph.D. Dissertation. Hong Kong.

Lee, S. Y. M., C. Ying, and C.-R. Huang. 2010. Emotion Cause Events: Corpus Construction and Analysis. In *Proceedings of The Seventh International Conference on Language Resources and Evaluation (LREC 2010).* May 19-21. Malta.

Lee, S. Y. M. and C.-R. Huang. 2009. Explicit Epistemic Markup of Causes in Emotion Constructions. The Fifth International Conference on Contemporary Chinese Grammar. Hong Kong. November 27 - December 1.

Masum, S. M., H. Prendinger, and M. Ishizuka. 2007. Emotion Sensitive News Agent: An Approach Towards User Centric Emotion Sensing from the News. In *Proceedings of the IEEE/WIC/ACM International Conference on Web Intelligence.*

Mihalcea, R. and H. Liu. 2006. A Corpus-based Approach to Finding Happiness. In *Proceedings of the AAAI Spring Symposium on Computational Approaches to Weblogs.*

Ortony A., G. L. Clone, and A. Collins. 1988. *The Cognitive Structure of Emotions.* New York: Cambridge University Press.

Picard, R.W. 1995. *Affective Computing.* Cambridge. MA: The MIT Press.

Plutchik, R. 1980. *Emotions: A Psychoevolutionary Synthesis.* New York: Harper & Row.

Saurí, R., J. Littman, R. Knippen, R. Gaizauskas, A. Setzer, and J. Pustejovsky. 2004. *TimeML Annotation Guidelines.* http://www.timeml.org.

Spinoza, B. 1985. *Ethics.* In E. Curley, *The Collected Works of Spinoza.* Princeton, N.J.: Princeton University Press. Vol 1.

Talmy, L. 2000. *Toward a Cognitive Semantics.* Vol. 1and 2. Cambridge: MIT Press.

Tokuhisa, R., K. Inui, and Y. Matsumoto. 2008. Emotion Classification Using Massive Examples Extracted from the Web. In *Proceedings of COLING.*

Turner, J. H. 1996. The Evolution of Emotions in Humans: A Darwinian-Durkheimian Analysis. *Journal for the Theory of Social Behaviour*, 26:1-34.

Turner, J. H. 2000. *On the Origins of Human Emotions: A Sociological Inquiry into the Evolution of Human Affect.* California: Stanford University Press.

Wierzbicka, A. 1999. *Emotions Across Languages and Cultures: Diversity and Universals.* Cambridge: Cambridge University Press.

Wishful Thinking
Finding suggestions and 'buy' wishes from product reviews

J. Ramanand
BFS Innovations
Cognizant Technology Solutions
Pune, India
ramanand.janardhanan
@cognizant.com

Krishna Bhavsar
BFS Innovations
Cognizant Technology Solutions
Pune, India
krishna.bhavsar
@cognizant.com

Niranjan Pedanekar
BFS Innovations
Cognizant Technology Solutions
Pune, India
niranjan.pedanekar
@cognizant.com

Abstract

This paper describes methods aimed at solving the novel problem of automatically discovering 'wishes' from (English) documents such as reviews or customer surveys. These wishes are sentences in which authors make suggestions (especially for improvements) about a product or service or show intentions to purchase a product or service. Such 'wishes' are of great use to product managers and sales personnel, and supplement the area of sentiment analysis by providing insights into the minds of consumers. We describe rules that can help detect these 'wishes' from text. We evaluate these methods on texts from the electronic and banking industries.

1 Introduction

Various products and business services are used by millions of customers each day. For the makers of these products & services, studying these customer experiences is critical to understanding customer satisfaction and making decisions about possible improvements to the products. Thanks to the advent of weblogs, online consumer forums, and product comparison sites, consumers are actively expressing their opinions online. Most of these reviews are now available on the web, usually at little or no cost. Moreover, these are available for a variety of domains, such as financial services, telecom services, consumer goods etc.

Automated analysis of opinions using such reviews could provide a cheaper and faster means of obtaining a sense of such customer opinions, thus supplementing more traditional survey methods. In addition, automated analysis can significantly shorten the time taken to find insights into the customer's mind and actions.

Sentiment analysis of texts such as product reviews, call center notes, and customer surveys aims to automatically infer opinions expressed by people with regards to various topics of interest. A sentiment analysis exercise classifies the overall opinion of a review document into positive, neutral, or negative classes. It may also identify sentiments at a finer granularity, i.e. recognizing the mix of opinions about the topic(s) expressed in the text. However, industry analysts (Strickland, 2009) report some common problems with the results of these exercises:

1. The results (usually numerical scores split across positive, negative, neutral classes) are hard to meaningfully interpret.
2. These results are more useful to certain roles and domains. Brand, reputation, and service managers in media and retail industries find sentiment analysis more useful than product managers or sales teams in various industries.
3. The results do not *'indicate user action'* i.e. opinions do not help identify a future action of the author based on the comments. An example of this is: does the consumer indicate that he intends to stop using a service after a negative experience?
4. The reader of the report often asks *"what do I do next?"* i.e. the results are not always 'actionable'. There is a gap between understanding the results and taking an appropriate action.

Proceedings of the NAACL HLT 2010 Workshop on Computational Approaches to Analysis and Generation of Emotion in Text, pages 54–61,
Los Angeles, California, June 2010.

This has led to interest in identifying aspects indirectly related to sentiment analysis, such as gauging possible loss of clientele or tapping into desires to purchase a product. Many of these methods attempt to identify *'user intent'*.

In this paper, we propose rule-based methods to identify two kinds of 'wishes' – one, the desire to see improvement in a product, and the other to purchase a product. These methods have been designed & tested using a variety of corpora containing product reviews, customer surveys, and comments from consumer forums in domains such as electronics and retail banking. From our reading, there has been only one published account of identifying 'wishes' (including suggestions) and no known work on identifying purchasing wishes. We hope to build approaches towards more comprehensive identification of such content.

The paper is organized as follows. We begin by discussing some of the work related to this upcoming area. Section 3 details our characterization of wishes. Section 4 describes the corpora used for these methods. We discuss our proposed algorithms and rules in Sections 5 & 6, including a discussion of the results. Finally, we wrap up with our conclusions and directions for future work.

2 Related Work

The principal context of our work is in the area of sentiment analysis, which is now a widely researched area because of the abundance of commentaries from weblogs, review sites, and social networking sites. In particular, we are interested in the analysis of product reviews (Dave et al., 2003; Hu and Liu, 2004), as well as its application to more service-oriented industries such as banks.

We have built a sentiment analyzer that can analyze product and service reviews from a variety of domains. This also accepts social networking commentaries, customer surveys and news articles. The implementation follows a lexicon-based approach, similar to the one described in Ding et al. (2008), using lexicons for product attributes and opinion words for basic sentiment analysis.

Our work is not a sub-task of sentiment analysis, but supplements the area. A similar example of a classification task that works on the sentence level and is also related to sentiment analysis is Jindal and Liu (2006) which aims to identify comparisons between two entities in texts such as product reviews.

Goldberg et al. (2009) introduced the novel task of identifying wishes. This used a "WISH" corpus derived from a web site that collected New Year's wishes. Goldberg et al. (2009) studied the corpus in detail, describing the nature, geography, and scope of topics found in them. The paper also looked at building 'wish detectors', which were applied on a corpus of political comments and product reviews. A mix of manual templates and SVM-based text classifiers were used. A method to identify more templates was also discussed.

Our task, though similar to the above problem, has some novel features. In particular, there are two significant differences from Goldberg et al. (2009). We are interested in two specific kinds of wishes: sentences that make suggestions about existing products, and sentences that indicate the writer is interested in purchasing a product. (These are described in detail in Section 3.) Secondly, our interest is limited to product reviews, and not to social or political wishes.

In Requirements Engineering, some methods of analyzing requirement documents have used linguistic techniques to understand and correlate requirements. These are somewhat related to our task, aiming to detect desired features in the project to be executed. och Dag et al. (2005) has some useful discussions on this topic.

Kröll and Strohmaier (2009) study the idea of Intent Analysis, noting a taxonomy of Human Intentions, which could be useful in future discussions on the topic.

3 What are Wishes

3.1 Defining Wishes

A dictionary definition (Goldberg et al. (2009)) of a *"wish"* is *"a desire or hope for something to happen."* Goldberg et al. (2009) discuss different types of wishes, ranging from political to social to business. In our case, we limit our interest to comments about products and services. In particular, we are interested in two specific kinds of wishes.

3.2 Suggestion Wishes

These are sentences where the commenter wishes for a change in an existing product or service. These range from specific requests for new product features and changes in existing behaviour, or an indication that the user is unhappy with the current experience. Examples[1]:

1. *I'd love for the iPod shuffle to also mirror as a pedometer.*
2. *It would be much better if they had more ATMs in my area.*

We also include sentences that do not fully elaborate on the required change, but could serve as a pointer to a nearby region that may contain the required desire. Examples of these:

1. *I wish they'd do this.*
2. *My wish list would be as follows:*

It is important to note the difference between our definition of wishes and that in Goldberg et al. (2009). That study seeks to discover any sentence expressing any desire. For instance, Goldberg et al. (2009) marks the following as wishes:

1. *I shouldn't have been cheap, should have bought a Toshiba.*
2. *hope to get my refund in a timely manner.*

In our approach, we do not treat these as wishes since they do not suggest any improvements.

In some cases, improvements could be inferred from a negative opinion about the product. The implication is that the customer would be happier if the problem could be fixed. Examples:

1. *"My only gripe is the small size of the camera body"* which implies *"I wish the camera was bigger"*.
2. *"The rubber flap that covers the usb port seems flimsy"* which implies *"I wish the rubber flap was more robust"*.

We do not address such implicit wishes.

3.3 Purchasing Wishes

These are sentences where the author explicitly expresses the desire to purchase a product. In some cases, a preferred price range is also indicated.

Examples:

1. *I have a Canon digital rebel xt, I am looking for a lens that will take sports actions football shots at night.*
2. *I want to purchase a cell phone range 12-15000/-... please suggest me some good and stylish phones?*
3. *We are also thinking of buying a condo in a few months...*

4 Corpora for Design and Evaluation

4.1 Suggestion Wishes

As part of building and testing our in-house sentiment analyzer, we collected a variety of texts from different sources such as popular consumer review sites (such as Epinions.com and MouthShut.com) and weblogs. These primarily belonged to the domains of electronics and retail banking. Of these, we chose reviews about the Apple iPod and a collection of banking reviews about five leading US banks. We also used customer surveys conducted for two products of a financial services company[2]. The sizes of the corpora are summarized in Table 1.

Some observations about these texts:

1. The texts are in American or British English and are largely well-formed.

2. They cover both reviews of products and descriptions of customer service.

3. The customer surveys consisted of sections for positives and negatives feedback, with an optional 'suggestions' section.

4. Wish sentences in the reviews were infrequent (on average, less than 1% of the total sentences). The surveys had a much larger presence of wishes (about 5% on average).

In addition, Goldberg et al. (2009) has made available a WISH corpus, which is a sample of 7614 sentences consisting of sentences from political discussions and product reviews. Since we are only interested in the latter, we evaluated our algorithm only on the product review sentences (1235 in number). 3% (41 sentences[3]) of these have been labeled as wishes.

[1] All sentences are taken from review sites such as epinions.com

[2] Anonymous for confidentiality reasons

[3] In the WISH corpus, 149 (12%) are marked as wishes; however we only chose those wishes that suggest improvements.

In a pre-processing step, individual sentences in the corpora were identified using GATE's (Cunningham, 2002) sentence splitter.

4.2 Purchasing Wishes

Similar to our collection of sentences for suggestions, we collected texts from review sites and consumer forums (such as Alibaba.com and Yahoo! Answers) that not only reviewed products and shared complaints but also allowed users to post requests for purchases.

The corpus consisted of 1579 sentences about the following products: Apple iPhone, Cameras, Desktop PCs, and a mix of Credit Cards from four leading Indian and American banks.

5 Finding Suggestions

5.1 Approach

The input to our system consists of the following:

1. Datasets containing sentences.
2. ATTRLEX[4]: A lexicon of product attributes for each of the domains. (e.g. the iPod attributes were words like *'battery'*, *'interface'* etc.)
3. POSLEX: A lexicon of positive opinions (words such as *'good'*, *'better'*, *'fast'*).
4. NEGLEX: A lexicon of negation words (these are words that invert the opinion of a sentence. e.g: *'not'*, *'wouldn't'*)

We began by manually classifying sentences in samples from each of the corpora as 'wishes' or 'non-wishes'. We then looked for common phrases and words across all these wishes to derive patterns and rules.

Initial analysis led to some proto-rules. These rules were then refined by using further analysis and in some cases, decision trees. The rules are grouped as follows.

5.1.1 Rules based on modal verbs

A majority of the wishes had pivotal phrases involving modal verbs such as *"would"*, *"could"*, *"should"* etc. Examples:

1. *It would be a much more valuable service if they would fix this flaw.*
2. *It might be nice if one could drag-and-drop music files and have the iPod reconstruct its index on-the-fly.*
3. *I would prefer the unit to have a simple on off switch.*

This led to the following rules:

a. modal verb + auxiliary verb + positive opinion word

Match sentences which contain the pattern:
<modal verb> <auxiliary verb> {window of size 3} <positive opinion word>

Where

Modal verb belongs to {*may, might, could, would, will, should*}
Auxiliary verb belongs to {*be, have been*}
Positive Opinion word belongs to POSLEX

The positive word should appear to the right of the modal verb in a pre-defined window size (usually 3 to 5).

b. modal verb + preference verb

Match sentences which contain the pattern:
<modal verb> {window of size 3} <preference verb>

Where

Modal verb belongs to {*may, might, would, will*}
Preference verb belongs to {*love, like, prefer, suggest*}

c. Other rules

Match sentences containing:
"should be able" or
"should come with" or
"could come with"

5.1.2 The *"needs to"* rule

Sentences containing the phrase *"needs to"* are candidate wishes, such as in the examples:

1. *Apple needs to step it up and get better longer lasting batteries.*
2. *Their customer service representatives need to be educated in assisting customers.*
3. *need to be able to configure the boxes.*

[4] These lexicons were built by semi-automated means using components built for our in-house sentiment analyzer which help detect opinions and attributes for a domain from related texts

For this pattern, we created a decision tree model with the following features:
1. Presence of negation word to the left of *"needs to"*
2. Presence of a *'product attribute'* word to the left
3. Whether the sentence is interrogative
4. Subject of the sentence from the list: {*I, you, s/he, we, this, that, those, it, they, one, someone, somebody, something*}

Based on analysis and the combination suggested by the decision tree experiments, we formulated rules. Some of these rules are as follows:
1. Interrogative sentences or those with a negation word to the left of *"need to"* are not wishes.
2. If the product attribute is present (usually as the subject), the sentence is a wish.
3. If the subject of the sentence is one of *"this, that, these"*, the sentence is likely to be a wish. When the subject is one of *"I, you, one"*, the sentence is not a wish.

5.1.3 Other rules

Sentences containing the patterns:
1. *"I wish"*: along with filters such as the subject (*"they, you, product"*) etc. can be matched as wishes.
2. *"hopefully"* or *"I hope"*
3. *"should be able to"* or *"should come with"*

These rules match very infrequently in the dataset. A summary of rule accuracy can be seen in Table 3.

5.2 Results

5.2.1 Precision of Rules

Type	Total sen-tences	No. of predicted wishes	No. of correct wishes	Precision
iPod	21147	90	53	58.89%
Banking	15408	75	23	30.67%
Product 1	4240	224	187	83.48%
Product 2	6850	355	284	80.00%
WISH corpus	1236	28	16	57.14%

Table 1 Precision of wish identification for various data sets

5.2.2 Recall of Rules

Recall was calculated on a 10% random sample from each data set, except in case of the WISH corpus, where all sentences were taken into account.

Type	No. of correctly predicted wishes in the sample	No. of actual wishes in the sample	Recall
iPod	7	14	50.0%
Banking	3	5	60.0%
Product 1	24	45	53.3%
Product 2	28	70	40.0%
WISH corpus	16	41	39.0%

Table 2 Recall of wish identification

5.2.3 Rule Analysis

This table analyses performance of the top 3 most frequently matched rules. For each type of data, the first row shows the number of wishes predicted by each rule. The succeeding row shows the corresponding precision.

Type/Rule	Modal, aux, positive opinion	Modal, preference	"Needs to"	Others
iPod	24	8	7	14
	57%	53%	43%	82%
Banking	14	17	7	2
	37%	85.0%	50%	28.5%
Product 1	89	56	25	17
	87%	83.6%	71%	85%
Product 2	146	25	50	30
	90%	71.4%	71%	90.9%
WISH Corpus	7	2	3	4
	63.6%	50%	50%	57.1%

Table 3 Rule Analysis

5.3 Comments on Results

Wishes occur very infrequently in reviews, where authors may or may not choose to talk about improvements. Surveys produced more wishes because of the design and objectives of the survey. Also, the language used in suggesting improvements was more consistent across authors, making it easier to catch them. Wishes could be made about existing product attributes, but several wish-

wishes were about newer aspects. This could help product managers envisage features that their customers are asking for.

Experiments on the banking reviews showed the worst results. The dataset had very few wishes and the language used was usually part of a narrative, which threw up a lot of false positives. It could also be that the nature of the collected dataset was such that it did not contain sufficient number of wishes.

Some of the false positives were difficult to avoid. Take an example such as:
I wish it will be a better year.

Though it is a 'wish' in general, this does not fit our definition of product suggestion though it fits a rule well. More semantic or contextual analysis may be required in this case. We do not filter out sentences that do not refer to already published product attributes since authors may be talking about adding completely new features, such as in the case:
I wish it will be in magazine form next year.

Of the rules, the first rule (modal + auxiliary + positive opinion word) had the highest contribution to make. The second rule was more consistent in detecting correct wishes. Incidentally, the "needs to" rule for banking reviews outperforms the results for iPod sentences – the only time this happens.

Different patterns may be applicable for different domains and types of texts. A possible approach to improving results would be to have a 'rule selection' phase were rules that fall below a certain threshold are discarded.

6 Finding Buy Wishes

6.1 Approach

Similar to finding suggestions, we assembled a corpus of sentences for various products and services, this time from forums that also contain buy-sell sections. These may contain comments like:
1. I am trying to find where I can purchase the complete 1st season of Army Wives-can you help me?
2. I am seriously looking for a new bank...
3. I want to give a new year's present to my 5 year old nephew. My budget is 1500 Rupees.

We derived proto-rules and refined them by manual analysis and decision trees. The pattern of each rule is:

...*<rule phrase> <common sub-rule>*...

If a sentence contains such a pattern, it is deemed to be a buy wish.

To begin, we describe a common sub-rule that is used with all rules.

6.1.1 Buy Identification common sub-rule

This depends on the following three aspects:

a. A *'buy verb'* from among {*find, buy, purchase, get, acquire*} should be present

b. Absence of a negation word (from NEGLEX) to the left of rule phrase

c. Subjects:

The subject should not be one of these: {*you, one, they, someone, those*}

The subject could be one of these: {*I, we, me*}

6.1.2 Rule phrases

Rule phrases are one of the following

1. *"want to"*
2. *"desire to"*
3. *"would like to"*
4. *"where can/do I"*
5. *"place to"*
6. *"going to"*
7. *"looking to/for"*
8. *"searching to/for"*
9. *"interested in"*

Of these, in rules involving phrases 7, 8, and 9, we also check if there are any past tense verbs preceding rule phrase. In such cases, we do not classify the sentence as a wish. For phrase 5, interrogative sentences are also ignored.

6.2 Results

6.2.1 Precision

Type	Total sentences	No. of predicted wishes	No. of correct wishes	Precision
iPhone	193	43	41	95.34%
iPod	176	48	37	79.54%
Credit Cards	865	6	4	66.67%

Canon Cameras	170	40	39	97.50%
Desktop PCs	175	36	34	94.44%

Table 4 Precision of wish identification for various data sets

6.2.2 Recall[5]

Type	No. of expected wishes	No. of correctly predicted wishes	Recall
iPhone	80	41	51.25%
iPod	54	37	68.51%
Canon Camera	65	39	60.00%
Desktop PCs	66	34	51.52%

Table 5 Recall of wish identification

6.2.3 Rule Analysis

This table analyses the precision of the tope three rules that matched the most sentences.

Rule Phrase	No. of matched sentences	No. of correct matches	*Precision*
Looking for	98	85	86.73%
Want to	24	22	91.67%
Interested In	6	6	100%

Table 6 Rule Analysis

6.3 Comments on Results

Buy wishes tend to occur only in forums where buyers can advertise their search and hope to receive advice or meet prospective sellers. In addition to sites dedicated to specific products, social networks such as Twitter[6] also provide such a platform. This is in contrast to regular weblogs.

The results for all the electronic products showed a precision of about 80% or more. As in the case of suggestion wishes, wishes were very rare in the credit cards postings.

The recall in all cases was above 50%. Buy wish sentences matching The *"looking for"* and *"want to buy/purchase"* rules were common. An observation was that in some cases, people would simply list the expected attributes of the product they were looking for. Because of the nature of the forum, other users would interpret it as a buy/sell request. We could not separate these sentences from other kinds of sentences in the data set.

In most cases, the sentences were terse and used phrases like *"we need"* and *"seeking"*. Further expanding the rule phrases & sub-phrases to include their synonyms is likely to improve recall.

7 Conclusions and Future Work

This paper described two novel problems in the world of opinion and intention mining, that of identifying 'wishes' relating to improvements in products and for purchasing them. These are likely to be directly useful to business users. We build approaches towards such detections, by the use of English-language patterns. To the best of our knowledge, this is the first attempt at solving such problems.

The approach for identifying suggestions works best for texts that contain explicit wishes, especially customer surveys. They work reasonably well for (electronic) product reviews. In contrast, reviews about banking services tend to contain narratives and have more implicit opinions and wishes. Similarly, the algorithm to detect buy wishes works well for electronic product reviews in comparison to banking products.

Wish statements appear very infrequently in reviews. Existing sentiment analysis corpora may not be sufficient to use in creating wish detectors. Augmenting corpora such as the WISH dataset or creating even more robust and representative corpora would be a must for such exercises. A possible source could be the "Make A Wish" foundation.

One of the possible future directions could be to look at tense and mood analysis of sentences. Wish sentences come under the 'optative' mood. Techniques that help identify such a mood could provide additional hints to the nature of the sentence. More features related to parts of speech and semantic roles could be explored.

We also plan to look at machine learning approaches, but the availability of good quality training data is a limiting factor.

The emergence of social networking sites may provide more challenges for such detectors. Sites like Twitter are already being used to advertise

[5] The credit cards set had very few actual wishes (less than 10) with which to carry out a meaningful recall exercise
[6] http://twitter.com

intentions to buy or sell. However, the nature of discourse in these media is markedly different to regular reviews and forums due to size restrictions.

Any system that helps business users to identify new customers or engage with existing ones would need to tap into all these emerging channels. The need for such detectors is likely to increase in the future, thus providing further motivation to study this nascent area.

References

Hamish Cunningham, Diana Maynard, Kalina Bontcheva, and Tablan, Valentin. *GATE: A framework and graphical development environment for robust NLP tools and applications.* 2002

Kushal Dave, Steve Lawrence, and David M. Pennock. *Mining the peanut gallery: Opinion extraction and semantic classification of product reviews.* Proceedings of the 12th international conference on World Wide Web. 2003.

Minqing Hu and Bing Liu. *Mining and summarizing customer reviews.* Proceedings of the tenth ACM SIGKDD international conference on Knowledge discovery and data mining. 2004.

Andrew B. Goldberg, Nathanael Fillmore, David Andrzejewski, Zhiting Xu, Z, Bryan Gibson, and Xiaojin Zhu. *May all your wishes come true: A study of wishes and how to recognize them.* Proceedings of Human Language Technologies: The 2009 Annual Conference of the North American Chapter of the Association for Computational Linguistics. 2009.

Nitin Jindal and Bing Liu. *Identifying comparative sentences in text documents.* Proceedings of the 29th annual international ACM SIGIR conference on Research and development in information retrieval. 2006.

Mark Kröll and Markus Strohmaier, M. *Analyzing human intentions in natural language text.* Proceedings of the fifth international conference on Knowledge capture. 2009.

Johan Natt och Dag, Vincenzo Gervasi, Sjaak Brinkkemper, and Björn Regnell, B. *A linguistic engineering approach to large-scale requirements management.* Managing Natural Language Requirements in Large-Scale Software Development. Vol 22-1. 2005.

Marta Strickland. *Five Reasons Sentiment Analysis Won't Ever Be Enough.* http://threeminds.organic.com/2009/09/five_reasons_sentiment_analysi.html. 2009.

Xiaowen Ding, Bing Liu, and Philip S.Yu. *A holistic lexicon-based approach to opinion mining.* Proceedings of the international conference on Web search and web data mining. 2008.

Evaluation of Unsupervised Emotion Models to Textual Affect Recognition

Sunghwan Mac Kim
School of Electrical
and Information Engineering
University of Sydney
Sydney, Australia
skim1871@uni.sydney.edu.au

Alessandro Valitutti
Department of Cognitive Science
and Education
University of Trento
Trento, Italy
a.valitutti@email.unitn.it

Rafael A. Calvo
School of Electrical
and Information Engineering
University of Sydney
Sydney, Australia
rafa@ee.usyd.edu.au

Abstract

In this paper we present an evaluation of new techniques for automatically detecting emotions in text. The study estimates categorical model and dimensional model for the recognition of four affective states: *Anger*, *Fear*, *Joy*, and *Sadness* that are common emotions in three datasets: SemEval-2007 "Affective Text", ISEAR (International Survey on Emotion Antecedents and Reactions), and children's fairy tales. In the first model, WordNet-Affect is used as a linguistic lexical resource and three dimensionality reduction techniques are evaluated: Latent Semantic Analysis (LSA), Probabilistic Latent Semantic Analysis (PLSA), and Non-negative Matrix Factorization (NMF). In the second model, ANEW (Affective Norm for English Words), a normative database with affective terms, is employed. Experiments show that a categorical model using NMF results in better performances for SemEval and fairy tales, whereas a dimensional model performs better with ISEAR.

1 Introduction

Supervised and unsupervised approaches have been used to automatically recognize expressions of emotion in text such as *happiness*, *sadness*, *anger*, etc… Supervised learning techniques have the disadvantage that large annotated datasets are required for training. Since the emotional interpretations of a text can be highly subjective, more than one annotator is needed, and this makes the process of the annotation very time consuming and expensive. For this reason, unsupervised methods are normally preferred in the realm of Natural Language Processing (NLP) and emotions.

Supervised and unsupervised techniques have been compared before. (Strapparava and Mihalcea 2008) describe the comparison between a supervised (Naïve Bayes) and an unsupervised (Latent Semantic Analysis - LSA) method for recognizing six basic emotions.

These techniques have been applied to many areas, particularly in improving Intelligent Tutoring Systems. For example, (D'Mello, Craig et al. 2008) used LSA but for detecting utterance types and affect in students' dialogue within Autotutor. (D'Mello, Graesser et al. 2007) proposed five categories for describing the affect states in student-system dialogue.

Significant differences arise not only between these two types of techniques but also between different emotion models, and these differences have significant implications in all these areas. While considering emotions and learning, (Kort, Reilly et al. 2001) proposed (but provided no empirical evidence) a model that combines two emotion models, placing categories in a valence-arousal plane. This mixed approach has also been used in other domains such as blog posts where (Aman and Szpakowicz 2007) studied how to identify emotion categories as well as emotion intensity. To date, many researchers have, however, utilized and evaluated supervised methods, mainly based on the categorical emotion model.

In this study, the goal is to evaluate the merits of two conceptualizations of emotions (a *categorical model* and a *dimensional model*) in which an unsupervised approach is used. The evaluation incorporates three dimensionality re-

Proceedings of the NAACL HLT 2010 Workshop on Computational Approaches to Analysis and Generation of Emotion in Text, pages 62–70,
Los Angeles, California, June 2010. ©2010 Association for Computational Linguistics

duction methods and two linguistic lexical resources.

The rest of the paper is organized as follows: In Section 2 we present representative research of the emotion models used to capture the affective states of a text. Section 3 describes the techniques of affect classification utilizing lexical resources. More specifically, it describes the role of emotion models and lexical resources in the affect classification. In addition, we give an overview of the dimension reduction methods used in the study. In Section 4 we go over the affective datasets used. Section 5 provides the results of the evaluation, before coming to our discussion in Section 6.

2 Emotion Models

There are two significantly different models for representing emotions: the *categorical model* and *dimensional model* (Russell 2003).

The categorical model assumes that there are discrete emotional categories such as Ekman's six basic emotions - *anger*, *disgust*, *fear*, *joy*, *sadness*, and *surprise* - (Ekman 1992). There are a number of primary and unrelated emotions in the model. Each emotion is characterized by a specific set of features, expressing eliciting conditions or responses. Some researchers have argued that a different set of emotions is required for different domains. For instance, the following emotion classes are used in the field of teaching and education: *boredom*, *delight*, *flow*, *confusion*, *frustration*, and *surprise*. The advantage of such a representation is that it represents human emotions intuitively with easy to understand emotion labels.

A second approach is the dimensional model, which represents affects in a dimensional form (Russell 2003). Emotional states are related each other by a common set of dimensions (e.g. valence or arousal) and are generally defined in a two or three dimensional space. Each emotion occupies some location in this space. A valence dimension indicates *positive* and *negative* emotions on different ends of the scale. The arousal dimension differentiates *excited* vs. *calm* states. Sometimes a third, dominance dimension is used to differentiate if the subject feels in control of the situation or not.

The categorical model and the dimensional model have two different methods for estimating the actual emotional states of a person. In the former, a person is usually required to choose one emotion out of an emotion set that represents the best feeling. On the other hand, the latter exploits rating scales for each dimension like the Self Assessment Manikin (SAM) (Lang 1980), which consists of pictures of manikins, to estimate the degree of valence, arousal, and dominance.

3 Automatic Affect Classification

3.1 Categorical classification with features derived from WordNet-Affect

WordNet-Affect (Strapparava and Valitutti 2004) is an affective lexical repository of words referring to emotional states. WordNet-Affect extends WordNet by assigning a variety of affect labels to a subset of synsets representing affective concepts in WordNet (emotional synsets). In addition, WordNet-Affect has an additional hierarchy of affective domain labels. There are publicly available lists relevant to the six basic emotion categories extracted from WordNet-Affect and we used four of the six lists of emotional words among them for our experiment.

In addition to WordNet-Affect, we exploited a Vector Space Model (VSM) in which terms and textual documents can be represented through a term-by-document matrix. More specifically, terms are encoded as vectors, whose components are co-occurrence frequencies of words in corpora documents. Frequencies are weighted according to the log-entropy with respect to a *tf-idf* weighting schema (Yates and Neto 1999). Finally, the number of dimensions is reduced through the dimension reduction methods.

The vector-based representation enables words, sentences, and sets of synonyms (i.e. WordNet synsets) to be represented in a unifying way with vectors. VSM provides a variety of definitions of distance between vectors, corresponding to different measures of semantic similarity. In particular, we take advantage of cosine angle between an input vector (input sentence) and an emotional vector (i.e. the vector representing an emotional synset) as similarity measures to identify which emotion the sentence connotes.

3.2 Dimension Reduction Methods

The VSM representation can be reduced with techniques well known in Information Retrieval: LSA, Probabilistic LSA (PLSA), or the Non-negative Matrix Factorization (NMF) representations.

Cosine similarities can be defined in these representations, and here, as other authors have done, we use a rule that if the cosine similarity does not exceed a threshold, the input sentence is labeled as "neutral", the absence of emotion. Otherwise, it is labeled with one emotion associated with the closest emotional vector having the highest similarity value. We use a predetermined threshold (t = 0.65) for the purpose of validating a strong emotional analogy between two vectors (Penumatsa, Ventura et al. 2006).

If we define the similarity between a given input text, *I*, and an emotional class, E_j, as sim(*I*, E_j), the categorical classification result, CCR, is more formally represented as follows:

$$\mathrm{CCR}(I) = \begin{cases} \arg\max_j \left(\mathrm{sim}(I, E_j)\right) & \text{if } \mathrm{sim}(I, E_j) \geq t \\ \text{"}neutral\text{"} & \text{if } \mathrm{sim}(I, E_j) < t \end{cases}$$

One class with the maximum score is selected as the final emotion class.

Dimensionality reduction in VSM reduces the computation time and reduces the noise in the data. This enables the unimportant data to dissipate and underlying semantic text to become more patent. We will review three statistical dimensionality reduction methods (LSA, PLSA, and NMF) that are utilized in a category-based emotion model.

Latent Semantic Analysis (LSA) is the earliest approach successfully applied to various text manipulation areas (Landauer, Foltz et al. 1998). The main idea of LSA is to map terms or documents into a vector space of reduced dimensionality that is the latent semantic space. The mapping of the given terms/document vectors to this space is based on singular vector decomposition (SVD). It is known that SVD is a reliable technique for matrix decomposition. It can decompose a matrix as the product of three matrices.

$$A = U\Sigma V^T \approx U_k \Sigma_k V_k^T = A_k \quad (1)$$

where A_k is the closest matrix of rank *k* to the original matrix. The columns of V_k represent the coordinates for documents in the latent space.

Probabilistic Latent Semantic Anlaysis (PLSA) (Hofmann 2001) has two characteristics distinguishing it from LSA. PLSA defines proper probability distributions and the reduced matrix does not contain negative values. Based on the combination of LSA and some probabilistic theories such as Bayes rules, the PLSA allows us to find the *latent topics*, the association of documents and topics, and the association of terms and topics. In the equation (2), *z* is a *latent class variable* (i.e. discrete emotion category), while *w* and *d* denote the elements of term vectors and document vectors, respectively.

$$P(d,w) = \sum_z P(z)P(w|z)P(d|z) \quad (2)$$

where $P(w|z)$ and $P(d|z)$ are topic-specific word distribution and document distribution, individually. The decomposition of PLSA, unlike that of LSA, is performed by means of the likelihood function. In other words, $P(z)$, $P(w|z)$, and $P(d|z)$ are determined by the maximum likelihood estimation (MLE) and this maximization is performed through adopting the Expectation Maximization (EM) algorithm. For document similarities, each row of the $P(d|z)$ matrix is considered with the low-dimensional representation in the semantic topic space.

Non-negative Matrix Factorization (NMF) (Lee and Seung 1999) has been successfully applied to semantic analysis. Given a non-negative matrix *A*, NMF finds non-negative factors *W* and *H* that are reduced-dimensional matrices. The product *WH* can be regarded as a compressed form of the data in *A*.

$$A \approx WH = \sum WH \quad (3)$$

W is a basis vector matrix and *H* is an encoded matrix of the basis vectors in the equation (3). NMF solves the following minimization problem (4) in order to obtain an approximation *A* by computing *W* and *H* in terms of minimizing the Frobenius norm of the error.

$$\min_{W,H} \|A - WH\|_F^2, \quad s.t.\ W,H \geq 0 \quad (4)$$

where $W, H \geq 0$ means that all elements of *W* and *H* are non-negative. This non-negative peculiarity is desirable for handling text data that always require non-negativity constraints. The classification of documents is performed based on the columns of matrix *H* that represent the documents.

3.3 Three-dimensional estimation with features derived from ANEW

Dimensional models have been studied by psychologists often by providing a stimulus (e.g. a photo or a text), and then asking subjects to report on the affective experience. ANEW (Bradley and Lang 1999) is a set of normative emotional ratings for a collection of English words (N=1,035), where after reading the words, subjects reported their emotions in a three dimensional representation. This collection provides the rated values for valence, arousal, and dominance for each word rated using the Self Assessment Manikin (SAM). For each word *w*, the normative database provides coordinates $\overline{w}$ in an affective space as:

$$\bar{w} = (valence, arousal, dominance) = ANEW(w) \quad (5)$$

The occurrences of these words in a text can be used, in a naïve way, to weight the sentence in this emotional plane. This is a naïve approach since words often change their meaning or emotional value when they are used in different contexts.

As a counterpart to the categorical classification above, this approach assumes that an input sentence pertains to an emotion based on the least distance between each other on the Valence-Arousal-Dominance (VAD) space. The input sentence consists of a number of words and the VAD value of this sentence is computed by averaging the VAD values of the words:

$$\overline{sentence} = \frac{\sum_{i=1}^{n} \bar{w}}{n} \quad (6)$$

where n is the total number of words in the input sentence.

Since not many words are available in this normative database, a series of synonyms from WordNet-Affect are used in order to calculate the position of each emotion. These emotional synsets are converted to the 3-dimensional VAD space and averaged for the purpose of producing a single point for the target emotion as follows:

$$\overline{emotion} = \frac{\sum_{i=1}^{k} \bar{w}}{k} \quad (7)$$

where k denotes the total number of synonyms in an emotion. *Anger*, *fear*, *joy*, and *sadness* emotions are mapped on the VAD space. Let A_c, F_c, J_c, and S_c be the centroids of four emotions. Then the centroids, which are calculated by the equation (7), are as follows: $A_c = (2.55, 6.60, 5.05)$, $F_c = (3.20, 5.92, 3.60)$, $J_c = (7.40, 5.73, 6.20)$, and $S_c = (3.15, 4.56, 4.00)$. Apart from the four emotions, we manually define *neutral* to be (5, 5, 5). If the centroid of an input sentence is the most approximate to that of an emotion, the sentence is tagged as the emotion (with the nearest neighbor algorithm). The centroid $\overline{sentence}$ might be close to an $\overline{emotion}$ on the VAD space, even if they do not share any terms in common. We define the distance threshold (empirically set to 4) to validate the appropriate proximity like the categorical classification.

4 Emotion-Labeled Data

Three emotional datasets, with sentence-level emotion annotations, were employed for the evaluation described in the next section. The first dataset is "Affective Text" from the SemEval 2007 task (Strapparava and Mihalcea 2007).[1] This dataset consists of news headlines excerpted from newspapers and news web sites. Headlines are suitable for our experiments because headlines are typically intended to express emotions in order to draw the readers' attention. This dataset has six emotion classes: *anger*, *disgust*, *fear*, *joy*, *sadness* and *surprise*, and is composed of 1,250 annotated headlines. The notable characteristics are that SemEval dataset does not only allow one sentence to be tagged with multiple emotions, but the dataset also contains a *neutral* category in contrast to other datasets.

We also use the ISEAR (International Survey on Emotion Antecedents and Reactions) dataset, which consists of 7,666 sentences (Scherer and Wallbott 1994), with regard to our experiments.[2] For building the ISEAR, 1,096 participants who have different cultural backgrounds completed questionnaires about experiences and reactions for seven emotions including *anger*, *disgust*, *fear*, *joy*, *sadness*, *shame* and *guilt*.

The annotated sentences of the third dataset are culled from fairy tales (Alm 2009). Emotions are particularly significant elements in the literary genre of fairy tales. The label set with five emotion classes is as follows: *angry-disgusted*, *fearful*, *happy*, *sad* and *surprised*. There are 176 stories by three authors: B. Potter, H.C. Andersen, and Grimm's. The dataset is composed of only sentences with affective high agreements, which means that annotators highly agreed upon the sentences (four identical emotion labels).

Emotion	SemEval	ISEAR	Fairy tales	Total
Anger	62	2,168	218	2,448
Fear	124	1,090	166	1,380
Joy	148	1,090	445	1,683
Sadness	145	1,082	264	1,491

Table 1: Number of sentences for each emotion

In our study, we have taken into account four emotion classes (*Anger*, *Fear*, *Joy* and *Sadness*) which are in the intersection among three datasets (SemEval, ISEAR and Fairy tales). The number of sentences for each emotion and each

[1] The dataset is publicly available at http://www.cse.unt.edu/~rada/affectivetext.

[2] Available at http://www.unige.ch/fapse/emotion/databanks/isear.html

Data set		SemEval			ISEAR			Fairy tales		
Emotion		Prec.	Rec.	F1	Prec.	Rec.	F1	Prec.	Rec.	F1
Anger	MCB	0.000	0.000	-	0.399	**1.000**	0.571	0.000	0.000	-
	CLSA	0.089	0.151	0.112	0.468	0.970	**0.631**	0.386	**0.749**	0.510
	CPLSA	0.169	**0.440**	0.244	0.536	0.397	0.456	0.239	0.455	0.313
	CNMF	**0.294**	0.263	**0.278**	0.410	0.987	0.579	**0.773**	0.560	**0.650**
	DIM	0.161	0.192	0.175	**0.708**	0.179	0.286	0.604	0.290	0.392
Fear	MCB	0.000	0.000	-	0.000	0.000	-	0.000	0.000	-
	CLSA	0.434	0.622	0.511	0.633	0.038	0.071	**0.710**	0.583	0.640
	CPLSA	0.000	0.000	0.000	0.000	0.000	0.000	0.000	0.000	0.000
	CNMF	**0.525**	**0.750**	**0.618**	**0.689**	0.029	0.056	0.704	**0.784**	**0.741**
	DIM	0.404	0.404	0.404	0.531	**0.263**	**0.351**	0.444	0.179	0.255
Joy	MCB	0.309	**1.000**	0.472	0.000	0.000	-	0.407	**1.000**	0.579
	CLSA	0.455	0.359	0.402	0.333	0.061	0.103	**0.847**	0.637	0.727
	CPLSA	0.250	0.258	0.254	0.307	0.381	0.340	0.555	0.358	0.436
	CNMF	**0.773**	0.557	0.648	**0.385**	0.005	0.010	0.802	0.761	0.781
	DIM	0.573	0.934	**0.710**	0.349	**0.980**	**0.515**	0.661	0.979	**0.789**
Sadness	MCB	0.000	0.000	-	0.000	0.000	-	0.000	0.000	-
	CLSA	0.472	0.262	0.337	0.500	0.059	0.106	0.704	0.589	0.642
	CPLSA	0.337	0.431	0.378	0.198	**0.491**	0.282	0.333	0.414	0.370
	CNMF	0.500	**0.453**	**0.475**	0.360	0.009	0.017	**0.708**	**0.821**	**0.760**
	DIM	**0.647**	0.157	0.253	**0.522**	0.249	**0.337**	0.408	0.169	0.240

Table 3: Emotion identification results

dataset used in our experiment is shown in Table 1. In addition, sample sentences from the annotated corpus appear in Table 2.

Dataset	Sentences tagged with *Sadness/Sad*
SemEval	Bangladesh ferry sink, 15 dead.
ISEAR	When I left a man in whom I really believed.
Fairy tales	The flower could not, as on the previous evening, fold up its petals and sleep; it dropped sorrowfully.

Table 2: Sample sentences labeled with sadness/sad from the datasets

5 Experiments and Results

The goal of the affect classification is to predict a single emotional label given an input sentence. Four different approaches were implemented in Matlab. A categorical model based on a VSM with dimensionality reduction variants, (LSA, PLSA, and NMF), and a dimensional model, each with evaluated with two similarity measures (cosine angle and nearest neighbor). Stopwords were removed in all approaches. A Matlab toolkit (Zeimpekis and Gallopoulos 2005), was used to generate the term-by-sentence matrix from the text.

The evaluation in Table 3 shows Majority Class Baseline (MCB) as the baseline algorithm. The MCB is the performance of a classifier that always predicts the majority class. In SemEval and Fairy tales the majority class is *joy*, while *anger* is the majority emotion in case of ISEAR. The five approaches were evaluated on the dataset of 479 news headlines (SemEval), 5,430 responses to questions (ISEAR), and 1,093 fairy tales' sentences. We define the following acronyms to identify the approaches:

- CLSA: LSA-based categorical classification
- CPLSA: PLSA-based categorical classification
- CNMF: NMF-based categorical classification
- DIM: Dimension-based estimation

The measure of accuracies used here were: Cohen's Kappa (Cohen 1960), average precision, recall, and F-measure. While the kappa scores are useful in obtaining an overview of the reliability of the various classification approaches, they do not provide any insight on the accuracy at the category level for which precision, recall, and F-measure are necessary.

5.1 Precision, Recall, and F-measure

Classification accuracy is usually measured in terms of precision, recall, and F-measure. Table 3 shows these values obtained by five approaches for the automatic classification of four emotions. The highest results for a given type of scoring and datasets are marked in bold for each individual class. We do not include the accuracy values in our results due to the imbalanced proportions of categories (see Table 1). The accuracy metric does not provide adequate information, whereas precision, recall, and F-measure can effectively evaluate the classification performance with respect to imbalanced datasets (He and Garcia 2009).

As can be seen from the table, the performances of each approach hinge on each dataset and emotion category, respectively. In the case of the SemEval dataset, precision, recall and F-measure for CNMF and DIM are comparable. DIM approach gives the best result for *joy*, which has a relatively large number of sentences. In ISEAR, DIM generally outperforms other approaches except for some cases, whereas CNMF has the best recall score after the baseline for the *anger* category. Figure 1 indicates the results of 3-dimensional and 2-dimensional attribute evaluations for ISEAR. When it comes to fairy tales, CNMF generally performs better than the other techniques. *Joy* also has the largest number of data instances in fairy tales and the best recall ignoring the baseline and F-measure are obtained with the approach based on DIM for this affect category. CNMF gets the best emotion detection performance for *anger*, *fear*, and *sadness* in terms of the F-measure.

Figure 2 and Table 4 display results among different approaches obtained on the three different datasets. We compute the classification performance by macro-average, which gives equal weight to every category regardless of how many sentences are assigned to it.[3] This measurement prevents the results from being biased given the imbalanced data distribution. From this summarized information, we can see that CPLSA performs less effectively with several low performance results across all datasets. CNMF is superior to other methods in SemEval and Fairy tales datasets, while DIM surpasses the others in ISEAR. In particular, CPLSA outperforms CLSA and CNMF in ISEAR because their performances are relatively poor. The result implies that statistical models which consider a probability distribution over the latent space do not always achieve sound performances. In addition, we can infer that models (CNMF and DIM) with non-negative factors are appropriate for dealing with these text collections.

Another notable result is that the precision, recall, and F-measure are generally higher in fairy tales than in the other datasets. These sentences in the fairy tales tend to have more emotional terms and the length of sentences is longer. The nature of fairy tales makes unsupervised models yield better performance (see Table 2). In addition, affective high agreement sentence is another plausible contributing reason for the encouraging experimental results.

In summary, categorical NMF model and dimensional model show the better emotion identification performance as a whole.

5.2 Cohen's Kappa

The kappa statistic measures the proportion of agreement between two raters with correction for chance. The kappa score is used as the metric to compare the performance of each approach. Figure 3 graphically depicts the mean kappa scores and its standard errors obtained from the emotion classification. Comparisons between four approaches are shown across all three datasets. MCB is excluded in the comparison because the mean kappa score of MCB is 0.

Let MK_{CLSA}, MK_{CPLSA}, MK_{CNMF}, and MK_{DIM} be the mean kappa scores of four methods. The highest score (MK_{CNMF} = 0.382) is achieved by the CNMF when the dataset is SemEval. In fairy tales, the CNMF method (MK_{CNMF} = 0.652) also displays better result than the others (MK_{CLSA} = 0.506, MK_{DIM} = 0.304). On the contrary, the achieved results are significantly different in the case of the ISEAR dataset in comparison with the aforementioned datasets. The DIM (MK_{DIM}= 0.210) clearly outperforms all methods. The kappa score of the CPLSA approach (MK_{CPLSA} = 0.099) is quantitatively and significantly higher than the CLSA (MK_{CLSA} = 0.031) and CNMF (MK_{CNMF} = 0.011). Kappa score for the NMF-based methods is remarkably lower than the other three approaches.

According to (Fleiss and Cohen 1973), a kappa value higher than 0.4 means a fair to good level of agreement beyond chance alone and it is

[3] Macro-averaging scores are defined as:
$P_m = \frac{1}{C}\sum_{i=1}^{C} p_i$, $R_m = \frac{1}{C}\sum_{i=1}^{C} r_i$, $F_m = \frac{1}{C}\sum_{i=1}^{C} f_i$
where C is total number of categories, and p_i, r_i, and f_i stand for precision, recall, and F-measure, respectively, for each category i.

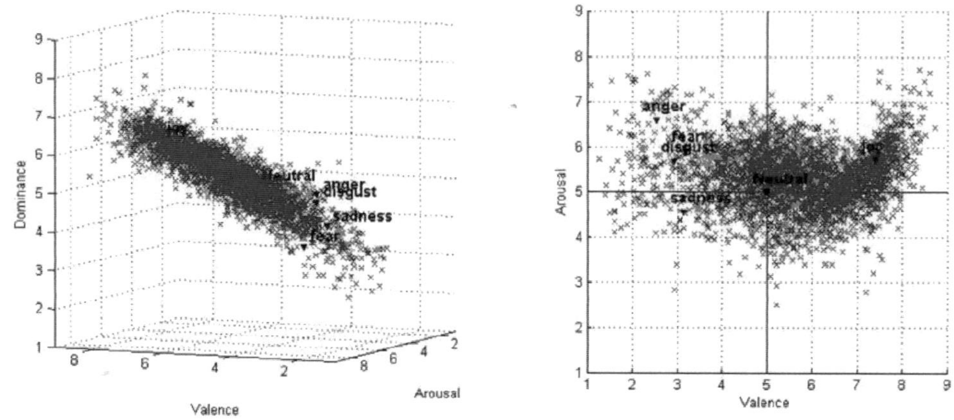

Figure 1: Distribution of the ISEAR dataset in the 3-dimensional and 2-dimensional sentiment space. The blue 'x' denotes the location of one sentence corresponding to valence, arousal, and dominance.

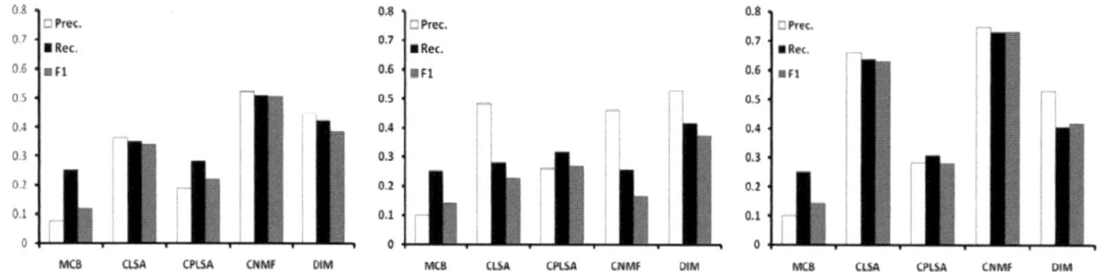

(a) (b) (c)

Figure 2: Comparisons of Precision, Recall, and F-measure: (a) SemEval; (b) ISEAR; (c) Fairy tales.

Data set	SemEval			ISEAR			Fairy tales		
	Prec.	Rec.	F1	Prec.	Rec.	F1	Prec.	Rec.	F1
MCB	0.077	0.250	0.118	0.100	0.250	0.143	0.102	0.250	0.145
CLSA	0.363	0.348	0.340	0.484	0.282	0.228	0.662	0.640	0.630
CPLSA	0.189	0.282	0.219	0.260	0.317	0.270	0.282	0.307	0.280
CNMF	**0.523**	**0.506**	**0.505**	0.461	0.258	0.166	**0.747**	**0.731**	**0.733**
DIM	0.446	0.422	0.386	**0.528**	**0.417**	**0.372**	0.530	0.404	0.419

Table 4: Overall average results

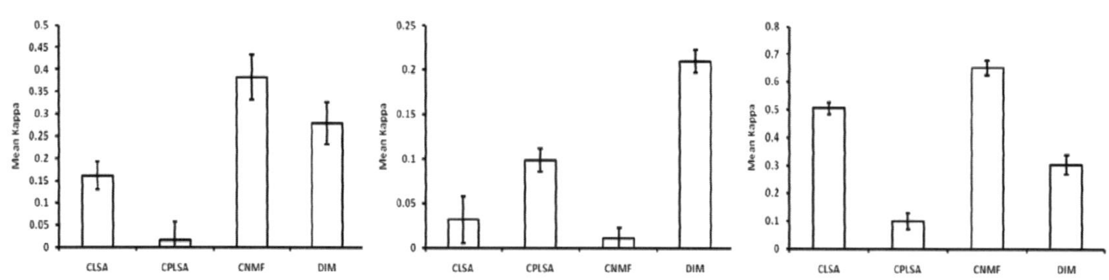

(a) (b) (c)

Figure 3: Comparisons of Mean Kappa: (a) SemEval; (b) ISEAR; (c) Fairy tales.

an acceptable level of agreement. On the basis of this definition, the kappa score obtained by our best classifier (MK_{CNMF} = 0.652) would be reasonable. Most of the values are too low to say that two raters (human judges and computer approaches) agreed upon the affective states. However, we have another reason with respect to this metric in the experiment. We make use of the kappa score as an unbiased metric of the reliability for comparing four methods. In other words, these measures are of importance in terms of the relative magnitude. Hence, the kappa results are meaningful and interpretable in spite of low values. We can observe that the NMF-based categorical model and the dimensional model both experienced higher performance.

5.3 Frequently occurring words

The most frequent words used in fairy tales for each emotion are listed in Table 5. We choose this dataset since there are varying lexical items and affective high agreement sentences, as mentioned in Section 5.1. Stemming is not used because it might hide important differences as between '*loving*' and '*loved*'. CNMF and DIM were selected for the comparison with the Gold Standard because they were the two methods with the better performance than the others. Gold Standard is the annotated dataset by human raters for the evaluation of algorithm performance. The words most frequently used to describe anger across all methods include: *cried*, *great*, *tears*, *king*, *thought*, and *eyes*. Those used to describe fear include: *heart*, *cried*, *mother*, *thought*, *man*, and *good*. Joy contains *happy*, *good*, and *cried* whereas sadness has only *cried* for three methods.

There is something unexpected for the word frequencies. We can observe that the association between frequently used words and emotion categories is unusual and even opposite. For instance, a '*joy*' is one of the most frequent words referred to for *sadness* in the Gold Standard. In CNMF and DIM, a '*good*' is employed frequently with regard to *fear*. Moreover, some words occur with the same frequency in more categories. For example, the word '*cried*' is utilized to express *anger*, *fear*, and *joy* in the Gold Standard, CNMF, and DIM. In order to find a possible explanation in the complexity of language used in the emotional expression, some sentences extracted from fairy tales are listed below:

"The cook was frightened when he heard the order, and said to Cat-skin, You must have let a hair fall into the soup; if it be so, you will have a ***good*** beating." – which expresses *fear*

"When therefore she came to the castle gate she saw him, and ***cried*** aloud for joy." – which is the expression for *joy*

"Gretel was not idle; she ran screaming to her master, and ***cried***: You have invited a fine guest!" – which is the expression for *angry-disgusted*

From these examples, we can observe that in these cases the affective meaning is not simply propagated form the lexicon, but is the effect of the linguistic structure at a higher level.

6 Conclusion

We compared the performances of three techniques, based on the categorical representation of emotions, and one based on the dimensional representation. This paper has highlighted that the NMF-based categorical classification performs

Model	Emotion	Top 10 words
Gold Standard	Anger	king, thought, eyes, great, cried, looked, joy, mother, wife, tears
	Fear	great, cried, good, happy, thought, man, heart, poor, child, mother
	Joy	thought, mother, good, cried, man, day, wept, beautiful, back, happy
	Sadness	cried, fell, father, mother, back, joy, dead, danced, wife, tears
CNMF	Anger	great, cried, eyes, mother, poor, joy, king, heart, thought, tears
	Fear	cried, king, happy, good, man, heart, thought, father, boy, mother
	Joy	mother, thought, cried, king, day, great, home, joy, good, child
	Sadness	thought, cried, good, great, looked, mother, man, time, king, heart
DIM	Anger	eyes, fell, heart, tears, cried, good, stood, great, king, thought
	Fear	king, cried, heart, mother, good, thought, looked, man, child, time
	Joy	eyes, man, children, danced, cried, good, time, happy, great, wedding
	Sadness	cried, thought, great, king, good, happy, sat, home, joy, found

Table 5: Most frequent 10 words from fairy tales

the best among categorical approaches to classification. When comparing categorical against dimensional classification, the categorical NMF model and the dimensional model have better performances. Nevertheless, we cannot generalize inferences on which of these techniques is the best performer because results vary among datasets. As a future work, we aim at performing a further investigation on this connection in order to identify more effective strategies applicable to a generic dataset. Furthermore, we aim at exploring improvements in the methodology, employed in this work, and based on the combination of emotional modeling and empirical methods.

Acknowledgments

This research is partially sponsored by a Norman I. Price Scholarship from the University of Sydney.

References

C. O. Alm (2009). Affect in Text and Speech, VDM Verlag Dr. Müller.

S. Aman and S. Szpakowicz (2007). Identifying expressions of emotion in text. Text, Speech and Dialogue.

M. M. Bradley and P. J. Lang (1999). Affective norms for English words (ANEW): Instruction manual and affective ratings. University of Florida: The Center for Research in Psychophysiology.

J. Cohen (1960). A coefficient of agreement for nominal scales. Educational and psychological measurement 20(1): 37-46.

S. D'Mello, A. Graesser, and R. W. Picard (2007). Toward an affect-sensitive AutoTutor. IEEE Intelligent Systems 22(4): 53-61.

S. D’Mello, S. Craig, A. Witherspoon, B. Mcdaniel, and A. Graesser (2008). Automatic detection of learner’s affect from conversational cues. User Modeling and User-Adapted Interaction 18(1): 45-80.

P. Ekman (1992). An argument for basic emotions. Cognition & Emotion 6(3): 169-200.

J. L. Fleiss and J. Cohen (1973). The equivalence of weighted kappa and the intraclass correlation. Educational and psychological measurement 33: 613-619.

H. He and E. A. Garcia (2009). Learning from Imbalanced Data. IEEE Transactions on Knowledge and Data Engineering 21(9): 1263.

T. Hofmann (2001). Unsupervised learning by probabilistic latent semantic analysis. Machine Learning 42(1): 177-196.

B. Kort, R. Reilly, and R. W. Picard (2001). An affective model of interplay between emotions and learning: Reengineering educational pedagogy-building a learning companion. IEEE International Conference on Advanced Learning Technologies, 2001. Proceedings.

T. K. Landauer, P. W. Foltz, and D. Laham (1998). An introduction to latent semantic analysis. Discourse processes, Citeseer. 25: 259-284.

P. J. Lang (1980). Behavioral treatment and bio-behavioral assessment: Computer applications. Technology in mental health care delivery systems: 119-137.

D. D. Lee and H. S. Seung (1999). Learning the parts of objects by non-negative matrix factorization. Nature 401(6755): 788-791.

P. Penumatsa, M. Ventura, A.C. Graesser, M. Louwerse, X. Hu, Z. Cai, and D.R. Franceschetti (2006). The Right Threshold Value: What Is the Right Threshold of Cosine Measure When Using Latent Semantic Analysis for Evaluating Student Answers? International Journal on Artificial Intelligence Tools, World Scientific Publishing.

J. A. Russell (2003). Core affect and the psychological construction of emotion. Psychological review 110(1): 145-172.

K. R. Scherer and H. G. Wallbott (1994). Evidence for universality and cultural variation of differential emotion response patterning. Journal of Personality and Social Psychology 66: 310-328.

C. Strapparava and R. Mihalcea (2007). Semeval-2007 task 14: Affective text. Proceedings of the 4th International Workshop on Semantic Evaluations, Association for Computational Linguistics.

C. Strapparava and R. Mihalcea (2008). Learning to identify emotions in text. SAC '08: Proceedings of the 2008 ACM symposium on Applied computing, Fortaleza, Ceara, Brazil, ACM.

C. Strapparava and A. Valitutti (2004). WordNet-Affect: an affective extension of WordNet. Proceedings of LREC.

R. B. Yates and B. R. Neto (1999). Modern information retrieval. ACM P.

Zeimpekis D. and E. Gallopoulos (2005). TMG: A MATLAB toolbox for generating term-document matrices from text collections. Grouping multidimensional data: Recent advances in clustering: 187-210.

Identifying Emotions, Intentions, and Attitudes in Text Using a Game with a Purpose

Lisa Pearl
Department of Cognitive Sciences
University of California, Irvine
3151 Social Science Plaza
Irvine, CA 92697, USA
lpearl@uci.edu

Mark Steyvers
Department of Cognitive Sciences
University of California, Irvine
3151 Social Science Plaza
Irvine, CA 92697, USA
msteyver@uci.edu

Abstract

Subtle social information is available in text such as a speaker's emotional state, intentions, and attitude, but current information extraction systems are unable to extract this information at the level that humans can. We describe a methodology for creating databases of messages annotated with social information based on interactive games between humans trying to generate and interpret messages for a number of different social information types. We then present some classification results achieved by using a small-scale database created with this methodology.

1 Introduction

A focus of much information extraction research has been identifying surface-level semantic content (e.g., identifying who did what to whom when). In recent years, research on sentiment analysis and opinion mining has recognized that more subtle information can be communicated via linguistic features in the text (see Pang and Lee (2008) for a review), such as whether text (e.g., a movie review) is positive or negative (Turney 2002, Pang, Lee, and Vaithyanathan 2002, Dave, Lawrence, and Pennock 2003, Wiebe et al. 2004, Kennedy and Inkpen 2006, Agarwal, Biadsy, and Mckeown 2009, Greene and Resnik 2009, among many others). However, other subtle information available in text, such as a speaker's emotional states (e.g., anger, embarrassment), intentions (e.g., persuasion, deception), and attitudes (e.g., disbelief, confidence), has not been explored as much, though there has been some work in detecting emotion (e.g., Subasic and Huettner 2001, Alm, Roth, and Sproat 2005, Nicolov et al. 2006, Abbasi 2007) and detecting deception (e.g., Annolli, Balconi, and Ciceri 2002, Zhou et al. 2004, Gupta and Skillicorn 2006, Zhou and Sung 2008). This latter kind of social information is useful for identifying the "tone" of a message, i.e., for understanding the underlying intention behind a message's creation, and also for predicting how this message will be interpreted by humans reading it.

A technical barrier to extracting this kind of social information is that there are currently no large-scale text databases that are annotated with social information from which to learn the relevant linguistic cues. That is, there are few examples of social information "ground truth" - text annotated with human perceptions of the social information contained within the text. Given the success of sentiment analysis, we believe this social information could also be retrievable once the relevant linguistic cues are identified.

One way to create the necessary annotated data is to draw from computational social science (Lazer et al. 2009), and make use of human-based computation (Kosurokoff 2001, von Ahn 2006, among others) since humans are used to transmitting social information through language. In this paper, we describe a methodology for creating this kind of database, and then present the results from a small-scale database created using this methodology[1]. In addition, we show one example of us-

[1]The database can be obtained by downloading it from http://www.socsci.uci.edu/~lpearl/CoLaLab/projects.html or contacting Lisa Pearl at lpearl@uci.edu.

Proceedings of the NAACL HLT 2010 Workshop on Computational Approaches to Analysis and Generation of Emotion in Text, pages 71–79, Los Angeles, California, June 2010.

ing this database by training a Sparse Multinomial Logistic Regression classifier (Krishnapuram et al. 2005) on these data.

2 Reliable databases of social information

2.1 The need for databases

In general, reliable databases are required to develop reliable machine learning algorithms. Unfortunately, very few databases annotated with social information exist, and the few that do are small in size. A recent addition to the Linguistic Data Consortium demonstrates this: The Language Understanding Annotation Corpus (LUAC) by Diab et al. (2009) includes text annotated with *committed belief*, which "distinguishes between statements which assert belief or opinion, those which contain speculation, and statements which convey fact or otherwise do not convey belief." This is meant to aid in determining which beliefs can be ascribed to a communicator and how strongly the communicator holds those beliefs. Nonetheless, this is still a small sample of the possible social information contained in text. Moreover, the LUAC contains only about 9000 words across two languages (6949 English, 2183 Arabic), which is small compared to the corpora generally available for natural language processing (e.g., the English Gigaword corpus (Graff 2003) contains 1756504 words).

Another tack taken by researchers has been to use open-source data that are likely to demonstrate certain social information by happenstance, e.g., online gaming forums with games that happen to involve the intent to deceive (e.g., Zhou and Sung 2008: Mafia game forums). While these data sets are larger in size, they do not have the breadth of coverage in terms of what social information they can capture because, by nature, the games only explicitly involve one kind of social information (e.g., intentions: deception); other social information cannot reliably be attributed to the text. In general, real world data sets present the problem of ground truth, i.e., knowing for certain which emotions, intentions, and attitudes are conveyed by a particular message.

However, people can often detect social information conveyed through text (perhaps parsing it as the "tone" of the message). For example, consider the following message: "*Come on...you have to buy this.*" From only the text itself, we can readily infer that the speaker intends to persuade the listener. Human-based computation can leverage this ability from the population, and use it to construct a reliable database of social information. Interestingly, groups of humans are sometimes capable of producing much more precise and reliable results than any particular individual in the group. For example, Steyvers et al. (2009) has shown that such "wisdom of crowds" phenomena occur in many knowledge domains, including human memory, problem solving, and prediction. In addition, Snow et al. (2008) have demonstrated that a relatively small number of non-expert annotations in natural language tasks can achieve the same results as expert annotation.

2.2 Games with a purpose

One approach is to use a *game with a purpose* (GWAP) (von Ahn and Dabbish 2004, von Ahn 2006, von Ahn, Kedia, and Blum 2006) that is designed to encourage people to provide the information needed in the database. GWAPs are currently being used to accumulate information about many things that humans find easy to identify (see *http://www.gwap.com/gwap/* for several examples), such as objects in images (von Ahn and Dabbish 2004), the musical style of songs, impressions of sights and sounds in videos, and common sense relationships between concepts (von Ahn, Kedia, and Blum 2006). In addition, as the collected data comes from and is vetted by a large number of participants, we can gauge which messages are reliable examples of particular social information and which are confusing examples.

2.3 A GWAP for social information in text

We designed a GWAP to create a database of messages annotated with social information, where unpaid participants provide knowledge about the social information in text. The GWAP encourages participants to both generate messages that reflect specific social information and to label messages created by other participants as reflecting specific social information. Participants are given points for every message they create that is correctly labeled by another participant, and for every message created by another participant that they correctly label.

Message generators were instructed to generate a

message expressing some particular social information type (such as *persuading*), and were allowed to use a displayed picture as context to guide their message, so they would not need to rely completely on their own imaginations. All context pictures used in our GWAP were meant to be generic enough that they could be a basis for a message expressing a variety of social information types. Context pictures were randomly assigned when participants were asked to generate messages; this meant that, for example, a picture could be used to generate a persuasive message and be used again later to generate a deceptive message. Generators were also warned not to use "taboo" words that would make the social information too easy to guess [2], but were encouraged to express the social information as clearly as possible. The generator was told that if another participant perceived the correct social information type from the message, the generator would be rewarded with game points.

Message annotators were instructed to guess which social information type was being expressed by the displayed message. They were also shown the image the generator used as context for the message, and were rewarded with points for successful detection of the intended social information.

As an example of the GWAP in action, one participant might generate the message "*Won't you consider joining our campaign? It's for a good cause.*" for the social information of *persuading*; a different participant would see this message and might label it as an example of *persuading*. A participant can only label a message with one social information type (e.g., a participant could not choose both *persuading* and *formal* for the same message).[3]

With enough game players, many messages are created that clearly reflect different social information. Without any of the participants necessarily having expert knowledge or training, we expect that the cumulative knowledge to be quite reliable (for example, see Steyvers et al. (2009) and work by von Ahn (von Ahn and Dabbish 2004, von Ahn 2006, von Ahn, Kedia, and Blum 2006) for other successful cases involving the "wisdom of the crowds", and Snow et al. (2008) for non-expert annotation in natural language tasks such as affect recognition). Because the same text can be evaluated by many different people, this can reduce the effect of idiosyncratic responses from a few individuals.

An advantage of this kind of database is that many different kinds of social information can be generated and labeled by the participants so that the database contains examples of many different kinds of social information in text, even if only a single label is given to a particular message (perhaps expressing that message's most obvious social information from the perspective of the labeler). We can gauge how clearly a message reflects social information by how often it is labeled by others as reflecting that social information. In addition, by the very nature of the GWAP, we can also assess which social information is easily confused by humans, e.g., politeness with embarrassment, or confidence with deception. This can aid the development of models that extract social information and could also identify messages likely to be ambiguous to humans.

2.4 A GWAP study

Below we report data from an offline GWAP that involves eight types of social information indicative of several social aspects that we thought would be of interest: politeness (indicates emotional state, attitude), rudeness (indicates emotional state, attitude), embarrassment (indicates emotional state), formality (indicates attitude), persuading (indicates intent), deception (indicates intent), confidence (indicates emotional state, attitude), and disbelief (indicates attitude). Fifty eight English-speaking adults participated in the GWAP, consisting of a mix of undergraduate students, graduate students, the authors, friends of the students, and friends of the authors, in order to simulate the varied mix of participants in an online GWAP. The undergraduate students were compensated with course credit. Together, these 58 participants created 1176 messages and made 3198 annotations. Note that a participant would label

[2] Taboo words were chosen as morphological variants of the social information type description. For example, *persuade*, *persuades*, *persuaded*, and *persuading* were considered taboo words for "persuading". Future versions of the GWAP could allow the taboo word list to be influenced by which words are often associated with a particular social information type.

[3] We note that this is a restriction that might be relaxed in future versions of the GWAP. For instance, participants might decide whether a message expresses a social information type or not from their perspective, so the task is more like binary classification for each social information type.

more messages than that participant would be asked to generate, and more than one participant would label the same message (though no participant would label a message that s/he created, nor would any participant label the same message more than once). Participants were encouraged to play the GWAP multiple times if they were inclined, to simulate the experience of playing a favorite game. There was no limit on message length, though most participants tended to keep messages fairly brief. Some sample messages (with the participants' own spelling and punctuation) that were correctly and incorrectly labeled are shown in Table 1.

Social Information Generated *Labeled*	**Message**
deception *deception*	"Oh yeah...your hair looks really great like that...yup, I love it...it, uh, really suits you..."
embarrassment *embarrassment*	"Oh... we're not dating. I would never date him... he's like a brother to me.."
disbelief *disbelief*	"Are you and him really friends?"
rudeness *persuading*	"James, Bree doesn't like you. She never did and never will!"
deception *persuading*	"I wasn't going to take anything from your storeroom, I swear! Really, I won't try to get inside again!'
politeness *deception*	"Your orange hair matches your sweater nicely"

Table 1: Sample messages from the offline GWAP.

The GWAP as currently designed allows us to gauge two interesting aspects of social information transmission via text. First, we can assess our non-expert participants' performance. Second, we can assess the messages themselves.

For the participants, we can gauge their accuracy as message generators by measuring how often a message they created was successfully perceived as expressing the intended social information type (that is, their "expressive accuracy"). On average, message generators were able to generate reliable messages 56% of the time. Figure 1 displays the expressive accuracy of participants, while also showing how many messages participants generated. Most participants created less than 30 messages, and were accurate more than half the time.

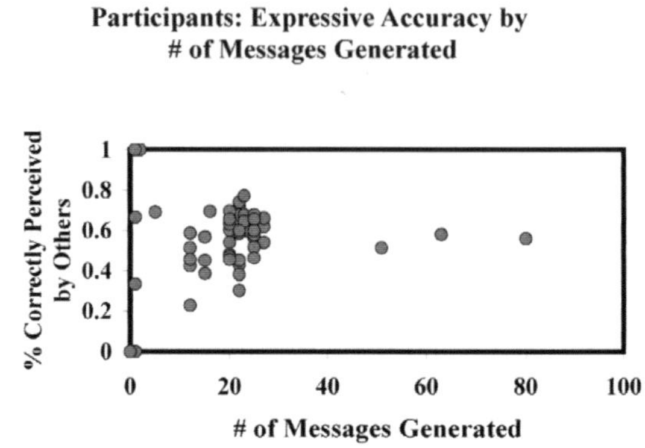

Figure 1: Expressive accuracy of GWAP participants.

At the same time, we can also gauge the accuracy of the participants as non-expert annotators by measuring how often a participant perceived the intended social information (that is, their "perceptive accuracy"). On average, annotators were able to perceive the intended social information 58% of the time. Figure 2 displays the perceptive accuracy, while also showing how many messages participants annotated. Most participants annotated around 20 messages or between 80 and 100 messages and were accurate more than half the time. Average inter-annotator agreement was 0.44, calculated using Fleiss' Kappa (Fleiss 1971), suggesting moderate agreement.

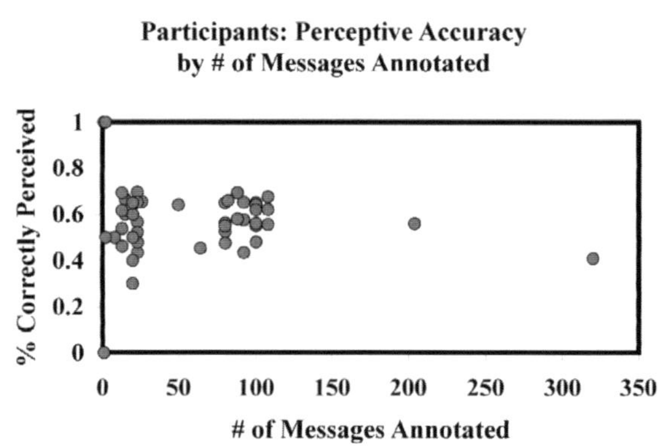

Figure 2: Perceptive accuracy of GWAP participants.

Turning to the messages, we can gauge how often messages were able to successfully express a particular social information type, and how often they were confused as expressing some other type. Table 2 shows a confusion matrix of social information derived from this database.

	deception	politeness	rudeness	embarrassment	confidence	disbelief	formality	persuading
deception	**.37**	.07	.10	.03	.09	.10	.04	.20
politeness	.05	**.53**	.05	.02	.03	.01	.20	.10
rudeness	.04	.01	**.78**	.02	.04	.04	.03	.03
embarrassment	.07	.09	.05	**.56**	.02	.13	.05	.03
confidence	.04	.04	.03	.01	**.67**	.05	.02	.13
disbelief	.10	.05	.05	.04	.07	**.62**	.02	.06
formality	.02	.34	.04	.02	.06	.03	**.39**	.10
persuading	.09	.06	.03	.01	.12	.03	.04	**.61**

Table 2: Confusion matrix for the human participants. The rows represent the intended social information for a message while the columns represent the labeled social information, averaged over messages and participants.

The matrix shows the likelihood that a message will be labeled as expressing specific social information (in a column), given that it has been generated with specific social information in mind (in a row), averaged over messages and participants. In other words, we show the probability distribution $p(labeled|generated)$. The diagonal probabilities indicate how often a message's social information was correctly labeled for each social information type; this shows how often social information transmission was successful. Messages were perceived correctly by human participants about 57% of the time. More particular observations about the data in Table 2 are that people are more likely to correctly identify a message expressing rudeness ($p = .78$) and confidence ($p = .67$) and less likely to correctly identify a message expressing deception ($p = .37$) or formality ($p = .39$). Also, we can see that a deceptive message can often be mistaken for a persuading message ($p = 0.20$), a formal message mistaken for a polite message ($p = 0.34$), a message expressing disbelief mistaken for a message expressing deception ($p = .10$), and a persuading message mistaken for a deceptive message ($p = .09$) or confidence ($p = .12$), among other observations. Some of these may be expected, e.g., confusing confidence with persuading since someone who is trying to persuade will likely be confident about the topic, or formality with politeness since many formal expressions are used to indicate politeness (e.g., *"if you would be so kind"*). Others may be unexpected a priori, such as mistaking disbelief for deception.

2.5 Human reliability and message reliability

Given that humans were believed to be good at identifying social information in text, the low perceptive accuracy rates for participants and low annotation accuracy rates for messages may seem unexpected. However, we believe it indicates that some messages are better than others at expressing social information in a way obvious to humans. That is, messages confusing to human participants (e.g., the lower three examples in Table 1, as well as the confusing messages represented by the probabilities in Table 2) would be consistently mislabeled.

It may be that some messages are created such that many annotators agree with each other, but they all perceive a social information type other than the one intended.[4] In a similar vein, messages with low inter-annotator agreement may simply be poorly generated messages that should be removed from the database. To this end, we can assess how often majority annotator agreement correlates with perception of the message's intended social information type. Table 3 shows the confusion matrix for messages where over 50% of the annotators agreed with each other on which social information type was intended, and at least two annotators labeled the message. A total of 866 messages satisfied these criteria.

The confusion matrix, as before, shows the likelihood that a message will be labeled as expressing specific social information (in a column), given that it has been generated with specific social information in mind (in a row), averaged over messages and participants. The diagonal probabilities indicate how often a message's social information was correctly labeled for each social information type; this shows how often social information transmission was successful. The messages in this subset were perceived correctly by human participants about 71% of the time, a significant improvement over 57%. This demonstrates how even a modest pooling of non-expert opinion can significantly in-

[4]Messages consistently perceived as expressing a different social information type than intended should perhaps be considered as actually expressing that social information type rather than the intended one.

	deception	politeness	rudeness	embarrassment	confidence	disbelief	formality	persuading
deception	**.45**	.05	.10	.01	.07	.07	.03	.21
politeness	.03	**.71**	.03	.00	.01	.00	.13	.09
rudeness	.03	.00	**.92**	.00	.01	.02	.02	.00
embarrassment	.04	.08	.05	**.69**	.00	.11	.01	.02
confidence	.01	.04	.02	.01	**.82**	.01	.01	.09
disbelief	.05	.03	.02	.02	.05	**.82**	.00	.02
formality	.02	.34	.02	.01	.03	.03	**.46**	.10
persuading	.03	.05	.01	.00	.05	.03	.01	**.82**

Table 3: Confusion matrix for the human participants, where the majority of participants agreed on a message's intended social information and at least two participants labeled the message. The rows represent the intended social information for a message while the columns represent the labeled social information, averaged over messages and participants.

crease the accuracy of social information identification in text.

We can observe similar trends to what we saw in Table 2, in many cases sharpened from what they were previously. People are still more likely to identify messages expressing rudeness ($p = .92$) and confidence ($p = .82$), though they are also now more likely to accurately identify persuading ($p = .82$). The ability to identify politeness ($p = .71$) and embarrassment ($p = .69$) has also improved, though a polite message can still be mistaken for a formal message ($p = .13$). Formality ($p = .46$) and deception ($p = .45$) remain more difficult to identify, with formal messages mistaken for politeness ($p = .34$) and deceptive messages mistaken for persuading ($p = .21$) and rudeness (p=.10) [5]. Note, however, that messages of disbelief and persuading are now rarely mistaken for deceptive messages ($p = .05$ and $p = .03$, respectively). It is likely then that the confusions arising in this data set are more representative of the actual confusion humans encounter when perceiving these social information types.

Identifying messages likely to be misperceived by humans is useful for two reasons. First, from a cognitive standpoint, we can identify what features of those messages are the source of the confusion if the messages are consistently misperceived, which tells us what linguistic cues humans are (mistakenly) keying into. This then leads to designing better machine learning algorithms that do not key into those misleading cues. Second, this aids the design of cognitive systems that predict how a message is likely to be interpreted by humans, and can warn a human reader if a message's intent is likely to be interpreted incorrectly.

3 Training a classifier with the database

To demonstrate the utility of the created database for developing computational approaches to social information identification in text, we applied a Sparse Multinomial Logistic Regression (SMLR) classifier (Krishnapuram et al. 2005) to the the subset of messages where two or more participants labeled the message and more than 50% of the participants perceived the intended social information type. This subset consisted of 624 messages (these messages make up the messages in the diagonals of table 3). While we realize that there are many other machine learning techniques that could be used, we thought this classifier would be a reasonable one to start with to demonstrate the utility of the database. As a first pass measure for identifying diagnostic linguistic cues, we examined a number of fairly shallow features:

- unigrams, bigrams, and trigrams
- number of word types, word tokens, and sentences
- number of exclamation marks, questions marks, and punctuation marks
- average sentence and word length
- word type to word token ratio
- average word log frequency for words appearing more than once in the database

[5] We note that people's precision on deceptive messages was higher: 0.67. That is, when they labeled a message as deceptive, it was deceptive 2/3 of the time. However, the probabilities in Table 3 represent deceptive message recall, i.e., how well they were able to label all deceptive messages as deceptive.

The use of shallow linguistic features seemed a reasonable first investigation as prior research involving linguistic cues for identifying information in text has often used word-level cues. For example, positive and negative affect words (e.g., *excellent* vs. *poor*) have been used in sentiment analysis to summarize whether a document is positive or negative (Turney 2002, Pang, Lee, and Vaithyanathan 2002, among others). In deception detection research, informative word-level cues include counting first and third person pronoun usage (e.g., *me* vs. *them*) (Anolli, Balconi, and Ciceri 2002), and noting the number of "exception words" (e.g., *but*, *except*, *without*) (Gupta and Skillicorn 2006). In addition, informative shallow text properties have also been identified (Zhou et al. 2004), such as (a) number of verbs, words, noun phrases, and sentences, (b) average sentence and word length, and (c) word type to word token ratio.

The SMLR classifier model was trained to produce the label (one of eight) corresponding to the generated social information using all the text features as input. Using a 10-fold cross-validation procedure, the model was trained on 90% of the messages and tested on the remaining 10%. The sparse classifier favors a small number of features in the regression solution and sets the weight of a large fraction of features to zero. Some of the non-zero weights learned by the model for each social information type are listed below (though each type has other features that also had non-zero weights). Positive weights indicate positive correlations while negative weights indicate negative correlations. Cues that are negatively correlated are *italicized*. Bigrams and trigrams are indicated by + in between the relevant words (e.g., no+way). BEGIN and END indicate the beginning and the end of the message, respectively.

- **deception**: *#-of-question-marks (-0.5)*, actually (1.4), at+all (0.6), if (0.8), *me (-0.9)*, *my (-0.2)*, not (1.6), of+course (1.1), trying+to (0.8), you+END (1.0)
- **politeness**: BEGIN+please (2.1), help (2.1), may+i (1.2), nice (2.3), nicely+END (1.1), so+sorry (1.5), would+you+like (1.0)
- **rudeness**: annoying (1.2), *good (-1.1)*, *great (-0.6)*, hurry+up (1.0), loud (2.7), mean (0.9), *pretty (-2.0)*, ugly (1.6)
- **embarrassment**: BEGIN+oh (2.0), can't+believe (1.0), can't+believe+i (0.6), forgot (2.1), *good (-.9)*, my (2.0), oh (1.1)
- **confidence**: i+believe (2.1), i+know (2.4), positive (3.5), really+good (2.9), sure (3.3), the+best (2.5), *think (-0.8)*
- **disbelief**: #-of-question-marks (2.4), BEGIN+are (3.8), *like (-0.6)*, never (1.4), no+way (3.0), shocked (1.1), such+a (1.1)
- **formality**: #-of-exclamation-marks (-0.8), BEGIN+excuse (2.1), *don't (-0.8)*, miss (4.1), mr (3.7), please (2.7), sir (5.1), very+nice (1.0)
- **persuading**: BEGIN+if+you (2.3), buy (1.3), come (3.5), have+to (1.6), we+can (1.3), would+look (2.9), you+should (3.4)

Some of the feature-label correlations discovered by the model fit with our intuitions about the social information types. For example, deceptive messages are negatively correlated with some of the first person pronouns (*me*, *my*), in accordance with Anolli, Balconi, and Ciceri (2002)'s results. Several polite and formal words appear correlated with polite and formal messages respectively (*may+i*, *nice*, *so+sorry*, *would+you+like*; *BEGIN+excuse*, *miss*, *mr*, *sir*), and formal messages tend not to include exclamation points. Negative words tend to be associated with rude messages (*annoying*, *loud*, *mean*, *ugly*), while positive words tend to be associated with confident messages (*really+good*, *sure*, *the+best*). Messages conveying disbelief tend to have more question marks and contain expressions of surprise (*never*, *no+way*, *shocked*), and persuasive messages tend to contain coercive expressions (*come*, *have+to*, *you+should*). As this is a relatively small data set, these cues are unlikely to be definitive – however, it is promising for the approach as a whole that the classifier can identify these cues using fairly shallow linguistic analyses.

We can also examine the classifier's ability to label messages, given the features it has deemed diagnostic for each social information type (i.e., those features it gave non-zero weight). For each message in the dataset, the classifier predicted what the intended social information type was. A correct prediction for a message's type matches the intended type for the message. A confusion matrix for the classifier based on the messages from the 624 message test set is shown in Table 4. Overall, the classifier was able to correctly label 59% of the messages. This is 12% less than humans were able to correctly label, but far better than chance performance (13%) and the performance of a simple algorithm that chooses the most frequent data type in the training set (17%).

The classifier shows some patterns similar to the human participants: (1) deception and formality are harder to detect than other social information types, (2) confidence and embarrassment are easier to detect than other social information types, and (3) formality is often mistaken for politeness ($p = .26$). However, some differences from the human participants are that deception is often mistaken for rudeness ($p = .19$) and politeness is often confused with rudeness and embarrassment, in addition to formality (all $p = .12$).

	deception	politeness	rudeness	embarrassment	confidence	disbelief	formality	persuading
deception	**.36**	.08	.19	.08	.08	.09	.06	.08
politeness	.05	**.49**	.12	.12	.05	.01	.12	.05
rudeness	.06	.06	**.63**	.04	.07	.07	.01	.07
embarrassment	.02	.01	.11	**.76**	.06	.03	.01	.00
confidence	.06	.01	.04	.08	**.68**	.02	.03	.08
disbelief	.08	.03	.08	.02	.09	**.56**	.02	.12
formality	.00	.26	.06	.03	.00	.06	**.43**	.15
persuading	.05	.06	.09	.03	.11	.03	.02	**.61**

Table 4: Confusion matrix for the machine learning classifier. The rows represent the intended social information for a message while the columns represent the labeled social information.

As the classifier's behavior was similar to human behavior in some cases, and the classifier used only these shallow linguistic features to make its decision, this suggests that humans may be keying into some of these shallower linguistic features when deciding a message's social information content. Given this, a classifier trained on such linguistic features may be able to predict which messages are likely to be ambiguous to humans.

4 Conclusion

We have described a methodology using GWAPs to create a database containing messages labeled with social information such as emotions, intentions, and attitudes, which can be valuable to the information extraction research community. Having implemented this methodology on a small scale, we discovered that non-expert annotators were able to identify the social information of interest fairly well when their collective perceptions were combined. However, we also noted that certain social information types are easily confusable by humans. We also used the database created by the GWAP to investigate shallow linguistic cues to social information in text and attempt to automatically label messages as expressing particular social information. The fact that the social information types we used in our GWAP can be identified automatically with some success suggests that these social information types are useful to pursue, though of course there are many other emotional states, attitudes, and intentions that could be explored in future work. In addition, other classifiers, particularly those using deeper-level properties like phrase structure, may be able to identify more subtle cues to social information in text. We also foresee extending the GWAP methodology to create large-scale databases both in English and in other languages in order to continue fostering the development of computational approaches to social information identification.

Acknowledgments

This paper has benefited from discussion and advice from Padhraic Smyth, Pierre Isabelle, and three anonymous reviewers. In addition, this work is supported by NSF grant BCS-0843896 to LP and CORCL grant MI 14B-2009-2010 to LP and MS.

References

Abbasi, A. 2007. Affect intensity analysis of dark web forums. *Proceedings of Intelligence and Security Informatics (ISI)*: 282-288.

Agarwal, A., Biadsy, F., and Mckeown, K. 2009. Contextual Phrase-Level Polarity Analysis using Lexical

Affect Scoring and Syntactic N-grams. *Proceedings of the 12th Conference of the European Chapter of the ACL*, Athens, Green: 24-32.

Alm, C. O., Roth, D., and Sproat, R. 2005. Emotions from text: Machine learning for text-based emotion prediction. *Proceedings of the Human Language Technology Conference and the Conference on Empirical Methods in Natural Language Processing (HLT/EMNLP)*.

Anolli, L., Balconi, M., and Ciceri, R. 2002. Deceptive Miscommunication Theory (DeMiT): A New Model for the Analysis of Deceptive Communication. In Anolli, L., Ciceri, R. and Rivs, G. (eds)., *Say not to say: new perspectives on miscommunication*. IOS Press: 73-100.

Dave, K., Lawrence, S., and Pennock, D. 2003. Mining the peanut gallery: Opinion extraction and semantic classication of product reviews, *Proceedings of WWW*: 519-528.

Diab, M., Dorr, B., Levin, L., Mitamura, T., Passonneau, R., Rambow, O., and Ramshaw, L. 2009. Language Understanding Annotation Corpus. LDC, Philadelphia.

Fleiss, J. L. 1971. Measuring nominal scale agreement among many raters. *Psychological Bulletin* 76(5): 378382.

Graff, D. 2003. English Gigaword. Linguistic Data Consortium, Philadelphia.

Greene, S. and Resnik, P. 2009. More than Words: Syntactic Packaging and Implicit Sentiment. *Human Language Technologies: The 2009 Annual Conference of the North American Chapter of the ACL*, Boulder, Colorado: 503-511.

Gupta, S. and Skillicorn, D. 2006. Improving a Textual Deception Detection Model, *Proceedings of the 2006 conference of the Center for Advanced Studies on Collaborative research*. Toronto, Canada.

Kennedy, A. and Inkpen, D. 2006. Sentiment classication of movie reviews using contextual valence shifters. Computational Intelligence, 22: 110-125.

Kosorukoff, A. 2001. Human-based Genetic Algorithm. *IEEE Transactions on Systems, Man, and Cybernetics*, SMC-2001: 3464-3469.

Krishnapuram, B., Figueiredo, M., Carin, L., and Hartemink, A. 2005. Sparse Multinomial Logistic Regression: Fast Algorithms and Generalization Bounds. *IEEE Transactions on Pattern Analysis and Machine Intelligence*, 27: 957-968.

Lazer, D., Pentland, A., Adamic, L., Aral, S., Barabsi, A., Brewer, D., Christakis, N., Contractor, N., Fowler, J., Gutmann, M., Jebara, T., King, G., Macy, M., Roy, D., and Val Alstyne, M. 2009. Computational Social Science, *Science*, 323: 721-723.

Nicolov, N., Salvetti, F., Liberman, M., and Martin, J. H. (eds.) 2006. *AAAI Symposium on Computational Approaches to Analysing Weblogs (AAAI-CAAW)*. AAAI Press.

Pang, B. and Lee, L. 2008. Opinion Mining and Sentiment Analysis. *Foundations and Trends in Information Retrieval* 2(1-2): 1-135.

Pang, B., Lee, L., and Vaithyanathan, S. 2002. Thumbs up? Sentiment Classification using Machine Learning Techniques. *Proceedings of the Conference on Empirical Methods in Natural Language Processing (EMNLP)*: 79-86.

Snow, R., O'Connor, B., Jurafsky, D., and Ng, A. 2008. Cheap and Fast - But is it Good? Evaluating Non-Expert Annotations for Natural Language Tasks. *Proceedings of the Conference on Empirical Methods in Natural Language Processing (EMNLP)*, 254-263.

Steyvers, M., Lee, M., Miller, B., and Hemmer, P. 2009. The Wisdom of Crowds in the Recollection of Order Information. In J. Lafferty, C. Williams (Eds.) *Advances in Neural Information Processing Systems*, 23, MIT Press.

Subasic, P. and Huettner A. 2001. A?ect analysis of text using fuzzy semantic typing. *IEEE Transactions on Fuzzy Systems*, 9: 483-496.

Turney, P. 2002. Thumbs Up or Thumbs Down? Semantic Orientation Applied to Unsupervised Classification of Reviews. *Proceedings of the Association for Computational Linguistics (ACL)*: 417-424.

von Ahn, L. 2006. Games With A Purpose. *IEEE Computer Magazine*, June 2006: 96-98.

von Ahn, L. and Dabbish, L. 2004. Labeling Images with a Computer Game. *Proceedings of the SIGCHI Conference on Human Factors in Computing Systems (Association for Computing Machinery, New York, 2004)*: 319-326.

von Ahn, L., Kedia, M. and Blum, M. 2006. Verbosity: A Game for Collecting Common-Sense Facts, *In Proceedings of the SIGCHI conference on Human Factors in computing systems*, Montral, Quebec, Canada.

Wiebe, J.M., Wilson, T., Bruce, R., Bell, M., and Martin, M. 2004. Learning subjective language. *Computational Linguistics*, 30: 277-308.

Zhou, L., Burgoon, J., Nunamaker, J., and Twitchell, D. 2004. Automating linguistics-based cues for detecting deception in text-based asynchronous computer-mediated communication. *Group Decision and Negotiation*, 13: 81-106.

Zhou, L. and Sung, Y. 2008. Cues to deception in online Chinese groups. *Proceedings of the 41st Annual Hawaii international Conference on System Sciences*, 146. Washington, DC: IEEE Computer Society.

@AM: Textual Attitude Analysis Model

Alena Neviarouskaya
University of Tokyo
7-3-1 Hongo, Bunkyo-ku
Tokyo 113-8656, Japan
lena@mi.ci.i.u-tokyo.ac.jp

Helmut Prendinger
Nat. Institute of Informatics
2-1-2 Hitotsubashi Chiyoda
Tokyo 101-8430, Japan
helmut@nii.ac.jp

Mitsuru Ishizuka
University of Tokyo
7-3-1 Hongo, Bunkyo-ku
Tokyo 113-8656, Japan
ishizuka@i.u-tokyo.ac.jp

Abstract

The automatic analysis and classification of text using fine-grained attitude labels is the main task we address in our research. The developed @AM system relies on compositionality principle and a novel approach based on the rules elaborated for semantically distinct verb classes. The evaluation of our method on 1000 sentences, that describe personal experiences, showed promising results: average accuracy on fine-grained level was 62%, on middle level – 71%, and on top level – 88%.

1 Introduction and Related Work

With rapidly growing online sources aimed at encouraging and stimulating people's discussions concerning personal, public or social issues (news, blogs, discussion forums, etc.), there is a great need in development of a computational tool for the analysis of people's attitudes. According to the Appraisal Theory (Martin and White, 2005), attitude types define the specifics of appraisal being expressed: affect (personal emotional state), judgment (social or ethical appraisal of other's behaviour), and appreciation (evaluation of phenomena).

To analyse contextual sentiment (polarity) of a phrase or a sentence, rule-based approaches (Nasukawa and Yi, 2003; Mulder et al., 2004; Moilanen and Pulman, 2007; Subrahmanian and Reforgiato, 2008), a machine-learning method using not only lexical but also syntactic features (Wilson et al., 2005), and a model of integration of machine learning approach with compositional semantics (Choi and Cardie, 2008) were proposed.

With the aim to recognize fine-grained emotions from text on the level of distinct sentences, researchers have employed a keyword spotting technique (Olveres et al., 1998; Chuang and Wu, 2004; Strapparava et al., 2007), a technique calculating emotion scores using Pointwise Mutual Information (PMI) (Kozareva et al., 2007), an approach inspired by common-sense knowledge (Liu et al., 2003), rule-based linguistic approaches (Boucouvalas, 2003; Chaumartin, 2007), machine-learning methods (Alm, 2008; Aman and Szpakowicz, 2008; Strapparava and Mihalcea, 2008), and an ensemble based multi-label classification technique (Bhowmick et al., 2009).

Early attempts to focus on distinct attitude types in the task of attitude analysis were made by Taboada and Grieve (2004), who determined a potential value of adjectives for affect, judgement and appreciation by calculating the PMI with the pronoun-copular pairs '*I was (affect)*', '*He was (judgement)*', and '*It was (appreciation)*', and Whitelaw et al. (2005), who used machine learning technique (SVM) with fine-grained semantic distinctions in features (attitude type, orientation) in combination with "bag of words" to classify movie reviews. However, the concentration only on adjectives, that express appraisal, and their modifiers, greatly narrows the potential of the Whitelaw et al.'s (2005) approach.

In this paper we introduce our system @AM (**AT**titude **A**nalysis **M**odel), which (1) classifies

Proceedings of the NAACL HLT 2010 Workshop on Computational Approaches to Analysis and Generation of Emotion in Text, pages 80–88,
Los Angeles, California, June 2010.

sentences according to the fine-grained attitude labels (nine affect categories (Izard, 1971): 'anger', 'disgust', 'fear', 'guilt', 'interest', 'joy', 'sadness', 'shame', 'surprise'; four polarity labels for judgment and appreciation: 'POS jud', 'NEG jud', 'POS app', 'NEG app'; and 'neutral'); (2) assigns the strength of the attitude; and (3) determines the level of confidence, with which the attitude is expressed. @AM relies on compositionality principle and a novel approach based on the rules elaborated for semantically distinct verb classes.

2 Lexicon for Attitide Analysis

We built the lexicon for attitude analysis that includes: (1) attitude-conveying terms; (2) modifiers; (3) "functional" words; and (4) modal operators.

2.1 The Core of Lexicon

As a core of lexicon for attitude analysis, we employ Affect database and extended version of SentiFul database developed by Neviarouskaya et al. (2009). The affective features of each emotion-related word are encoded using nine emotion labels ('anger', 'disgust', 'fear', 'guilt', 'interest', 'joy', 'sadness', 'shame', and 'surprise') and corresponding emotion intensities that range from 0.0 to 1.0. The original version of SentiFul database, which contains sentiment-conveying adjectives, adverbs, nouns, and verbs annotated by sentiment polarity, polarity scores and weights, was manually extended using attitude labels. Some examples of annotated attitude-conveying words are listed in Table 1. It is important to note here that some words could express different attitude types (affect, judgment, appreciation) depending on context; such lexical entries were annotated by all possible categories.

POS	Word	Category	Intensity
adjective	*honorable*	POS jud	0.3
	unfriendly	NEG aff (sadness)	0.5
		NEG jud	0.5
		NEG app	0.5
adverb	*gleefully*	POS aff (joy)	0.9
noun	*abnormality*	NEG app	0.25
verb	*frighten*	NEG aff (fear)	0.8
	desire	POS aff (interest)	1.0
		POS aff (joy)	0.5

Table 1. Examples of attitude-conveying words and their annotations.

2.2 Modifiers and Functional Words

The robust attitude analysis method should rely not only on attitude-conveying terms, but also on modifiers and contextual valence shifters (term introduced by Polanyi and Zaenen (2004)), which are integral parts of our lexicon.

We collected 138 modifiers that have an impact on contextual attitude features of related words, phrases, or clauses. They include:

1. Adverbs of degree (e.g., '*significantly*', '*slightly*' etc.) and adverbs of affirmation (e.g., '*absolutely*', '*seemingly*') that have an influence on the strength of attitude of the related words.
2. Negation words (e.g., '*never*', '*nothing*' etc.) that reverse the polarity of related statement.
3. Adverbs of doubt (e.g., '*scarcely*', '*hardly*' etc.) and adverbs of falseness (e.g., '*wrongly*' etc.) that reverse the polarity of related statement.
4. Prepositions (e.g., '*without*', '*despite*' etc.) that neutralize the attitude of related words.
5. Condition operators (e.g., '*if*', '*even though*' etc.) that neutralize the attitude of related words.

Adverbs of degree and adverbs of affirmation affect on related verbs, adjectives, or another adverb. Two annotators gave coefficients for intensity degree strengthening or weakening (from 0.0 to 2.0) to each of 112 collected adverbs, and the result was averaged (e.g., coeff('*perfectly*') = 1.9, coeff('*slightly*') = 0.2).

We distinguish two types of "functional" words that influence contextual attitude and its strength:

1. *Intensifying* adjectives (e.g., '*rising*', '*rapidly-growing*'), nouns (e.g., '*increase*', '*up-tick*'), and verbs (e.g., '*to grow*', '*to rocket*'), which increase the strength of attitude of related words.
2. *Reversing* adjectives (e.g., '*reduced*'), nouns (e.g., '*termination*', '*reduction*'), and verbs (e.g., '*to decrease*', '*to limit*', '*to diminish*'), which reverse the prior polarity of related words.

2.3 Modal Operators

Consideration of the modal operators in the tasks of opinion mining and attitude analysis is very important, as they indicate a degree of person's belief in the truth of the proposition, which is subjective in nature. Modal expressions point to likelihood and clearly involve the speaker's judgment (Hoye, 1997). Modals are distinguished by the *confidence level*.

We collected modal operators of two categories:

1. Modal verbs (13 verbs).
2. Modal adverbs (61 adverbs).

Three human annotators assigned the *confidence level*, which ranges from 0.0 to 1.0, to each modal verb and adverb; these ratings were averaged (e.g., conf(‘*vaguely*’) = 0.17, conf(‘*may*’) = 0.27, conf(‘*arguably*’) = 0.63, conf(‘*would*’) = 0.8, conf(‘*veritably*’) = 1.0).

3 Compositionality Principle

Words in a sentence are interrelated and, hence, each of them can influence the overall meaning and attitudinal bias of a statement. The algorithm for the attitude classification is designed based on the *compositionality principle*, according to which we determine the attitudinal meaning of a sentence by composing the pieces that correspond to lexical units or other linguistic constituent types governed by the rules of *polarity reversal, aggregation (fusion), propagation, domination, neutralization*, and *intensification*, at various grammatical levels.

Polarity reversal means that phrase or statement containing attitude-conveying term/phrase with prior positive polarity becomes negative, and vice versa. The rule of *polarity reversal* is applied in three cases: (1) negation word-modifier in relation with attitude-conveying statement (e.g., ‘*never*’ & POS(‘*succeed*’) => NEG(‘*never succeed*’)); (2) adverb of doubt in relation with attitude-conveying statement (e.g., ‘*scarcely*’ & POS(‘*relax*’) => NEG(‘*scarcely relax*’)); (3) functional word of *reversing* type in relation with attitude-conveying statement (e.g., adjective ‘*reduced*’ & POS(‘*enthusiasm*’) => NEG(‘*reduced enthusiasm*’)). In the case of judgment and appreciation, the use of *polarity reversal* rule is straightforward (‘POS jud’ <=> ‘NEG jud’, ‘POS app’ <=> ’NEG app’). However, it is not trivial to find pairs of opposite emotions in the case of a fine-grained classification, except for ‘joy’ and ‘sadness’. Therefore, we assume that (1) opposite emotion for three positive emotions, such as ‘interest’, ‘joy’, and ‘surprise’, is ‘sadness’ (‘POS aff’ => ‘sadness’); and (2) opposite emotion for six negative emotions, such as ‘anger’, ‘disgust’, ‘fear’, ‘guilt’, ‘sadness’, and ‘shame’, is ‘joy’ (‘NEG aff’ => ‘joy’).

The rules of *aggregation (fusion)* are as follows: (1) if polarities of attitude-conveying terms in adjective-noun, noun-noun, adverb-adjective, adverb-verb phrases have opposite directions, mixed polarity with dominant polarity of a descriptive term is assigned to the phrase (e.g., POS(‘*beautiful*’) & NEG(‘*fight*’) => POS-neg(‘*beautiful fight*’); NEG(‘*shamelessly*’) & POS(‘*celebrate*’) => NEG-pos(‘*shamelessly celebrate*’)); otherwise (2) the resulting polarity is based on the equal polarities of terms, and the strength of attitude is measured as a maximum between polarity scores (intensities) of terms (*max*(score1,score2)).

The rule of *propagation* is useful, as proposed in (Nasukawa and Yi, 2003), for the task of detection of local sentiments for given subjects. “Propagation” verbs propagate the sentiment towards the arguments; “transfer” verbs transmit sentiments among the arguments. The rule of *propagation* is applied when verb of “propagation” or “transfer” type is used in a phrase/clause and sentiment of an argument that has prior neutral polarity needs to be investigated (e.g., PROP-POS(‘*to admire*’) & ‘*his behaviour*’ => POS(‘*his behaviour*’); ‘*Mr. X*’ & TRANS(‘*supports*’) & NEG(‘*crime business*’) => NEG(‘*Mr. X*’)).

The rules of *domination* are as follows: (1) if polarities of verb (this rule is applied only for certain classes of verbs) and object in a clause have opposite directions, the polarity of verb is prevailing (e.g., NEG(‘*to deceive*’) & POS(‘*hopes*’) => NEG(‘*to deceive hopes*’)); (2) if compound sentence joints clauses using coordinate connector ‘*but*’, the attitude features of a clause following after the connector are dominant (e.g., ‘NEG(*It was hard to climb a mountain all night long*), *but* POS(*a magnificent view rewarded the traveler at the morning*).’ => POS(whole sentence)).

The rule of *neutralization* is applied when preposition-modifier or condition operator relate to the attitude-conveying statement (e.g., ‘*despite*’ & NEG(‘*worries*’) => NEUT(‘*despite worries*’)).

The rule of *intensification* means strengthening or weakening of the polarity score (intensity), and is applied when:

1. adverb of degree or affirmation relates to attitude-conveying term (e.g., Pos_score(‘*extremely happy*’) > Pos_score(‘*happy*’));
2. adjective or adverb is used in a comparative or superlative form (e.g., Neg_score(‘*sad*’) < Neg_score(‘*sadder*’) < Neg_score (‘*saddest*’)).

Our method is capable of processing sentences of different complexity, including simple, compound, complex (with complement and relative clauses), and complex-compound sentences. To understand how words and concepts relate to each other in a sentence, we employ Connexor Machinese Syntax parser (`http://www.connexor.eu/`) that returns lemmas, parts of speech, dependency functions, syntactic function tags, and morphological tags. When handling the parser output, we represent the sentence as a set of primitive clauses. Each clause might include Subject formation, Verb formation and Object formation, each of which may consist of a main element (subject, verb, or object) and its attributives and complements. For the processing of complex or compound sentences, we build a so-called "relation matrix", which contains information about dependences (e.g., coordination, subordination, condition, contingency, etc.) between different clauses in a sentence.

The annotations of words are taken from our attitude-conveying lexicon. The decision on most appropriate label, in case of words with multiple annotations (e.g., word '*unfriendly*' in Table 1), is made based on (1) the analysis of morphological tags of nominal heads and their premodifiers in the sentence (e.g., first person pronoun, third person pronoun, demonstrative pronoun, nominative or genitive noun, etc.); (2) the analysis of the sequence of hypernymic semantic relations of a particular noun in WordNet (Miller, 1990), which allows to determine its conceptual domain (e.g., "person, human being", "artifact", "event", etc.). For ex., '*I feel highly unfriendly attitude towards me*' conveys 'NEG aff' ('sadness'), while '*Shop assistant's behavior was really unfriendly*' and '*Plastic bags are environment unfriendly*' express 'NEG jud' and 'NEG app', correspondingly.

While applying the compositionality principle, we consecutively assign attitude features to words, phrases, formations, clauses, and finally, to the whole sentence.

4 Consideration of the Semantics of Verbs

All sentences must include a verb, because the verb tells us what action the subject is performing and object is receiving. In order to elaborate rules for attitude analysis based on the semantics of verbs, we investigated VerbNet (Kipper et al., 2007), the largest on-line verb lexicon that is organized into verb classes characterized by syntactic and semantic coherence among members of a class. Based on the thorough analysis of 270 first-level classes of VerbNet and their members, 73 verb classes (1) were found useful for the task of attitude analysis, and (2) were further classified into 22 classes differentiated by the role that members play in attitude analysis and by rules applied to them. Our classification is shown in Table 2.

Verb class (verb samples)
1 Psychological state or emotional reaction
1.1 Object-centered (oriented) emotional state (*adore, regret*)
1.2 Subject-driven change in emotional state (trans.) (*charm, inspire, bother*)
1.3 Subject-driven change in emotional state (intrans.) (*appeal to, grate on*)
2 Judgment
2.1 Positive judgment (*bless, honor*)
2.2 Negative judgment (*blame, punish*)
3 Favorable attitude (*accept, allow, tolerate*)
4 Adverse (unfavorable) attitude (*discourage, elude, forbid*)
5 Favorable or adverse calibratable changes of state (*grow, decline*)
6 Verbs of removing
6.1 Verbs of removing with neutral charge (*delete, remove*)
6.2 Verbs of removing with negative charge (*deport, expel*)
6.3 Verbs of removing with positive charge (*evacuate, cure*)
7 Negatively charged change of state (*break, crush, smash*)
8 Bodily state and damage to the body (*sicken, injure*)
9 Aspectual verbs
9.1 Initiation, continuation of activity, and sustaining (*begin, continue, maintain*)
9.2 Termination of activity (*quit, finish*)
10 Preservation (*defend, insure*)
11 Verbs of destruction and killing (*damage, poison*)
12 Disappearance (*disappear, die*)
13 Limitation and subjugation (*confine, restrict*)
14 Assistance (*succor, help*)
15 Obtaining (*win, earn*)
16 Communication indicator/reinforcement of attitude (*guess, complain, deny*)
17 Verbs of leaving (*abandon, desert*)
18 Changes in social status or condition (*canonize, widow*)
19 Success and failure
19.1 Success (*succeed, manage*)
19.2 Failure (*fail, flub*)
20 Emotional nonverbal expression (*smile, weep*)
21 Social interaction (*marry, divorce*)
22 Transmitting verbs (*supply, provide*)

Table 2. Verb classes defined for attitude analysis.

For each of our verb classes, we developed set of rules that are applied to attitude analysis on the phrase/clause-level. Some verb classes include verbs annotated by attitude type, prior polarity orientation, and the strength of attitude: "*Psychological state or emotional reaction*", "*Judgment*", "*Verbs of removing with negative charge*", "*Verbs of removing with positive charge*", "*Negatively charged change of state*", "*Bodily state and damage to the body*", "*Preservation*", and others. The attitude features of phrases, which involve positively or negatively charged verbs from such classes, are context-sensitive, and are defined by means of rules designed for each of the class.

As an example, below we provide short description and rules elaborated for the subclass "*Object-centered (oriented) emotional state*".

Features: subject experiences emotions towards some stimulus; verb prior polarity: positive or negative; context-sensitive.

Verb-Object rules (subject is ignored):

1. "Interior perspective" (subject's inner emotion state or attitude):

S & V+('*admires*') & O+('*his brave heart*') => (fusion, *max*(V_score,O_score)) => 'POS aff'.

S & V+('*admires*') & O-('*mafia leader*') => (verb valence dominance, V_score) => 'POS aff'.

S & V-('*disdains*') & O+('*his honesty*') => (verb valence dominance, V_score) => 'NEG aff'.

S & V-('*disdains*') & O-('*criminal activities*') => (fusion, *max*(V_score,O_score)) => 'NEG aff'.

2. "Exterior perspective" (social/ethical judgment):

S & V+('*admires*') & O+('*his brave heart*') => (fusion, *max*(V_score,O_score)) => 'POS jud'.

S & V+('*admires*') & O-('*mafia leader*') => (verb valence reversal, *max*(V_score,O_score)) => 'NEG jud'.

S & V-('*disdains*') & O+('*his honesty*') => (verb valence dominance, *max*(V_score,O_score)) => 'NEG jud'.

S & V-('*disdains*') & O-('*criminal activities*') => (verb valence reversal, *max*(V_score,O_score)) => 'POS jud'.

3. In case of neutral object => attitude type and prior polarity of verb, verb score (V_score).

Verb-PP (prepositional phrase) rules:

1. In case of negatively charged verb and PP starting with '*from*' => verb valence dominance:

S & V-('*suffers*') & PP-('*from illness*') => interior: 'NEG aff'; exterior: 'NEG jud'.

S & V-('*suffers*') & PP+ ('*from love*') => interior: 'NEG aff'; exterior: 'NEG jud'.

2. In case of positively charged verb and PP starting with '*in*'/'*for*', treat PP same as object (see above):

S & V+('*believes*') & PP-('*in evil*') => interior: 'POS aff'; exterior: 'NEG jud'.

S & V+('*believes*') & PP+('*in kindness*') => interior: 'POS aff'; exterior: 'POS jud'.

In the majority of rules the strength of attitude is measured as a maximum between attitude scores of a verb and an object (*max*(V_score,O_score)), because strength of overall attitude depends on both scores. For example, attitude conveyed by '*to suffer from grave illness*' is stronger than that of '*to suffer from slight illness*'.

In contrast to the rules of "*Object-centered (oriented) emotional state*" subclass, which ignore attitude features of a subject in a sentence, the rules elaborated for the "*Subject-driven change in emotional state (trans.)*" disregard the attitude features of object, as in sentences involving members of this subclass object experiences emotion, and subject causes the emotional state. For example (due to limitation of space, here and below we provide only some cases):

S('*Classical music*') & V+('*calmed*') & O-('*disobedient child*') => interior: 'POS aff'; exterior: 'POS app'.

S-('*Fatal consequences of GM food intake*') & V-('*frighten*') & O('*me*') => interior: 'NEG aff'; exterior: 'NEG app'.

The Verb-Object rules for the subclasses "*Positive judgment*" and "*Negative judgment*" (verbs from "*Judgment*" class relate to a judgment or opinion that someone may have in reaction to something) are very close to those defined for the subclass "*Object-centered (oriented) emotional state*". However, Verb-PP rules have some specifics: for both positive and negative judgment verbs, we treat PP starting with '*for*'/'*of*'/'*as*' same as object in Verb-Object rules. For example:

S('*He*') & V-('*blamed*') & O+('*innocent person*') => interior: 'NEG jud'; exterior: 'NEG jud'.

S('*They*') & V-('*punished*') & O('*him*') & PP-('*for his misdeed*') => interior: 'NEG jud'; exterior: 'POS jud'.

Verbs from classes "*Favorable attitude*" and "*Adverse (unfavorable) attitude*" have prior neutral polarity and positive or negative reinforcement, correspondingly, that means that they only impact on the polarity and strength of non-neutral phrase (object in a sentence written in active voice, or subject in a sentence written in passive voice, or PP in case of some verbs).

Rules:

1. If verb belongs to the "Favorable attitude" class and the polarity of phrase is not neutral, then the

attitude score of the phrase is intensified (we use symbol '^' to indicate intensification):

S('*They*') & [V pos. reinforcement]('*elected*') & O+('*fair judge*') => 'POS app'; O_score^.

S('*They*') & [V pos. reinforcement]('*elected*') & O-('*corrupt candidate*') => 'NEG app'; O_score^.

2. If verb belongs to the "Adverse (unfavorable) attitude" class and the polarity of phrase is not neutral, then the polarity of phrase is reversed and score is intensified:

S('*They*') & [V neg. reinforcement]('*prevented*') & O-('*the spread of disease*') => 'POS app'; O_score^.

S+('*His achievements*') & [V neg. reinforcement]('*were overstated*') => 'NEG app'; S_score^.

Below are examples of processing the sentences with verbs from "*Verbs of removing*" class.

"*Verbs of removing with neutral charge*":

S('*The tape-recorder*') & [V neutral rem.]('*automatically ejects*') & O-neutral('*the tape*') => neutral.

S('*The safety invention*') & [V neutral rem.]('*ejected*') & O('*the pilot*') & PP-('*from burning plane*') => 'POS app'; PP_score^.

"*Verbs of removing with negative charge*":

S('*Manager*') & [V neg. rem.]('*fired*') & O-('*careless employee*') & PP('*from the company*') => 'POS app'; *max*(V_score,O_score).

"*Verbs of removing with positive charge*":

S('*They*') & [V pos. rem.]('*evacuated*') & O('*children*') & PP-('*from dangerous place*') => 'POS app'; *max*(V_score,PP_score).

Along with modal verbs and modal adverbs, members of the "*Communication indicator/reinforcement of attitude*" verb class also indicate the confidence level or degree of certainty concerning given opinion.

Features: subject (communicator) expresses statement with/without attitude; statement is PP starting with '*of*', '*on*', '*against*', '*about*', '*concerning*', '*regarding*', '*that*', '*how*' etc.; ground: positive or negative; reinforcement: positive or negative.

Rules:

1. If the polarity of expressed statement is neutral, then the attitude is neutral:

S('*Professor*') & [V pos. ground, pos. reinforcement, confidence:0.83]('*dwelled*') & PP-neutral('*on a question*') => neutral.

2. If the polarity of expressed statement is not neutral and the reinforcement is positive, then the polarity score of the statement (PP) is intensified:

S('*Jane*') & [V neg. ground, pos. reinforcement, confidence:0.8]('*is complaining*') & PP-('*of a headache again*') => 'NEG app'; PP_score^; confidence:0.8.

3. If the polarity of expressed statement is not neutral and reinforcement is negative, then the polarity of the statement (PP) is reversed and score is intensified:

S('*Max*') & [V neg. ground, neg. reinforcement, confidence:0.2]('*doubt*') & PP-{'*that*' S+('*his good fortune*') & [V termination]('*will ever end*')} => 'POS app'; PP_score^; confidence:0.2.

In the last example, to measure the sentiment of PP, we apply rule for the verb '*end*' from the "*Termination of activity*" class, which reverses the non-neutral polarity of subject (in intransitive use of verb) or object (in transitive use of verb). For example, the polarity of the following sentence with positive PP is negative: '*They discontinued helping children*'.

5 Evaluation

In order to evaluate the performance of our algorithm, we conducted experiment on the set of sentences extracted from personal stories about life experiences that were anonymously published on the social networking website *Experience Project* (`www.experienceproject.com`). This website represents an interactive platform that allows people to share personal experiences, thoughts, opinions, feelings, passions, and confessions through the network of personal stories. With over 4 million experiences accumulated (as of February 2010), *Experience Project* is a perfect source for researchers interested in studying different types of attitude expressed through text.

5.1 Data Set Description

For our experiment we extracted 1000 sentences from various stories grouped by topics within 13 different categories, such as "Arts and entertainment", "Current events", "Education", "Family and friends", "Health and wellness", "Relationships and romance" and others, on the *Experience Project*. Sentences were collected from 358 distinct topic groups, such as "I still remember September 11", "I am intelligent but airheaded", "I think bullfighting is cruel", "I quit smoking", "I am a fashion victim", "I was adopted" and others.

TOP	POS					NEG								neutral
MID	POS aff			POS jud	POS app	NEG aff						NEG jud	NEG app	neutral
ALL	interest	joy	surprise	POS jud	POS app	anger	disgust	fear	guilt	sadness	shame	NEG jud	NEG app	neutral

Figure 1. Hierarchy of attitude labels.

We considered three hierarchical levels of attitude labels in our experiment (see Figure 1). Three independent annotators labeled the sentences with one of 14 categories from ALL level and a corresponding score (the strength or intensity value). These annotations were further interpreted using labels from MID and TOP levels. Fleiss' Kappa coefficient was used as a measure of reliability of human raters' annotations. The agreement coefficient on 1000 sentences was 0.53 on ALL level, 0.57 on MID level, and 0.73 on TOP level.

Only those sentences, on which at least two out of three human raters completely agreed, were included in the "gold standard" for our experiment. Three "gold standards" were created according to the hierarchy of attitude labels. Fleiss' Kappa coefficients are 0.62, 0.63, and 0.74 on ALL, MID, and TOP levels, correspondingly. Table 3 shows the distributions of labels in the "gold standards".

ALL level		MID level	
Label	**Number**	**Label**	**Number**
anger	45	POS aff	233
disgust	21	NEG aff	332
fear	54	POS jud	66
guilt	22	NEG jud	78
interest	84	POS app	100
joy	95	NEG app	29
sadness	133	neutral	87
shame	18	**total**	925
surprise	36		
POS jud	66	**TOP level**	
NEG jud	78	**Label**	**Number**
POS app	100	POS	437
NEG app	29	NEG	473
neutral	87	neutral	87
total	868	**total**	997

Table 3. Label distributions in the "gold standards".

5.2 Results

After processing each sentence from the data set by our system, we measured averaged accuracy, precision, recall, and F-score for each label within ALL, MID, and TOP levels. The results are shown in Table 4. The ratio of the most frequent attitude label in the "gold standard" was considered as the baseline. As seen from the obtained results, our algorithm performed with high accuracy significantly surpassing the baselines on all levels of attitude hierarchy (except 'neutral' category on the TOP level, which is probably due to the unbalanced distribution of labels in the "gold standard", where 'neutral' sentences constitute less than 9%).

ALL level				
Baseline	0.153			
Label	**Accuracy**	**Precision**	**Recall**	**F-score**
anger	0.621	0.818	0.600	0.692
disgust		0.818	0.857	0.837
fear		0.768	0.796	0.782
guilt		0.833	0.455	0.588
interest		0.772	0.524	0.624
joy		0.439	0.905	0.591
sadness		0.528	0.917	0.670
shame		0.923	0.667	0.774
surprise		0.750	0.833	0.789
POS jud		0.824	0.424	0.560
NEG jud		0.889	0.410	0.561
POS app		0.755	0.400	0.523
NEG app		0.529	0.310	0.391
neutral		0.559	0.437	0.490
MID level				
Baseline	0.359			
Label	**Accuracy**	**Precision**	**Recall**	**F-score**
POS aff	0.709	0.668	0.888	0.762
NEG aff		0.765	0.910	0.831
POS jud		0.800	0.424	0.554
NEG jud		0.842	0.410	0.552
POS app		0.741	0.400	0.519
NEG app		0.474	0.310	0.375
neutral		0.514	0.437	0.472
TOP level				
Baseline	0.474			
Label	**Accuracy**	**Precision**	**Recall**	**F-score**
POS	0.879	0.918	0.920	0.919
NEG		0.912	0.922	0.917
neutral		0.469	0.437	0.452

Table 4. Results of the system performance evaluation.

In the case of fine-grained attitude recognition (ALL level), the highest precision was obtained for 'shame' (0.923) and 'NEG jud' (0.889), while the highest recall was received for 'sadness' (0.917) and ‘joy’ (0.905) emotions at the cost of low precision (0.528 and 0.439, correspondingly). The algorithm performed with the worst results in recognition of ‘NEG app’ and ‘neutral’.

The analysis of a confusion matrix for the ALL level revealed the following top confusions of our system (see Table 5): (1) ‘anger’, ‘fear’, ‘guilt’, ‘shame’, ‘NEG jud’, ‘NEG app’ and ‘neutral’ were predominantly incorrectly predicted as ‘sadness’ (for ex., @AM resulted in ‘sadness’ for the sentence *‘I know we have several months left before the election, but I am already sick and tired of seeing the ads on TV’*, while human annotations were ‘anger’/‘anger’/‘disgust’); (2) ‘interest’, ‘POS jud’ and ‘POS app’ were mostly confused with ‘joy’ by our algorithm (e.g., @AM classified the sentence *‘It’s one of those life changing artifacts that we must have in order to have happier, healthier lives’* as ‘joy’(-ful), while human annotations were ‘POS app’/‘POS app’/‘interest’).

Actual label	Incorrectly predicted labels (%), in descending order
anger	sadness (28.9%), joy (4.4%), neutral (4.4%), NEG app (2.2%)
disgust	anger (4.8%), sadness (4.8%), NEG jud (4.8%)
fear	sadness (13%), joy (5.6%), POS app (1.9%)
guilt	sadness (50%), anger (4.5%)
interest	joy (33.3%), neutral (7.1%), sadness (3.6%), POS app (2.4%), fear (1.2%)
joy	interest (3.2%), POS app (3.2%), sadness (1.1%), surprise (1.1%), neutral (1.1%)
sadness	neutral (3.8%), joy (1.5%), anger (0.8%), fear (0.8%), guilt (0.8%), NEG app (0.8%)
shame	sadness (16.7%), fear (5.6%), guilt (5.6%), NEG jud (5.6%)
surprise	fear (5.6%), neutral (5.6%), joy (2.8%), POS jud (2.8%)
POS jud	joy (37.9%), POS app (9.1%), interest (4.5%), sadness (1.5%), surprise (1.5%), NEG jud (1.5%), neutral (1.5%)
NEG jud	sadness (37.2%), anger (3.8%), disgust (3.8%), neutral (3.8%)
POS app	joy (37%), neutral (9%), surprise (7%), interest (3%), POS jud (3%), sadness (1%)
NEG app	sadness (44.8%), fear (13.8%), disgust (3.4%), surprise (3.4%), neutral (3.4%)
neutral	sadness (29.9%), joy (13.8%), interest (3.4%), fear (2.3%), POS jud (2.3%), NEG app (2.3%), NEG jud (1.1%), POS app (1.1%)

Table 5. Data from a confusion matrix for ALL level.

Our system achieved high precision for all categories on the MID level (Table 4), with the exception of ‘NEG app’ and ‘neutral’, although high recall was obtained only in the case of categories related to affect (‘POS aff’, ‘NEG aff’). These results indicate that affect sensing is easier than recognition of judgment or appreciation from text.

TOP level results (Table 4) show that our algorithm classifies sentences that convey positive or negative sentiment with high accuracy (92% and 91%, correspondingly). On the other hand, ‘neutral’ sentences still pose a challenge.

The analysis of errors revealed that system requires common sense or additional context to deal with sentences like *‘All through my life I’ve felt like I’m second fiddle’* (“gold standard”: ‘sadness’; @AM: ‘neutral’) or *‘For me every minute on my horse is alike an hour in heaven!’* (“gold standard”: ‘joy’; @AM: ‘neutral’).

We also evaluated the system performance with regard to attitude intensity estimation. The percentage of attitude-conveying sentences (not considering neutral ones), on which the result of our system conformed to the fine-grained “gold standard” (ALL level), according to the measured distance between intensities given by human raters (averaged values) and those obtained by our system is shown in Table 6. As seen from the table, our system achieved satisfactory results in estimation of the strength of attitude expressed through text.

Range of intensity difference	Percent of sentences, %
[0.0 – 0.2]	55.5
(0.2 – 0.4]	29.5
(0.4 – 0.6]	12.2
(0.6 – 0.8]	2.6
(0.8 – 1.0]	0.2

Table 6. Results on intensity.

6 Conclusions

In this paper we introduced @AM, which is so far, to the best of our knowledge, the only system classifying sentences using fine-grained attitude types, and extensively dealing with the semantics of verbs in attitude analysis. Our composition approach broadens the coverage of sentences with complex contextual attitude. The evaluation results indicate that @AM achieved reliable results in the task of textual attitude analysis. The limitations include dependency on lexicon and on accuracy of the parser. The primary objective for the future research is to use the results of named-entity recognition software in our algorithm.

References

Cecilia O. Alm. 2008. *Affect in Text and Speech*. PhD Dissertation. University of Illinois at Urbana-Champaign.

Saima Aman and Stan Szpakowicz. 2008. Using Roget's Thesaurus for Fine-Grained Emotion Recognition. *Proceedings of the Third International Joint Conference on Natural Language Processing IJCNLP 2008*, Hyderabad, India, pp. 296-302.

Plaban Kumar Bhowmick, Anupam Basu, and Pabitra Mitra. 2009. Reader Perspective Emotion Analysis in Text through Ensemble based Multi-Label Classification Framework. *Computer and Information Science*, 2 (4): 64-74.

Anthony C. Boucouvalas. 2003. Real Time Text-to-Emotion Engine for Expressive Internet Communications. *Being There: Concepts, Effects and Measurement of User Presence in Synthetic Environments*, Ios Press, pp. 306-318.

Francois-Regis Chaumartin. 2007. UPAR7: A Knowledge-based System for Headline Sentiment Tagging. *Proceedings of the Fourth International Workshop on Semantic Evaluations (SemEval-2007)*, Prague, Czech Republic, pp. 422-425.

Yejin Choi and Claire Cardie. 2008. Learning with Compositional Semantics as Structural Inference for Subsentential Sentiment Analysis. *Proceedings of the Conference on Empirical Methods in Natural Language Processing*, pp. 793-801.

Ze-Jing Chuang and Chung-Hsien Wu. 2004. Multimodal Emotion Recognition from Speech and Text. *Computational Linguistic and Chinese Language Processing*, 9(2): 45-62.

Leo Hoye. 1997. *Adverbs and Modality in English*. New York: Addison Wesley Longman Inc.

Carroll E. Izard. 1971. *The Face of Emotion*. New York: Appleton-Century-Crofts.

Karin Kipper, Anna Korhonen, Neville Ryant, and Martha Palmer. 2007. A Large-scale Classification of English Verbs. *Language Resources and Evaluation*, 42 (1): 21-40.

Zornitsa Kozareva, Borja Navarro, Sonia Vazquez, and Andres Montoyo, A. 2007. UA-ZBSA: A Headline Emotion Classification through Web Information. *Proceedings of the Fourth International Workshop on Semantic Evaluations*, pp. 334-337.

Hugo Liu, Henry Lieberman, and Ted Selker. 2003. A Model of Textual Affect Sensing Using Real-World Knowledge. *Proceedings of the International Conference on Intelligent User Interfaces*, pp. 125-132.

James R. Martin and Peter R.R. White. 2005. *The Language of Evaluation: Appraisal in English*. Palgrave, London, UK.

George A. Miller. 1990. WordNet: An On-line Lexical Database. *International Journal of Lexicography*, Special Issue, 3 (4): 235-312.

Karo Moilanen and Stephen Pulman. 2007. Sentiment Composition. *Proceedings of the Recent Advances in Natural Language Processing International Conference*, pp. 378-382.

Matthijs Mulder, Anton Nijholt, Marten den Uyl, and Peter Terpstra. 2004. A Lexical Grammatical Implementation of Affect. *Proceedings of the Seventh International Conference on Text, Speech and Dialogue*, pp. 171-178.

Tetsuya Nasukawa and Jeonghee Yi. 2003. Sentiment Analysis: Capturing Favorability using Natural Language Processing. *Proceedings of the 2nd International Conference on Knowledge Capture*, pp. 70-77.

Alena Neviarouskaya, Helmut Prendinger, and Mitsuru Ishizuka. 2009. SentiFul: Generating a Reliable Lexicon for Sentiment Analysis. *Proceedings of the International Conference on Affective Computing and Intelligent Interaction*, IEEE, Amsterdam, Netherlands, pp. 363-368.

J. Olveres, M. Billinghurst, J. Savage, and A. Holden. 1998. Intelligent, Expressive Avatars. *Proceedings of the First Workshop on Embodied Conversational Characters*, pp. 47-55.

Livia Polanyi and Annie Zaenen. 2004. Contextual Valence Shifters. *Working Notes of the AAAI Spring Symposium on Exploring Attitude and Affect in Text: Theories and Applications*.

Carlo Strapparava and Rada Mihalcea. 2008. Learning to Identify Emotions in Text. *Proceedings of the 2008 ACM Symposium on Applied Computing*, Fortaleza, Brazil, pp. 1556-1560.

Carlo Strapparava, Alessandro Valitutti, and Oliviero Stock. 2007. Dances with Words. *Proceedings of the International Joint Conference on Artificial Intelligence*, Hyderabad, India, pp. 1719-1724.

V.S. Subrahmanian and Diego Reforgiato. 2008. AVA: Adjective-Verb-Adverb Combinations for Sentiment Analysis. *Intelligent Systems*, IEEE, 23 (4): 43-50.

Maite Taboada and Jack Grieve. 2004. Analyzing Appraisal Automatically. *Proceedings of American Association for Artificial Intelligence Spring Symposium on Exploring Attitude and Affect in Text*, pp.158-161.

Casey Whitelaw, Navendu Garg, and Shlomo Argamon. 2005. Using Appraisal Groups for Sentiment Analysis. *Proceedings of the 14th ACM International Conference on Information and Knowledge Management*, CIKM, Bremen, Germany, pp. 625-631.

Theresa Wilson, Janyce Wiebe, and Paul Hoffmann. 2005. Recognizing Contextual Polarity in Phrase-level Sentiment Analysis. *Proceedings of Human Language Technology Conference and Conference on Empirical Methods in Natural Language Processing*, Vancouver: ACL, pp. 347-354.

Generating Shifting Sentiment for a Conversational Agent

Simon Whitehead
University of Melbourne, Australia
srwhitehead@gmail.com

Lawrence Cavedon
RMIT University, Australia
lawrence.cavedon@rmit.edu.au

Abstract

We investigate techniques for generating alternative output sentences with varying sentiment, using (an approximation to) the Valentino method, based on SentiWordNet, of Guerini et al. We extend this method by filtering out unacceptable candidate sentences, using bigrams sourced from different corpora to determine whether lexical substitutions are appropriate in the given context. We also compare the generated candidates against human judgements of whether the desired sentiment shift has occurred: our results suggest limitations with the overall knowledge-based approach, and we propose potential directions for improvement.

1 Introduction

The design of more natural or *believable* conversational agents (Bates, 1994; Pelachaud and Bilvi, 2003) requires the need for such agents to communicate affectively, by the display of emotion or attitude towards objects, other agents, or states of affairs. More engaging or influential agents may seek to actually affect their conversational partner at a deeper level, for example, by influencing their emotional state (van der Sluis and Mellish, 2008). Previous work in this area has explored the use of gestures and facial expression (Caridakis et al., 2007) and rhythm and prosody of speech (Zovato et al., 2008) for expressing affect; however there has been little work on generation of affective language in dialogue.

Our general approach is inspired by (Fleischman and Hovy, 2002)'s work on generating different surface-level versions of utterance content, depending on an agent's appraisals towards objects, characters and events in its environment. While their approach is effective, it relies on manual creation of lexical alternatives, customized to the application domain. We are interested in approaches that will scale, and can be applied domain-independently.

While our ultimate aim is generation of language that relects emotional state, in this work we investigate the automatic generation of varying "sentiment" in output utterances; we focus on sentiment mainly due to the recent development of useful resources for this task. (Guerini et al., 2008)'s Valentino system is an approach to automatically generating candidate output utterances with different sentiment from an original; the authors suggest ECAs as a possible application scenario for their techniques. We explore this suggestion, implementing a *lexical substitution* (McCarthy and Navigli, 2007) approach to dialogue generation with sentiment, using the Valentino approach and associated resources. Lexical substitution approaches raise well-known challenges, and we investigate a number of techniques to address these in Section 4; for example, using bigrams and grammatical relations to determine which substitutions are acceptable based on their context in a sentence.[1]

Our techniques show improvement over naive lexical substitution; however, an evaluation with human subjects suggests that a deeper problem is that even "acceptable" candidate sentences generated by the method do not match human judgements with respect to sentiment shift: i.e., alternatives labeled as more positive (resp., negative) than the original by the system are often seen as a sentiment shift in the opposite direction by human judges (Section 5).

2 Background: Valentino

The *Valentino*[2] system (Guerini et al., 2008) is a tool developed from WordNet and SentiWordNet

[1] Guerini et al. suggest this as an area for further work.

[2] VALENced Text INOculator

Proceedings of the NAACL HLT 2010 Workshop on Computational Approaches to Analysis and Generation of Emotion in Text, pages 89–97,
Los Angeles, California, June 2010.

designed to produce more positively or negatively slanted versions of text. Input to the system consists of a short sentence, and a *target valence* (between -1 and 1), which indicates the *desired* polarity and magnitude of sentiment in the modified output text. Valentino uses a number of strategies for adding, removing, or substituting certain words in order to alter the overall sentiment of the sentence. Table 1 shows examples of Valentino output for different target valences, with modifications in italics.

To perform the word-substitution, (Guerini et al., 2008) created a resource of *OVVTs*[3]: vectors of semantically related terms which may substitute for one another. The OVVTs were constructed using structural analysis of WordNet, and are divided into adjectives, nouns, and verbs. (Guerini et al., 2008) also constructed a separate resource of *Modifier OVVTs* which list adverbs that can be used to modify verbs. Modifier OVVTs were created using verbs extracted from certain *FrameNet*[4] categories, then recording which adverbs occur next to these verbs in the British National Corpus (BNC). Each term in the Valentino resource was assigned a *sentiment valence*, which corresponds to the SentiWordNet score of its parent WordNet synset. Table 2 shows part of an OVVT containing the noun 'man'.[5]

Term	POS	Sense	Valence
hunk	n	1	0.375
man	n	1	0
dude	n	1	-0.125
beau	n	2	-0.125

Table 2: (Abridged) example of an OVVT

To generate a modified sentence, (Guerini et al., 2008) apply the following strategies to each word[6] until the sentence valence (total of term valences) meets the target:

1. **Paraphrase:** Lemmas with only one sense are replaced by their WordNet gloss, which is scored for sentiment using the OVVTs;
2. **Use of most frequent senses:** The OVVTs are searched using only the most frequent senses;
3. **Adjective modification:** Adjectives are replaced with their stronger/weaker alternatives such that the target valence is not exceeded;
4. **Verb modification:** Verbs are modified by inserting, removing, or replacing intensifier or downtoner adverbs.

The final sentence is rendered as surface text by transforming each of the inserted lemmas back into the original morphology.

(Guerini et al., 2008) suggest their system's potential application to dialogue generation in an ECA, enabling emotional variation. However, they do not present an evaluation of Valentino's effectiveness. We expect that not all output utterances generated using their method will be sensible in the context of a believable ECA, for the following reasons:

Unconventional Word Usage: Upon inspection, we found the OVVTs often contain several words which are no longer conventionally used (e.g. "beau"). For an ECA to be believable, we hypothesise that such unpopular words should not be considered as potential candidates for substitution.

Incorrect Grammatical Context: The naive version of the Valentino method assumes that all words in an OVVT can be substituted for one another regardless of their context in the sentence (see Table 3); Guerini et al. propose this as an area for future work. We explore semi-informed solutions using bigrams and grammatical relations to eliminate syntactically incorrect substitutions.

... Williams was not *interested* (in) girls
... Williams was not *concerned* (with) girls
... Williams was not *fascinated* (by) girls

Table 3: Illustration of grammatical context issues

3 Implementation

We implemented a lexical substitution approach to varying valence, closely following the Valentino approach described in (Guerini et al., 2008). We did

[3]We assume OVVT stands for Ordered Vector of Valenced Terms; this is not explicit in (Guerini et al., 2008).

[4]`http://framenet.icsi.berkeley.edu/`

[5]All our examples and evaluations are using a version of the OVVTs made available by Marco Guerini on May 13, 2009.

[6]Actually, to the lemma of each word.

Valence	Sentence
n/a	Bob admitted that John is absolutely the best guy
1.0	Bob *wholeheartedly admitted* that John is *absolutely a superb hunk*
0.5	Bob *openly admitted* that John is *highly* the *redeemingest signor*
0.0	Bob *admitted* that John is *highly a well-behaved sir*
-0.5	Bob *sadly confessed* that John is *nearly a well-behaved beau*
-1.0	Bob *harshly confessed* that John is *pretty an acceptable eunuch*

Table 1: Example of Valentino sentiment shifting (Guerini et al., 2008)

not implement all the above strategies—in particular, we did not implement paraphrasing, adverb modification, or morphology synthesis; rather we focused on developing techniques that would address the lexical substitution issues described above.

As with Valentino, we calculate *sentence valence* by summing the valences of all terms in the sentence which are present in the OVVTs[7]. However, as a variation on Valentino, we aggregated sentence shift into five broad categories: "major positive shift"; "minor positive shift"; "no shift"; "minor negative shift"; "major negative shift".

Since most OVVTs contain only lemmas, we first performed *lemmatisation* using the *MorphAdorner*[8] package. To locate a term in the OVVTs, we first search for the original word morphology, then if no match is found we try using the lemma.

As with (Guerini et al., 2008), we included candidates from multiple senses of a matching word; however, rather than stopping at the third most frequent sense, we explored up to sense forty so as to increase the number of possible substitutions for terms.[9] We performed a very naive version of word sense disambiguation (WSD) (see below), but lack of WSD was an issue (discussed later).

Alternative sentences were generated by modifying at most a single word; this reduces the explosion in the number of alternatives, but the methods described could just as easily apply to alternatives constructed by varying multiple words.

The novel aspect of our implementation was the "candidate filtering" techniques: i.e. techniques for deciding whether to accept a candidate replacement term as substitute in a given sentence; this was specifically designed to address the issues above. In the next section, we describe filtering techniques using simple bigrams and grammatical relations, and evaluate the effectiveness of each.

4 Evaluation: Candidate Filtering

The data set we used for this evaluation consisted of 25 sentences, randomly extracted from the BNC.[10] The sentences were sourced from the BNC to avoid any bias which may have been introduced had the test sentences been created manually. We required that each test sentence satisfy the following conditions[11]:

1. The sentence must contain between 6 and 10 words (to reflect length of a typical dialogue utterance);

2. The sentence must contain at least one term which is found in the OVVTs (otherwise it would be pointless for evaluation purposes); the term may have any valence.[12]

Our second filtering technique requires information about the grammatical relations between terms in a sentence (illustrated in Figure 1). For this, we used a version of the BNC which was pre-processed with the RASP parser (Briscoe et al., 2006).

Our gold standard for candidate acceptability was created using the first author's judgements.[13] In or-

[7] Since we ignore adverbs, we do not include these when scoring a sentence.

[8] `http://morphadorner.northwestern.edu/`

[9] Increasing this further increased the number of alternatives but did not improve performance.

[10] The size of our test data set was capped at 25 due to the time required to create the gold standard (i.e., judging 1030 substitutions consistently).

[11] These constraints reduced our sample set from the ~4.6 million sentences in the BNC to approx. 627,000 sentences.

[12] The sentence can theoretically be valence-shifted by substituting that term, regardless of the term's valence.

[13] With more time we would of course have preferred to use multiple annotators. However, the judgement task was simple

der to be judged as an ACCEPT by the annotator, a generated sentence needed to satisfy the following criteria (otherwise it was labelled REJECT):

1. **Semantic Equivalence:** The new sentence should convey reasonably equivalent semantics compared to the original: e.g., phrases such as 'young boy' and 'small boy' were considered acceptably close;[14]

2. **Grammatical Correctness:** The new sentence should not contain grammatical errors. For the gold standard, terms were *manually* converted into their original morphological form before annotation (e.g., if the lemma 'speak' replaced an instance of 'shouted', then it was converted to 'spoke').

4.1 Evaluation Methodology

To evaluate each candidate selection method, we performed the following procedure for each of our 25 test sentences:

1. Find all matching[15] terms and retrieve the valence score of each;

2. For each matching term:

   (a) Retrieve the corresponding list of alternative terms from the OVVTs;

   (b) Generate several different candidate sentences by substituting each alternative term into the original sentence;

   (c) Apply the chosen *candidate selection* technique to each generated sentence, and label each as ACCEPT or REJECT (for step 3);

3. Compare all system classifications to our gold standard (automatically), and mark each as either a true positive (TP), false positive (FP), true negative (TN), or false negative (FN).

We then used the TP, FP, TN and FN counts to compute the accuracy, precision, recall and F-score across all generated sentences. These metrics are used to compare the relative performance between each of our candidate selection methods.

We describe each of our techniques and the results; we present all the measurements in a single table (Table 5).[16]

4.2 Candidate filtering using bigrams

For each candidate sentence generated, we examined the bigrams including the newly substituted term. If both[17] bigrams appear in the BNC, we take this as an indication that the substitution is acceptable, and we accept the candidate sentence. Otherwise, the candidate is rejected. We pre-processed the BNC to extract 8,463,295 unique bigrams, formatted as `lemma/pos lemma/pos` pairs, where `lemma` is the lemmatised word, and `pos` is the WordNet POS. As a simple attempt to address word-sense disambiguation, we discriminated on POS[18] when extracting and matching these bigrams. For example, '`drive/n home/n`' and '`drive/v home/n`' would be considered separate bigrams, as the term 'drive' occurs with different POS in each. We chose to lemmatise all bigrams due to the relatively small size of the BNC. Also, we did not consider bigrams which are interrupted by sentence punctuation, as this indicates a phrase break.

We take this bigram approach as our baseline.[19] This simple technique has reasonable accuracy (0.752: see Table 5) but this is due largely to the high number of true negatives produced. The false negatives are mainly caused by the BNC's relatively limited bigram coverage.

To address this issue, we sourced our bigrams from the Google Web 1T Corpus, which covers approximately *one trillion* words of English text sourced from publicly accessible web pages. Compared with the BNC, it has much greater coverage, containing ~314 million bigrams. However, Web 1T does not contain POS information, and due to its size we did not lemmatise the bigrams. Using a

enough for us to believe it to be reliable.

[14]A fairly liberal view of "semantic equivalence" was taken; for example, for our purposes we consider all sentences in Table 1 to be more-or-less semantically equivalent.

[15]A matching term is defined as a term which has a corresponding entry in the OVVTs.

[16]Note that had we performed *no filtering*, all TN's would become FP's and all FN's would befome TP's.

[17]For terms beginning/ending a sentence (or phrase surrounded by punctuation), we only examine one bigram.

[18]We differentiated only adjectives, nouns, verbs, and adverbs; all other POS were considered equivalent for the purposes of bigram extraction.

[19]A lower baseline would be to perform no filtering.

smaller corpus, these differences may reduce coverage and bigram matching accuracy. However we hypothesise that using the Web 1T corpus, such limitations should be outweighed by its sheer size.

From Table 5, we see a substantial increase in recall over our previous baseline, which supports our hypothesis that using a larger corpus would increase true positives and reduce false negatives. However, the increased coverage of the Web 1T corpus brings with it more opportunities for false positives, the number of which has increased dramatically from our baseline, causing a reduction in precision and accuracy. Despite this, due to increased recall, we achieved an improvement in overall F-score.

Due to its web-based nature, the Web 1T corpus will contain more errors than a corpus sourced from published print, such as the BNC. Bigrams which occur infrequently may be a source of noise. We hypothesized that a substitution is acceptable if its replacement bigrams occur in some reasonable proportion to the original bigrams. Hence, we experimented with *bigram frequency ratios*, where a candidate is accepted only if its ratio exceeds a given threshold The ratio is calculated as f_r/f_o, where f_r and f_o represent the replacement and original bigram frequencies, respectively. We repeated our Web 1T bigrams experiment for several ratio thresholds between 0 and 0.9, and measured the changes in accuracy, precision and recall. Our results showed that frequency ratio thresholding can reduce false positives, leading to slightly increased precision for certain ratios. However, true positives are also reduced, and we sacrifice significant recall for only minor gains in precision.

4.3 Filter using grammatical relations

Candidate selection using bigrams is a somewhat naïve approach, as it considers only the surface text without regard for the underlying *grammatical relations* (GRs) between terms. To illustrate, consider the example shown in Table 4.

We observed that alternatives for 'lovely' such as 'picturesque' and 'scenic' were falsely rejected using BNC bigrams.[20] As bigrams, "picturesque family" and "scenic family" seem like unnatural ways

Context	on their *lovely* family holidays
Term	lovely
Alt.s	handsome, picturesque, pretty, splendid, scenic, resplendent, ...

Table 4: Sample context & replacements for 'lovely'

of describing a family. However, in this context 'lovely' modifies 'holiday', not 'family': this distinction is not picked up using simple bigrams. To address this limitation, we extended our bigram candidate selection technique to consider grammatical relations (GRs).

Our GR technique uses an input sentence in RASP format. We only change one term per sentence as before; however we first extract the term's GRs from the RASP annotation. We convert each binary[21] GR into a *GR-bigram* using the original ordering of terms in the sentence. Figure 1 illustrates the GRs for our example sentence, and how such translate into GR-bigrams.

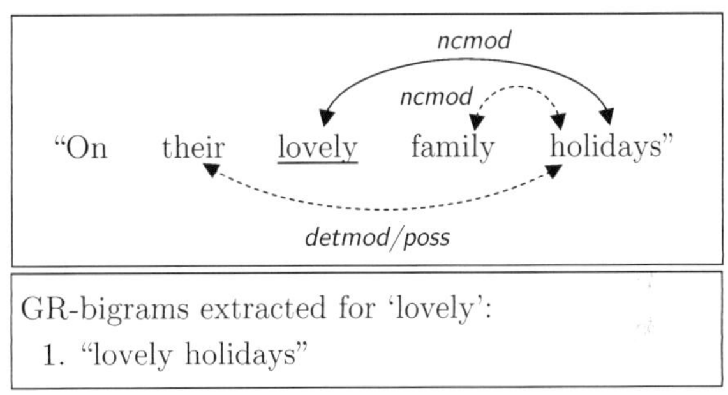

Figure 1: Grammatical relations and GR-bigrams

By converting GRs into bigrams, we can take advantage of Web 1T's extensive coverage. However, due to our restrictions on GR types, it is possible to obtain zero GR-bigrams for some words in a sentence. This happens when the word has no modifier or comparative relations associated with it. For these words, we revert to our bigram selection technique.

Our results for candidate selection using GRs are again shown in Table 5. Surprisingly, this technique performs worse than using regular bigrams for all metrics when compared to our baseline. We suspect our GR selection technique performs no better than

[20] These candidates were accepted using the Web 1T corpus.

[21] We only examine binary comparative and modifier GR types, as RASP provides many other syntactic relations which we deemed not relevant to our task.

Web 1T bigrams simply due to the corpus' extensive coverage, which leads to a similar amount of false positives.

Selection Technique	BNC Bigrams	Web 1T Bigrams		Web 1T GRs	
True positives	22	**55**	**150%**	54	145%
False positives	**45**	155	244%	169	276%
True negatives	**288**	178	-38%	164	-43%
False negatives	57	**24**	**-58%**	25	-56%
Accuracy	**0.752**	0.566	-25%	0.529	-30%
Precision	**0.328**	0.262	-20%	0.242	-26%
Recall	0.278	**0.696**	**150%**	0.684	145%
F-score	0.301	**0.381**	**26%**	0.358	19%

Table 5: Collated results for all experiments

4.4 Error Analysis

To explain our experimental results, we first look at how the performance changes between our different versions relative to the baseline (i.e., BNC Bigrams): see Table 5. Note first that, while all methods increased the number of true positives and decreased false negatives, any performance gains were simply drowned out by the massive increases in false positives that occurred: this is the main cause of our low precision and recall. For the following discussion, we focus on the use of Web IT bigrams, which was the best performing filtering technique.

Since false positives are the most important source of error to avoid in an ECA, we focus on these. We examined the false positive instances and categorised each error into the following four groups. The distribution of errors into these categories is shown in Table 6.

Category	No. FP	% of all FP
Change in Meaning	76	49.03%
Incorrect WSD	42	27.10%
Phrase/Metaphor	31	20.00%
Grammatical	6	3.87%
Total	155	100%

Table 6: Distribution of classification errors

4.4.1 Change in meaning

A major limitation of the OVVT resource is that several of the alternative terms simply cause too much semantic change even when the correct sense of the original term is detected. For example, some alternatives for 'winner' are words such as 'sleeper', 'upsetter', and 'walloper'. In the context of the phrase "Cash prizes will be offered to the winners", we will almost always prefer the generic 'winner'.

We suspect this limitation arises due to the methods used to construct the OVVTs; in particular the use of the WordNet `hyponym` and `hypernym` relations. For example, the 'thing' category in WordNet encompasses a multitude of more specific terms, such as 'ornament', 'structure', 'surface', and 'installation'. These terms all made their way into the OVVT for 'thing', yet they are rarely appropriate substitutions for 'thing'. Conversely, we may not wish to replace any specific terms with the more generic 'thing' as this removes too much meaning.

As this kind of error accounted for almost half of our false positives, addressing this limitation may lead to significant gains in performance. This likely requires a more conservative approach to constructing the OVVTs themselves, e.g., by incorporating corpus-based information, as per (Guerini et al., 2008)'s approach to constructing the Modifier-OVVTs): the technique for mining appropriate verb-adverb pairings from the BNC could be generalised to include other POS types.

Related to the problem of semantic change is the idea of context-dependent semantics. For example, certain qualifiers have opposing effects depending on the appraisal of the subject: consider a "long term *illness*" compared to a "long term *vacation*". One possible solution to this problem is to modify the way valences are calculated to take into account which terms modify one another.

4.4.2 Incorrect word-sense disambiguation

The WSD approach used in our work adapted from (Guerini et al., 2008) is only a crude approximation to a complex problem; the WSD-related problems could at least be alleviated by incorporating a more sophisticated WSD approach into the pipeline. However, even if we could determine the correct sense of each word, we are still left with the limitation that the OVVTs are not exhaustive in their coverage, with several word senses missing.

4.4.3 Phrases and metaphors

Several false positives were caused by phrases such as "long term". Metaphors were a similar cause for error, e.g. "stepping stone". Phrase and metaphor detection should improve our technique's performance, especially since the OVVTs contain several phrases; however, these are known difficult challenges in themselves.

4.4.4 Grammatical errors

A grammatical error occurs when the alternative term is acceptable *semantically*, yet further syntactic modification to the sentence is needed to preserve correct grammar: see Table 3.

An extension of our bigram approach could be to use a larger window around replaced words to assess the suitability of a substitution. Recent work has shown this technique could be used to rank potential substitutions in order of acceptability (Hawker, 2007) and is worth considering as future work.

4.4.5 Limitations of bigrams and corpus coverage

In some cases, our bigram selection technique is ineffective when the term being changed is flanked by *stop words*. In a corpus of sufficient size and coverage, the majority of terms will occur next to stop words far more often than they occur next to other, less common terms. Hence, bigrams containing stop words were a common source of false positives.

This limitation could be addressed in future work by extending our grammatical relation technique to include *ternary* GRs, which provide relations for noun-verb phrases such as "solution to fitness" and "solution to health". Given these, we could accept or reject based on the presence of the accompanying *tri*grams in the Web 1T corpus. As described in (Hawker, 2007), use of an even larger window, such as 4-grams and 5-grams around replaced terms may also address this issue, however the size of the Web 1T corpus for larger N-grams presents serious processing challenges.[22]

5 Evaluation: Sentiment Shift

The technqiues described above attempt to create acceptable candidates to shift sentiment. However, this leaves open the question as to whether the technique has its desired effect: i.e. appropriately shifting sentiment. We designed an experiment which aims to measure correlation between human judgements of the sentiment shift in our generated candidates, and our system's representation of sentiment shift.

We presented subjects with an original sentence, along with *one* of the generated candidates. Our six subjects had no specialised knowledge of the task and were all native English speakers. Subjects were asked to judge the modified sentence for *change* in sentiment relative to the original according to the five shift categories described earlier (i.e., major/minor positive/negative/no shift). In order to avoid bias and to clarify the task, we explained that *sentiment* should be separated from changes in meaning, or the reader's opinions about the sentences. Instead, we urged subjects to ask themselves the question: "Is the author of the second sentence saying what they're saying in a more positive or more negative way, compared to the first sentence?"

The sentences used were extracted from the BNC at random, using the restrictions listed above. We extracted 250 sentences to be used as the originals, each of which was used as input to our sentiment shifting system. For each original sentence, we produced all possible candidates using our best performing candidate selection method, Web 1T Bigrams. We also limited our generation to changing one term per sentence, as to not produce a combinatorial explosion in the number of candidates generated. This produced approximately 3000 modified candidates, including several candidates with no sentiment shift.

Upon inspection, we found many generated candidates contained the types of errors described above. Hence, we manually extracted original and modified sentences until we had a total of 50 originals, and 100 shifted sentences. In selecting which sentences to keep, we chose ones which sounded the most natural, or had the least amount of semantic change from the original. Manual selection was performed in order to prevent introducing any bias into judgements when a subject is confronted with a grammatically incorrect or unnatural sentence. We also aimed for a fairly even distribution of the shifted

[22](Hassan et al., 2007) describes a successful approach to lexical substitution that combines multiple knowledge sources.

sentences into the five sentiment shift intervals.[23]

5.1 Results and analysis

We performed a pairwise Kendall's Tau rank correlation (Kendall and Gibbons, 1962), which compares each human's judgements with the system's sentiment shift, for all 100 generated sentences. Kendall's Tau measures the correlation between two distributions on a scale of -1 to 1, with 1 indicating total agreement; -1 indicating total disagreement; and 0 indicating no (or random) correlation.

We measured the correlation using the five sentiment shift intervals, and also using judgement *polarities*, i.e. whether a score is positive, negative or zero. We only report on polarity results as the finer-grained comparison showed similar results with slightly less correlation.

Our results are shown in Table 7; Kendall's Tau correlations are shown above the shaded diagonal, while the corresponding p-values for statistical significance are shown below the diagonal.

Kendall's Tau Correlation

p-value	sys	h1	h2	h3	h4	h5	h6
sys		0.075	0.024	-0.099	0.034	0.022	-0.078
h1	0.413		0.276	0.423	0.417	0.339	0.249
h2	0.790	0.002		0.406	0.348	0.361	0.198
h3	0.273	0.000	0.000		0.418	0.300	0.343
h4	0.708	0.000	0.000	0.000		0.325	0.277
h5	0.810	0.000	0.000	0.001	0.000		0.189
h6	0.393	0.006	0.029	0.000	0.002	0.040	

Table 7: Kendall's Tau rank correlation between system (**sys**) and human (**hi**) judgement polarities

Although the correlation observed between inter-annotator judgements of polarity was fairly low, it is statistically significant in all cases using a confidence level of $p < 0.05$. While this indicates there was some agreement between human annotators, the relatively low correlation indicates that judging sentiment is a fairly subjective task. However, we saw no correlation between the human judgements and our system's representation of sentiment shift.

[23]Note: the judgement of which sentiment-shift category a sentence-pair fell into was made by the system (and subjects); the manual intervention in the experiment design was to remove unacceptable sentence-pairs.

The poor correlation between human and system polarities can possibly be attributed to a number of reasons. (Guerini et al., 2008) mention that in SentiWordNet, several of the WordNet synsets are valenced incorrectly, with many having a valence of zero, which we also observed in the OVVT resource. Our survey results suggest that SentiWordNet in its current form is not ideally suited to the task of generating sentiment in text using the Valentino method.

SentiWordNet may be effective when classifying the sentiment of *large* texts; the valence scores can be considered to reflect the degree to which each word represents a sentiment "feature". However, it is somewhat unrealistic to assume that every term will have the same effect on sentiment in all contexts; assigning words a 'universal' sentiment score seems non-intuitive, and a finer-grained representation of sentiment is needed for short texts such as dialogue utterances.

In sentiment *generation*, when choosing a replacement term from a set of alternatives, we are more interested in each candidate's effect on sentiment, *relative* to the other candidates. While a resource of semantically clustered terms is needed for this task (such as the OVVTs), terms within each cluster need to be ranked for sentiment in a *localised* way, taking account of positivity or negativity relative to other terms in the cluster. Upon inspection of several OVVTs, this ranking is a straightforward task for a human to perform (if time-consuming).

However, the context of a substitution often determines its effects of sentiment. Hence, we argue that future work in sentiment generation using knowledge-based techniques should extend existing resources to encompass ranking of candidates in a *contextual* way, rather than ranking them statically out of context. For example, an MRE-style (Traum et al., 2003) approach could be used which goes beyond scoring the overall sentiment of an utterance, but considers how sentiment (or *attitude*) is directed towards agents, objects and events.

Acknowledgements: We thank Marco Guerini for kindly providing us with the OVVTs resource, Tim Baldwin for helpful suggestions for the evaluation in Section 5, and the referees for valuable feedback. Cavedon's contribution was partially supported by the Australian Research Council under Linkage Grant LP0882013.

References

Joseph Bates. 1994. The Role of Emotion in Believable Agents. *Communications of the ACM*, 37(7):122–125.

Ted Briscoe, John Carroll, and Rebecca Watson. 2006. The Second Release of the RASP System. In *Proceedings of ACL*, pages 77–80, Sydney.

G. Caridakis, A. Raouzaiou, E. Bevacqua, M. Mancini, K. Karpouzis, L. Malatesta, and C. Pelachaud. 2007. Virtual Agent Multimodal Mimicry of Humans. *Language Resources and Evaluation*, 41(3):367–388.

Michael Fleischman and Eduard Hovy. 2002. Towards Emotional Variation in Speech-Based Natural Language Generation. In *Proceedings of the Second International Natural Language Generation Conference*, pages 57–64, New York.

Marco Guerini, Carlo Strapparava, and Oliviero Stock. 2008. Valentino: A Tool for Valence Shifting of Natural Language Texts. In *Proceedings of the 6th International Conference on Language Resources and Evaluation*, Marrakech.

Samer Hassan, Andras Csomai, Carmen Banea, Ravi Sinha, and Rada Mihalcea. 2007. Unt: Subfinder: combining knowledge sources for automatic lexical substitution. In *Proc. Fourth Int. Workshop on Semantic Evaluations (SemEval 2007)*, pages 410–413, Prague.

Tobias Hawker. 2007. USYD: WSD and Lexical Substitution Using the Web1T Corpus. In *Proc. 4th Int. Workshop on Semantic Evaluations (SemEval 2007)*, pages 446–453, Prague.

M.G. Kendall and J.D. Gibbons. 1962. *Rank Correlation Methods*. Griffin London.

Diana McCarthy and Roberto Navigli. 2007. SemEval-2007 task 10: English lexical substitution task. In *Proc. Fourth Int. Workshop on Semantic Evaluations (SemEval 2007)*, pages 48–53, Prague.

Catherine Pelachaud and Massimo Bilvi. 2003. Computational Model of Believable Conversational Agents. In *Communication in Multiagent Systems*, volume 2650 of *Lecture Notes in Computer Science*, pages 300–317. Springer.

David Traum, Michael Fleischman, and Eduard Hovy. 2003. NL Generation for Virtual Humans in a Complex Social Environment. In *In Proceedings of the AAAI Spring Symposium on Natural Language Generation in Spoken and Written Dialogue*, pages 151–158, Palo Alto.

Ielka van der Sluis and Chris Mellish. 2008. Towards Affective Natural Language Generation: Empirical Investigations. In *Proceedings of the Symposium on Affective Language in Human and Machine, AISB*, pages 9–16, Aberdeen.

E. Zovato, F. Tini Brunozzi, and M. Danieli. 2008. Interplay between pragmatic and acoustic level to embody expressive cues in a Text to Speech system. In *Proceedings of the Symposium on Affective Language in Human and Machine, AISB*, pages 88–91, Aberdeen.

Emotional Perception of Fairy Tales: Achieving Agreement in Emotion Annotation of Text

Ekaterina P. Volkova[1,2], **Betty J. Mohler**[2], **Detmar Meurers**[1], **Dale Gerdemann**[1], **Heinrich H. Bülthoff**[2]

[1] Universität Tübingen, Seminar für Sprachwissenschaft
19 Wilchelmstr., Tübingen, 72074, Germany
[2] Max Planck Institute for Biological Cybernetics
38 Spemannstr., Tübingen, 72076, Germany

Abstract

Emotion analysis (EA) is a rapidly developing area in computational linguistics. An EA system can be extremely useful in fields such as information retrieval and emotion-driven computer animation. For most EA systems, the number of emotion classes is very limited and the text units the classes are assigned to are discrete and predefined. The question we address in this paper is whether the set of emotion categories can be enriched and whether the units to which the categories are assigned can be more flexibly defined. We present an experiment showing how an annotation task can be set up so that untrained participants can perform emotion analysis with high agreement even when not restricted to a predetermined annotation unit and using a rich set of emotion categories. As such it sets the stage for the development of more complex EA systems which are closer to the actual human emotional perception of text.

1 Introduction

As a first step towards developing an emotion analysis (EA) system simulating human emotional perception of text, it is important to research the nature of the emotion analysis performed by humans and examine whether they can reliably perform the task. To investigate these issues, we conducted an experiment to find out the strategies people use to annotate selected folk fairy tale texts for emotions. The participants had to choose from a set of fifteen emotion categories, a significantly larger set than typically used in EA, and assign them to an unrestricted range of text.

To explore whether human annotators can reliably perform a task, inter-annotator agreement (IAA) (Artstein and Poesio, 2008) is the relevant measure. This measure can be calculated between every two individual annotations in order to find pairs or even teams of annotators whose strategies seem to be consistent and coherent enough so that they can be used further as the gold-standard annotation suited to train a machine learning approach for automatic EA analysis. A resulting EA system, capable of simulating human emotional perception of text, would be useful for information retrieval and many other fields.

There are two main aspects of the resulting annotations to be researched. First, how consistently can people perceive and locate the emotional aspect of fairy tale texts? Second, how do they express their perception of text by means of annotation strategies? In the next sections, we address these questions and provide details of an experiment we conducted to empirically advance our understanding of the issues.

2 Motivation and Aimed Application

Most existing EA systems are implemented for and used in specific predefined areas. The application field could be anything from extracting appraisal expressions (Whitelaw et al., 2005) to opinion mining of customer feedback (Lee et al., 2008). In our case, the intended application of the EA system predominantly is emotion enhancement of human-computer interaction, especially in virtual or augmented reality. Emotion enhancement of

Proceedings of the NAACL HLT 2010 Workshop on Computational Approaches to Analysis and Generation of Emotion in Text, pages 98–106,
Los Angeles, California, June 2010.

computer animation, especially when it deals with spoken or written text, is primarily done through manual annotation of text, even if a rich database of perceptually guided animations for behavioral scripts compilation is available (Cunningham and Wallraven, 2009). The resulting system of our project is meant to be a bridge between unprocessed input text (generated or provided) and visual and auditory information, coming from the virtual character, like generated speech, facial expressions and body language. In this way a virtual character would be able to simulate emotional perception and production of text in story telling scenarios.

3 Related Work

Although EA is often referred to as a developing field, the amount of work carried out during the last decades is phenomenal. This section is not meant as a full overview of the related research as that scope is too great for the length of this paper. To contextualize the research presented in this paper we focus on the projects that inspired us and fostered the ideas.

The work done by Alm (Alm and Sproat, 2005; Alm et al., 2005; Alm, 2008) is close to our project in its sprit and goals. Alm, (2008) aims at implementing affective text-to-speech system for storytelling scenarios. An EA system, detecting sentences with emotions expressed in written text is a crucial element for achieving this goal. The annotated corpus was composed of three sets of children's stories written by Beatrix Potter, H. C. Andersen, and the Brothers Grimm.

Like Liu et al. (2003), Alm (2008) uses several emotional categories, while most research in automatic EA works with pure polarities. The set of emotion categories used is essentially the list of *basic emotions* (Ekman, 1993), which has a justified preference for negative emotion categories. Ekmann's list of basic emotions was extended by Alm, since the emotion of surprise is validly taken as ambivalent and was thus split into *positive surprise* and *negative surprise*. The EA system described in Alm et al. (2005) is machine learning based, where the EA problem is defined as multi-class classification problem, with sentences as classification units.

Liu et al. (2003) have combined an emotion lexicon and handcrafted rules, which allowed them to create affect models and thus form a representation of the emotional affinity of a sentence. Their annotation scheme is also sentence-based. The EA system was tested on short user-composed text emails describing emotionally colored events.

In the research on recognizing contextual polarity done by Wilson et al. (2009) a rich prior-polarity lexicon and dependency parsing technique were employed to detect and analyze subjectivity on phrasal level, taking into account all the power of context, captured through such features as *negation*, *polarity modification* and *polarity shifters*. The work presents auspicious results of high accuracy scores for classification between neutrality and polarized private states and between negative and positive subjective phrases. A detailed account of several ML algorithms performance tests is discussed in thought-provoking manner. This work encouraged us to build a lexicon of subjective clues and use sentence structure information for future feature extraction and ML architecture training.

Another thought-provoking work by Polanyj (2006) shows the influence of the context on subjective clues. This is relevant to our project since we are collecting lexicons of subjective clues and the mechanisms of contextual influence may prove to be of value for future automatic EA system training.

Bethard et at. (2004) provide valuable information about corpus annotation for EA means and give accounts on the performance of various existing ML algorithms. They provide excellent analysis of automatic extraction of opinion proposition and their holders. For feature extraction, the authors employ such well-known resources as WordNet (Miller et al., 1990), PropBank (Kingsbury et al., 2002) and FrameNet (Baker et al., 1998). Several types of classification tasks involve evaluation on the level of documents. For example, detecting subjective sentences, expressions, and other opinionated items in documents representing certain press categories (Wiebe et al., 2004) and measuring strength of subjective clauses (Wilson et al., 2004). All these and many more helped us to decide upon our own strategies, provided many examples of corpus collection and annotation, feature extraction and ML techniques usage in ways specific for the EA task.

4 Experimental Setup

Having established the research context, we now turn to the questions we investigate in this paper: the use of an enriched category set and the flexible annotation units, and their influence on annotation quality. We describe the experiment we conducted and its main results. Each participant performed several tasks for each session. The first task always was a cognitive task on emotion categories taken outside the fairy tales context. The results are discussed in Sections 4.1 and 4.2. The next assignment discussed in Section 4.3 was to annotate a list of words for their inherent polarities. The third task was to read the text out loud to the experimenter. This allowed the participant to feel immersed into the story telling scenario and also get used to the text of the story they were about to annotate for the full set of emotion categories. The annotation process is described in Section 4.4. The last exercise was to read the full fairy tale text out loud again, with the difference that this time their voice and face were recorded by means of a microphone and a camera. The potential importance of the extra data sources like speech melody and facial expressions are further discussed in Section 8 as future work.

Ten German native speakers voluntarily participated in the experiment. The participants were divided into two groups and each participant worked on five of the eight texts. The fairy tale sets for each group overlapped in two texts, which allowed us to achieve a high number of individual annotations in a short amount of time and compare the performance of people working on different sets of texts (see Table 1). Each participant annotated their texts in five sessions, dealing with only one text per session. The fatigue effect was avoided as no annotator had more than one session a day.

User	Fairy Tale ID							
	JG	D	R	BR	FH	DS	BM	SJ
A_1	•	•	•	•	•			
A_2	•	•	•	•	•			
A_3	•	•	•	•	•			
A_4	•	•	•	•	•			
A_5	•	•	•	•	•			
A_6				•	•	•	•	•
A_7				•	•	•	•	•
A_8				•	•	•	•	•
A_9				•	•	•	•	•
A_{10}				•	•	•	•	•

Table 1: Annotation Sets

Positive	Negative
Entspannung (relief)	Unruhe (disturbance)
Freude (joy)	Trauer (sadness)
Hoffnung (hope)	Verzweiflung (despair)
Interesse (interest)	Ekel (disgust)
Mitgefühl (compassion)	Hass (hatred)
Überraschung (surprise)	Angst (fear)
Zustimmung (approval)	Ärger (anger)

Table 2: Emotion Categories Used in the Experiment

4.1 Determining Emotion Categories

First, we needed to define the set of emotions to be used in the experiment. Based on the current emotion theories from comparative literature and cognitive psychology (Ekman, 1993; Auracher, 2007; Fontaine et al., 2007), we compiled a set of fifteen emotion categories: seven positive, seven negative, and neutral (see Table 2). We chose an equal number of negative and positive emotions, since in our experiment the main focus is on the freedom and equality of choice of emotion categories. We aimed at the set to be comprehensive and we also expected the participants to be able to detect each of the emotions in the text as well as express them through speech melody and facial expressions.

The polarity of each category was determined experimentally. Participants were asked to decide on the underlying polarity of each emotion category and then to evaluate each emotion on an intensity scale [1:5], '5' marking extreme polarization, '1' being close to neutral. All participants were in full agreement concerning the underlying polarity of the emotions in the set, while the numerical values varied. It is important to note, that the category *Überraschung (surprise)* was stably estimated as *positive*. In English the word *surprise* is reported to be ambivalent (Alm and Sproat, 2005), but we found that in German its most common translation is clearly positive.

4.2 Emotion Categories Clustering

In the second part of the experiment we asked participants to organize the fifteen emotions into clusters. Each cluster was to represent a situation in which

Cluster	Polarity
{relief, hope, joy}	positive
{joy, surprise}	positive
{joy, approval}	positive
{approval, interest}	positive
{disgust, anger, hatred}	negative
{fear, despair, disturbance}	negative
{fear, disturbance, sadness}	negative
{sadness, compassion}	mixed

Table 3: Emotion Clusters

German Title	English Title	Abbr.
Arme Junge im Grab	Poor Boy in Grave	JG
Bremer Stadtmusikanten	Bremen Musicians	BM
Dornröschen	Little Briar-Rose	BR
Eselein	Donkey	D
Frau Holle	Mother Hulda	FH
Heilige Joseph im Walde	St. Joseph in Forest	SJ
Hund und Sperling	Dog and Sparrow	DS
Rätsel	Riddle	R

Table 4: Stories Used (the titles are shortened)

several emotions were equally likely to co-occur, e.g. a situation formulated by a participant as "*When a friend gives me a nicely wrapped birthday present and I am about to open it.*" was reported to involve such emotions as joy, interest and surprise. On average, each participant has formed 5 clusters with 3–4 items per cluster. The clusters were encoded as sets on unordered pairs of items. Pairs were filtered out if they were indicated by fewer than seven participants. As the result, the following eight clusters were obtained (see Table 3). For most clusters, the categories composing them share one polarity. The {*sadness, compassion*} cluster is the only exception.

It is important to note that the clusters were determined through this cognitive task, independently of the annotations. Since the annotators agree well on clustering the emotions, employing this information captures conceptual agreement between individual annotations even if the specific emotion categories for the same stretch of text do not coincide. However, we intend to keep the full set of emotions for the future corpus expansions.

4.3 Word list Annotation

For each text, we compiled its word list by taking the set of words contained in the text, normalizing each word to its lemma and filtering the set for most common German stop words (function words, pronouns, auxiliaries). Like full story texts, word lists were divided into two annotation sets. At each session, before seeing the full text of the fairy tale, the participant was to annotate each item of the corresponding word list for its inherent polarity. All the words were taken out their contexts and were neutral by default. The annotator's task was to label only those words that had the potential to change the polarity of the context in which they could occur. We purposefully did not limit the task to the words occurring in all texts in order to be able to investigate the stability of participants' decisions. Every annotator worked with five word lists, one for each fairy tale text. The total number of unique items for the first annotation set was 893 words and 823 words long for the second set; 267 and 236 words correspondingly occurred in more than one word list. These words could potentially be marked with different polarity categories, but in fact only about 15% of those words (4% from the total number of items on each of the word lists) were "unstable", namely, labeled with different polarities by the same annotator. The labels received in these cases were either {*positive, neutral*} or {*negative, neutral*}. These words were further "stabilized" by either choosing the most frequent label or the *neutral* label if the unstable word had received only two label instances. The results show that such annotation tasks could be used further for subjective clues lexicon collection.

4.4 Text Annotation

For the third and main part of the experiment, we selected eight Grimm's fairy tales, each 1200 – 1400 words long and written in Standard German (see Table 4). The texts were chosen based on their genre, for in spite of the depth of all the hidden and open references to human psyche and national traditions that were shown in works of (von Franz, 1996; Propp and Dundes, 1977), folk fairy tales are relatively uncomplicated in the plot-line and the characters' personalities. Due to this relative simplicity of the content, we expect the participants' emotional reactions to folk fairy tale texts to be more coherent than to other texts of fiction literature.

The task for the participants was to locate and mark stretches of text where an emotion was to be conveyed through the speech melody and/or facial expressions if the participant was to read the text out loud. To make the annotation process and its further analysis time-efficient and convenient for both, annotators and experimenters, a simple tool was developed. We created the Manual Emotion Annotation Tool (MEAT) which allows the user to annotate text for emotion by selecting stretches of text and labeling it with one of fifteen emotion categories. The application also has a special mode for word list annotation, where only the three polarity categories are available: positive, negative and neutral. The user can always undo their labels or change them until they are satisfied with the annotation and can submit the results. The main part of the experiment resulted in fifty individual annotations which produced 150 annotation pairs.

5 Analyzing Inter-annotator Agreement

For each of the 150 pairs (two texts annotated by ten annotators, six texts annotated by five annotators), the IAA rate was calculated. However, the calculation of IAA is not as straightforward in this situation as it might seem. In many types of corpus annotation, e.g., in POS tagging, there are previously identified discrete elements. In this experiment we intentionally have no predefined units, even if this makes the IAA calculation more difficult. Consider the following examples:

(1) A_1: "... [the evil wolf]$_X$ ate the girl"
A_2: "... the [evil wolf ate the girl]$_X$"

(2) A_1: "... [the evil wolf]$_X$ ate the girl"
A_2: "... [the evil wolf]$_Y$ ate the girl"

(3) A_1: "... [the evil wolf]$_X$ ate the girl"
A_2: "... the evil wolf ate [the girl]$_X$"

(4) A_1: "... [the evil wolf]$_X$ ate [the girl]$_Z$"
A_2: "... [the evil wolf ate the girl]$_X$"

In example (1) both annotators marked certain stretches of text with the same category *X*, but the annotations do not completely coincide, there is only an overlap. This situation is similar to that in syntactic annotation, where one needs to distinguish between bracketing and labeling of the constituent and measures such as Parseval (Carroll et al., 2002) have been much debated.

Both annotators in example (1) recognize *evil wolf* as marked for *X* and thus this example should be counted towards agreement, while examples (2) and (3) should not. A second type of evaluation arises if the emotion clusters are taken into account. According to this evaluation type, example (2) is counted towards agreement if the categories *X* and *Y* belong to the same cluster.

Example (4) provides an illustration of how IAA is accounted for in a more complex case. Annotator A_1 has marked two stretches of text with two different emotion categories, while annotator A_2 has united both stretches under the same emotion category. Both annotators agree that *the evil wolf* is marked for *X*, but disagree on the emotion category for *the girl*. In order to avoid the crossing brackets problem (Carroll et al., 2002), we treat *the evil wolf ate* as agreement, and *the girl* as disagreement. Although *ate* was left unmarked by one of the annotators, it is counted towards agreement because it is next to a stretch of text on which both annotators agree. Stretches of text the annotators agree or disagree upon also receive weight values: the higher the number of words that belong to open word classes in a stretch, the higher its weight.

The general calculation formulae for the IAA measure are taken from (Artstein and Poesio, 2008):

$$\kappa = \frac{A_o - A_e}{1 - A_e}$$

$$A_o = \frac{1}{i} \sum_{i \in I} arg_i$$

$$A_e = \frac{1}{I^2} \sum_{k \in K} n_{c_1 k} n_{c_2 k}$$

A_o is the observed agreement, A_e is the expected agreement, I is the number of annotation items, K is the set of all categories used by both annotators, n_{ck} is the number of items assigned by annotator c to category k.

6 Analyzing Annotation Strategies

Analysis of IAA, presented in Section 5 can answer the first question we aim to investigate: How consistently do people perceive and locate the emotional aspect of fairy tale texts? The second issue necessary for investigation is the annotation strategies people use to express their emotional perception of text. In our experiment conditions, the resulting strategies can be investigated via three aspects: *a*) length of user-defined flexible units *b*) emotional

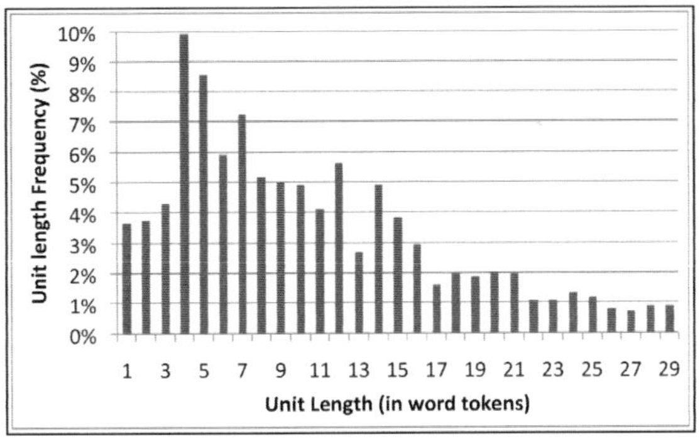

Figure 1: Annotator Defined Unit Length Rating

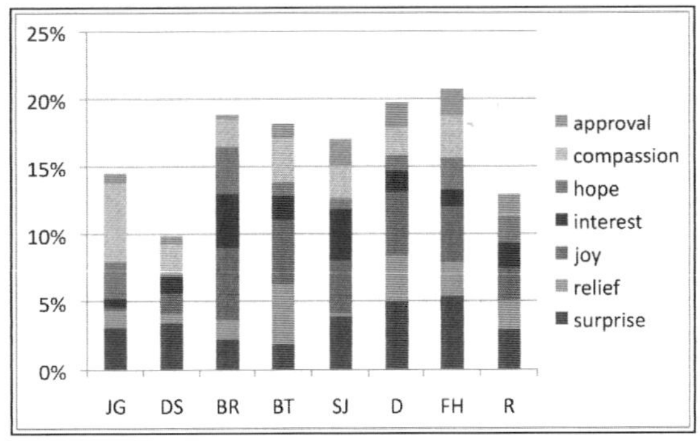

Figure 2: Distribution of Positive Emotion Categories in Texts

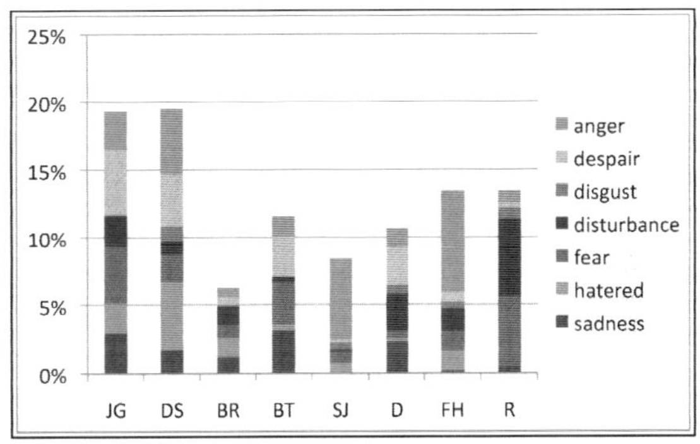

Figure 3: Distribution of Negative Emotion Categories in Texts

composition of fairy tales *c*) emotional flow of the fairy tales. In this section we give a brief account of our findings concerning the given aspects.

The participants were always free to select text stretches of the length they considered to be appropriate for a specific emotional category label. The only guideline they received was to mark the entire stretch of text which, according to their judgement, was marked by the chosen emotion category and, if read without the surrounding context, would still allow one to clearly perceive the applied emotion category label. As Figure 1 shows, the most frequent unit length consists of four to seven word tokens, which corresponds to short phrases, e.g., a verb phrase with a noun phrase argument. We consider the findings to be encouraging, since this observation could be used favorably for the automatic EA system training.

Emotional composition of a fairy tale helps to reveal the overall character of the text and establish if the story is abundant with various emotions or is overloaded with only a few. For our overall research goal, we would prefer the former kind of stories, since they would build a rich training corpus. Figures 2 and 3 give an overview on the average shares various emotion categories hold over the eight texts. It is important to note that 65%– 75% of the text was left neutral. The results show that most stories are rich in positive rather than negative emotions, with two exceptions we would like to elaborate upon. The stories *The Poor Boy in the Grave* and *The Dog and the Sparrow* belonged to different annotation sets and thus no annotator dealt with both stories. These texts were selected partially for their potential overcharge with negative emotions. The hypothesis proved to be true, since the annotators have labeled on average 20% of text with negative emotions, like *hatred* and *sadness*. The only positive emotion category salient for the *The Poor Boy in the Grave* story is *compassion*, which is also mostly triggered by sad events happening to a positive character.

The emotional flow in the fairy tales is illustrated by the graph presented in Figure 4. In order to build it, we used the numerical evaluations obtained in the first part of the experiment and described in section 4.1. For each fairy tale text, each word token was mapped to the absolute value of the average numerical evaluation of its emotional categories assigned by all participants. The word tokens also received its relative position in the text, where the first word was at position 0.0 and the last at 1.0. Thus, the emotional trajectories of all texts were correlated despite the fact that their actual lengths differed. The polynomial fit graph, taken over thus acquired emotional flow common for all fairy tale texts has a wave-shaped form and is similar to the

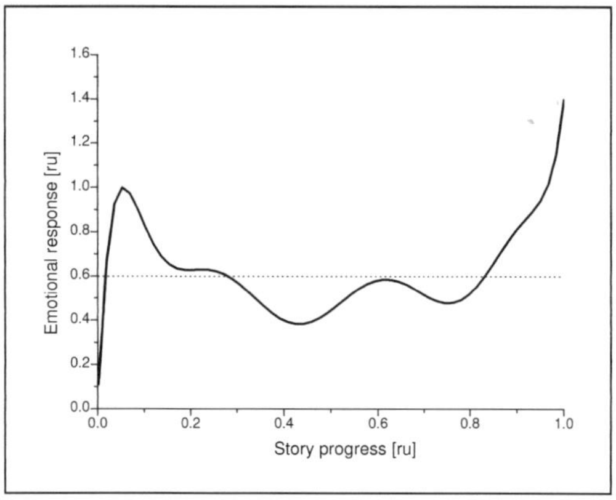

Figure 4: Emotional Trajectory over all Stories

emotional trajectory reported by Alm and Sproat (2005). The emotional charge increases and falls steeply in the beginning of the fairy tale, then cycles though rise and fall phases (which do not exceed in their intensity the average rate of 0.6) and then ascents steeply at the end of the story. We agree with the explanation of such a trajectory, given by Propp and Dundes (1977) and also elaborated by Alm and Sproat (2005) — the first emotional intensity peak in the story line corresponds to the rising action, after the main characters have been introduced and the plot develops through a usually unexpected event. At the end of the story the intensity is highest, regardless whether the denouement is a happy ending or a tragedy. The fact that the fairy tale texts we chose for the experiment are relatively short is probably responsible for the steep peak of intensity in the very beginning of the story — the stories are too short to include a proper exposition. However, we need to investigate further how much of this is a property of texts themselves and how much — the perception (and thus annotation) of emotions.

7 Results

The IAA scores were calculated using the emotion clusters information, for according to the results, participants would often stably use different emotions from same clusters at the same stretch of text.

Four out of ten participants, two from each group (marked gray in Table 1), had very low IAA scores ($\kappa < 0.40$ average per participant), a high proportion of unmarked text, and they used few emotion categories ($<$ 7 categories average per participant), so for the evaluation part their data was discarded. The final IAA evaluation was calculated on all the annotation pairs obtained from the six remaining participants (marked black in table 1), whose average agreement score in the original set of participants was originally higher than 0.50. The total number of annotation pairs amounted to 48: two texts annotated by all the six annotators, six texts annotated by three annotators for each of the two annotation sets.

According to the interpretation of κ by (Landis and Koch, 1977), the annotator agreement was *moderate* on average (0.53), and some pairs approached the *almost perfect* IAA rate (0.83). The IAA rates, calculated on the full set of fifteen emotions, without taking the emotion clusters into consideration, gave a *moderate* IAA rate on average (0.34) and reached *substantial* level (0.62) at maximum. The κ rates are considerably high for the hard task and are comparable with the results presented in (Alm and Sproat, 2005). The word lists have a somewhat lower κ IAA (0.45 on average, 0.72 at maximum), which is due to the low number of categories and the heavy bias towards the *neutral* category. The observed agreement on word lists is considerably high: 0.81 on average, reaching 0.91 at maximum.

While our approach may seem very similar to the one of Alm (2005), there are some important differences. We gave the participants the freedom of using flexible annotation units, which allowed the annotators to define the source of emotion more precisely and mark several emotions in one sentence. In fact, in 39% of all annotated sentences represented a mixture of the *neutral* category and "polarized" categories, 20% of which included more than one "polarized" categories. Another difference is the rich set of emotion categories, with equal number of *positive* and *negative* items. The results show that people can successfully use the large set to express their emotional perception of text (e.g., see Figures 3 and 2).

Other important findings include the fact that short phrases are the naturally preferred annotation unit among our participants and that the emotional trajectory of a general story line corresponds to the one proposed by Propp and Dundes (1977).

8 Future Work

8.1 Corpus Expansion

In the near future, we will expand the collections of annotated text in order to compile a substantially large training corpus. We plan to work further with three annotators that have formed a natural team, since their group has always attained the highest annotation scores for their annotation set, exceeding the highest scores in the other annotation set. The task defined for the three annotators is similar to the experiment described in the paper, with several differences. For the corpus expansion we chose 85 stories by the Grimm Brothers 1400 – 4500 tokens long. We expect that longer texts have more potential space for an emotionally rich plot. Each text will be annotated by two people, the third annotator will tie-break disagreements by choosing the most appropriate of the conflicting categories, similar to the method described by (Alm and Sproat, 2005). It is also probable that a basic annotation unit will be defined and imposed on the annotators, for, as the studies discussed in Section 6 show, short phrases are a language unit most often naturally chosen by annotators.

Each of the annotators will also work with a single word list, compiled from all texts and filtered for the most common stop-words. Each of the words on the word list should be annotated with its inherent polarity (positive, negative or neutral). Since each word on the list is free of its context, the lists provide valuable information about the word and its context interaction in full texts, which can be further used for machine learning architecture training.

We also plan to keep the fifteen emotion categories and their clustering, since it gives the annotator more freedom of expression and simultaneously allows the researches to find the common cognitive ground behind the labels if they vary within one cluster

8.2 Feature Extraction and Machine Learning Architecture Training

When the corpus is large enough, the relevant features will be extracted automatically by means of existing NLP tools, followed by training a machine learning architecture, most probably TiMBL (Daelemans et al., 2004), to map textual units to the emotion categories. It is yet to be determined which features to use, one compulsory parameter is that all the features should be available through automatic processing tools. This is crucial, since the resulting EA system has to be fully automated with no manual work involved.

8.3 Extra Information Sources and their Potential Contribution

We also plan to collect data from other information sources, like video and audio recordings, by inviting amateur actors for story-telling sessions. This will allow emotion retrieval from the speech melody, facial expressions and body language. The manual annotation and the extra data sources can be aligned by means of Text and Speech Aligner (Rapp, 1995), which allows to track correspondences between them. This alignment would most certainly benefit the facial and body animation of the virtual characters, since there is no clear understanding of time correlation between emotions labeled in written text and the ones expressed through speech and facial clues in a story telling scenario. An EA system could also be perfected through a careful analysis of recorded speech and video of story telling sessions — regular recurrence of subjectivity of certain contexts will be even more significant if the transmission of the emotions from the story teller to the listener via mentioned information sources is successful.

9 Conclusions

In this paper, we reported on an experiment investigating the inter-annotator agreement levels which can be achieved by untrained human annotators performing emotion analysis of variable units of text. While EA is a very difficult task, our experiment shows that even untrained annotators can have high agreement rates, even given considerable freedom in expressing their emotional perception of text. To the best of our knowledge, this is the first attempt at emotion analysis that operates on flexible, annotator defined units and uses a relatively rich inventory of emotion categories. We consider the resulting IAA rates to be high enough to accept the annotations as suitable for gold-standard corpus compilation in the frame of this research. As such, we view this work as the first step towards the development of a more complex EA system, which aims to simulate the actual human emotional perception of text.

References

C.O. Alm and R. Sproat. 2005. Emotional sequencing and development in fairy tales. In *Proceedings of the First International Conference on Affective Computing and Intelligent Interaction (ACII05)*. Springer.

C.O. Alm, D. Roth, and R. Sproat. 2005. Emotions from text: Machine learning for text-based emotion prediction. In *Proceedings of HLT/EMNLP*, volume 2005.

C.O. Alm. 2008. Affect in Text and Speech. *lrc.cornell.edu*.

R. Artstein and M. Poesio. 2008. Inter-coder agreement for computational linguistics. *Computational Linguistics*, 34(4):555–596.

Jan Auracher. 2007. *... wie auf den allmächtigen Schlag einer magischen Rute. Psychophysiologische Messungen zur Textwirkung*. Ars poetica ; 3. Dt. Wiss.-Verl.

C.F. Baker, C.J. Fillmore, and J.B. Lowe. 1998. The berkeley framenet project. In *Proceedings of the 17th international conference on Computational linguistics-Volume 1*, pages 86–90. Association for Computational Linguistics Morristown, NJ, USA.

Steven Bethard, Hong Yu, Ashley Thornton, Vasileios Hatzivassiloglou, and Dan Jurafsky. 2004. Automatic extraction of opinion propositions and their holders. In *2004 AAAI Spring Symposium on Exploring Attitude and Affect in Text*, page 2224.

J. Carroll, A. Frank, D. Lin, D. Prescher, and H. Uszkoreit. 2002. Beyond Parseval-Towards improved evaluation measures for parsing systems. In *Workshop at the 3rd International Conference on Language Resources and Evaluation LREC-02., Las Palmas*.

D. W. Cunningham and C. Wallraven. 2009. Dynamic information for the recognition of conversational expressions. *Journal of Vision*, 9(13:7):1–17, 12.

Walter Daelemans, Jakub Zavrel, Ko van der Sloot, and Antal van den Bosch. 2004. Timbl: Tilburg memory based learner, version 5.1, reference guide. ilk technical report 04-02. Technical report.

P. Ekman. 1993. Facial Expression and Emotion. *American Psychologist*, 48(4):384–392.

JR Fontaine, KR Scherer, EB Roesch, and PC Ellsworth. 2007. The world of emotions is not two-dimensional. *Psychological science: a journal of the American Psychological Society/APS*, 18(12):1050.

P. Kingsbury, M. Palmer, and M. Marcus. 2002. Adding semantic annotation to the Penn Treebank. In *Proceedings of the Human Language Technology Conference*, pages 252–256. Citeseer.

J.R. Landis and G.G. Koch. 1977. The measurement of observer agreement for categorical data. *Biometrics*, 33(1):159–174.

D. Lee, O.R. Jeong, and S. Lee. 2008. Opinion mining of customer feedback data on the web. In *Proceedings of the 2nd international conference on Ubiquitous information management and communication*, page 230235, New York, New York, USA. ACM.

Hugo Liu, Henry Lieberman, and Ted Selker. 2003. A model of textual affect sensing using real-world knowledge. In *Proceedings of the 8th international conference on Intelligent user interfaces - IUI '03*, page 125, New York, New York, USA. ACM Press.

G.A. Miller, R. Beckwith, C. Fellbaum, D. Gross, and K.J. Miller. 1990. Introduction to Wordnet: An on-line lexical database*. *International Journal of lexicography*, 3(4):235.

L. Polanyi and A. Zaenen. 2006. Contextual valence shifters. *Computing Attitude and Affect in Text: Theory and Applications*, page 110.

V.I.A. Propp and A. Dundes. 1977. *Morphology of the Folktale*. University of Texas Press.

S. Rapp. 1995. Automatic phonemic transcription and linguistic annotation from known text with Hidden Markov Models. In *Proceedings of ELSNET Goes East and IMACS Workshop*. Citeseer.

M.L. von Franz. 1996. *The interpretation of fairy tales*. Shambhala Publications.

C. Whitelaw, N. Garg, and S. Argamon. 2005. Using appraisal groups for sentiment analysis. In *Proceedings of the 14th ACM international conference on Information and knowledge management*, page 631. ACM.

J. Wiebe, T. Wilson, R. Bruce, M. Bell, and M. Martin. 2004. Learning subjective language. *Computational linguistics*, 30(3):277–308.

T. Wilson, J. Wiebe, and R. Hwa. 2004. Just how mad are you? Finding strong and weak opinion clauses. In *Proceedings of the National Conference on Artificial Intelligence*, pages 761–769. Menlo Park, CA; Cambridge, MA; London; AAAI Press; MIT Press; 1999.

T. Wilson, J. Wiebe, and P. Hoffmann. 2009. Recognizing Contextual Polarity: an exploration of features for phrase-level sentiment analysis. *Computational Linguistics*, 35(3):399433, September.

Experiments on Summary-based Opinion Classification

Elena Lloret
Department of Software
and Computing Systems
University of Alicante
Apdo. de Correos 99
E-03080, Alicante, Spain
elloret@dlsi.ua.es

Horacio Saggion
Department of Infomation and
Communication Technologies
Grupo TALN
Universitat Pompeu Fabra
C/Tánger, 122-134, 2nd floor
08018 Barcelona, Spain
horacio.saggion@upf.edu

Manuel Palomar
Department of Software
and Computing Systems
University of Alicante
Apdo. de Correos 99
E-03080, Alicante, Spain
mpalomar@dlsi.ua.es

Abstract

We investigate the effect of text summarisation in the problem of *rating-inference* – the task of associating a fine-grained numerical rating to an opinionated document. We set-up a comparison framework to study the effect of different summarisation algorithms of various compression rates in this task and compare the classification accuracy of summaries and documents for associating documents to classes. We make use of SVM algorithms to associate numerical ratings to opinionated documents. The algorithms are informed by linguistic and sentiment-based features computed from full documents and summaries. Preliminary results show that some types of summaries could be as effective or better as full documents in this problem.

1 Introduction

Public opinion has a great impact on company and government decision making. In particular, companies have to constantly monitor public perception of their products, services, and key company representatives to ensure that good reputation is maintained. Recent cases of public figures making headlines for the wrong reasons have shown how companies take into account public opinion to distance themselves from figures which can damage their public image. The Web has become an important source for finding information, in the field of business intelligence, business analysts are turning their eyes to the Web in order to monitor public perception on products, services, policies, and managers. The field of sentiment analysis has recently emerged (Pang and Lee, 2008) as an important area of research in Natural Language Processing (NLP) which can provide viable solutions for monitoring public perception on a number of issues; with evaluation programs such as the *Text REtrieval Conference* track on blog mining [1], the *Text Analysis Conference* [2] track on opinion summarisation, and the *DEfi Fouille de Textes* program (Grouin et al., 2009) advances in the state of the art have been produced. Although sentiment analysis involves various different problems such as identifying subjective sentences or identifying positive and negative opinions in text, here we concentrate on the opinion classification task; and more specifically on *rating-inference*, the task of identifying the author's evaluation of an entity with respect to an ordinal-scale based on the author's textual evaluation of the entity (Pang and Lee, 2005). The specific problem we study in this paper is that of associating a fine-grained rating (1=worst,...5=best) to a review. This is in general considered a difficult problem because of the fuzziness inherent of mid-range ratings (Mukras et al., 2007). A considerable body of research has recently been produced to tackle this problem (Chakraborti et al., 2007; Ferrari et al., 2009) and reported figures showing accuracies ranging from 30% to 50% for such complex task; most approaches derive features for the classification task from the full document. In this research we ask whether extracting features from document summaries could help a classification system. Since text summaries are meant to contain the essential content of a document (Mani, 2001), we investigate whether filtering noise through text summarisation is of any help in the rating-inference task. In re-

[1]http:trec.nist.gov/

[2]http://www.nist.gov/tac/

Proceedings of the NAACL HLT 2010 Workshop on Computational Approaches to Analysis and Generation of Emotion in Text, pages 107–115,
Los Angeles, California, June 2010.

cent years, text summarisation has been used to support both manual and automatic tasks; in the SUMMAC evaluation (Mani et al., 1998), text summaries were tested in document classification and question answering tasks where summaries were considered suitable surrogates for full documents; Bagga and Baldwin (1998) studied summarisation in the context of a cross-document coreference task and found that summaries improved the performance of a clustering-based coreference mechanism; more recently Latif and McGee (2009) have proposed text summarisation as a preprocessing step for student essay assessment finding that summaries could be used instead of full essays to group "similar" quality essays. Summarisation has been studied in the field of sentiment analysis with the objective of producing opinion summaries, however, to the best of our knowlegde there has been little research on the study of document summarisation as a text processing step for opinion classification. This paper presents a framework and extensive experiments on text summarisation for opinion classification, and in particular, for the rating-inference problem. We will present results indicating that some types of summaries could be as effective or better than the full documents in this task.

The remainder of the paper is organised as follows: Section 2 will compile the existing work with respect to the inference-rating problem; Section 3 and Section 4 will describe the corpus and the NLP tools used for all the experimental set-up. Next, the text summarisation approaches will be described in Section 5, and then Section 6 will show the experiments conducted and the results obtained together with a discussion. Finally, we will draw some conclusions and address further work in Section 7.

2 Related Work

Most of the literature regarding sentiment analysis addresses the problem either by detecting and classifying opinions at a sentence level (Wilson et al., 2005; Du and Tan, 2009), or by attempting to capture the overall sentiment of a document (McDonald et al., 2007; Hu et al., 2008). Traditional approaches tackle the task as binary classification, where text units (e.g. words, sentences, fragments) are classified into *positive vs. negative*, or *subjective vs. objective*, according to their polarity and subjectivity degree, respectively. However, sentiment classification taking into account a finer granularity has been less considered. Rating-inference is a particular task within sentiment analysis, which aims at inferring the author's numerical rating for a review. For instance, given a review and 5-star-rating scale (ranging from 1 -the worst- to 5 -the best), this task should correctly predict the review's rating, based on the language and sentiment expressed in its content.

In (Pang and Lee, 2005), the rating-inference problem is analysed for the movies domain. In particular, the utility of employing label and item similarity is shown by analysing the performance of three different methods based on SVM (one vs. all, regression and metric labeling), in order to infer the author's implied numerical rating, which ranges from 1 up to 4 stars, depending on the degree the author of the review liked or not the film. The approach described in (Leung et al., 2006) suggests the use of collaborative filtering algorithms together with sentiment analysis techniques to obtain user preferences expressed in textual reviews, focusing also on movie reviews. Once the opinion words from user reviews have been identified, the polarity of those opinion words together with their strength need to be computed and mapped to the rating scales to be further input to the collaborative input algorithms.

Apart from these approaches, this problem is stated from a different point of view in (Shimada and Endo, 2008). Here it is approached from the perspective of rating different details of a product under the same review. Consequently, they rename the problem as "*seeing several stars*" instead of only one, corresponding to the overall sentiment of the review. Also, in (Baccianella et al., 2009) the rating of different features regarding hotel reviews (cleanliness, location, staff, etc.) is addressed by analysing several aspects involved in the generation of product review's representations, such as part-of-speech and lexicons. Other approaches (Devitt and Ahmad, 2007), (Turney, 2002) face this problem by grouping documents with closer stars under the same category, i.e. positive or negative, simplifying the task into a binary classification problem.

Recently, due to the vast amount of on-line information and the subjectivity appearing in documents, the combination of sentiment analysis and summarisation task in tandem can result in great benefits for stand-alone applications of sentiment analysis, as well as for the potential uses of sentiment analysis as part of other NLP applications (Stoyanov and Cardie, 2006). Whilst there is much literature combining sentiment analysis and text summarisation focusing on generating opinion-oriented summaries for the new textual genres, such as blogs (Lloret et al., 2009), or reviews (Zhuang et al., 2006), the use of summaries as substitutes of full documents in tasks such as rating-inference has been not yet explored to the best of our knowledge. In contrast to the existing literature, this paper uses summaries instead of full reviews to tackle the rating-inference task in the financial domain, and we carry out a preliminary analysis concerning the potential benefits of text summaries for this task.

3 Dataset for the Rating-inference Task

Since there is no standard dataset for carrying out the rating-inference task, the corpus used for our experiments was one associated to a current project on business intelligence we are working on. These data consisted of 89 reviews of several English banks (Abbey, Barcalys, Halifax, HSBC, Lloyds TSB, and National Westminster) gathered from the Internet. In particular the documents were collected from *Ciao*[3], a Website where users can write reviews about different products and services, depending on their own experience.

Table 1 lists some of the statistical properties of the data. It is worth stressing upon the fact that the reviews have on average 2,603 words, which means that we are dealing with long documents rather than short ones, making the rating-inference task even more challenging. The shortest document contains 1,491 words, whereas the longest document has more than 5,000 words.

# Reviews	Avg length	Max length	Min length
89	2,603	5,730	1,491

Table 1: Corpus Statistics

Since the aim of the task we are pursuing focuses on classifying correctly the star for a review (ranging from 1 to 5 stars), it is necessary to study how many reviews we have for each class, in order to see whether we have a balanced distribution or not. Table 2 shows this numbers for each star-rating. It is worth mentioning that one-third of the reviews belong to the 4-star class. In contrast, we have only 9 reviews that have been rated as 3-star, consisting of the 10% of the corpus, which is a very low number.

Star-rating	# reviews	%
1-star	17	19
2-star	11	12
3-star	9	10
4-star	28	32
5-star	24	27

Table 2: Class Distribution

4 Natural Language Processing Tools

Linguistic analysis of textual input is carried out using the General Architecture for Text Engineering (GATE) – a framework for the development and deployment of language processing technology in large scale (Cunningham et al., 2002). We make use of typical GATE components: tokenisation, parts of speech tagging, and morphological analysis to produce document annotations. From the annotations we produce a number of features for document representation. Features produced from the annotations are: *string* – the original, unmodified text of each token; *root* – the lemmatised, lower-case form of the token; *category* – the part-of-speech (POS) tag, a symbol that represents a grammatical category such as determiner, present-tense verb, past-tense verb, singular noun, etc.; *orth* – a code representing the token's combination of upper- and lower-case letters. In addition to these basic features, "sentiment" features based on a lexical resource are computed as explained below.

4.1 Sentiment Features

SentiWordNet (Esuli and Sebastiani, 2006) is a lexical resource in which each synset (set of synonyms) of WordNet (Fellbaum, 1998) is associated with three numerical scores obj (how objective the word is), pos (how positive the word is), and neg (how negative the word is). Each of the scores ranges from 0 to 1, and their sum equals 1. SentiWordNet word values have been semi-automatically computed based on the use of weakly supervised classi-

[3]http://www.ciao.co.uk/

fication algorithms. In this work we compute the "general sentiment" of a word in the following way: given a word w we compute the number of times the word w is more positive than negative (positive > negative), the number of times is more negative than positive (positive < negative) and the total number of entries of word w in SentiWordNet, therefore we can consider the overall positivity or negativity a particular word has in SentiWordNet. We are interested in words that are generally "positive", generally "negative" or generally "neutral" (not much variation between positive and negative). For example a word such as "good" has many more entries where the positive score is greater than the negativity score while a word such as "unhelpful" has more negative occurrences than positive. We use this aggregated scores in our classification experiments. Note that we do not apply any word sense disambiguation procedure here.

4.2 Machine Learning Tool

For the experiments reported here, we adopt a Support Vector Machine (SVM) learning paradigm not only because it has recently been used with success in different tasks in natural language processing (Isozaki and Kazawa, 2002), but it has been shown particularly suitable for text categorization (Kumar and Gopal, 2009) where the feature space is huge, as it is in our case. We rely on the support vector machines implementation distributed with the GATE system (Li et al., 2009) which hides from the user the complexities of feature extraction and conversion from documents to the machine learning implementation. The tool has been applied with success to a number of datasets for opinion classification and rating-inference (Saggion and Funk, 2009).

5 Text Summarisation Approach

In this Section, three approaches for carrying out the summarisation process are explained in detail. First, a generic approach is taken as a basis, and then, it is adapted into a query-focused and a opinion-oriented approach, respectively.

5.1 Generic Summarisation

A generic text summarisation approach is first taken as a core, in which three main stages can be distinguished: i) document preprocessing; ii) relevance detection; and ii) summary generation. Since we work with Web documents, an initial preprocessing step is essential to remove all unnecessary tags and noisy information. Therefore, in the first stage the body of the review out of the whole Web page is automatically delimitated by means of patterns, and only this text is used as the input for the next summarisation stages. Further on, a sentence relevance detection process is carried out employing different combinations of various techniques. In particular, the techniques employed are:

Term frequency (*tf*): this technique has been widely used in different summarisation approaches, showing the the most frequent words in a document contain relevant information and can be indicative of the document's topic (Nenkova et al., 2006)

Textual entailment (*te*): a *te* module (Ferrández et al., 2007) is used to detect redundant information in the document, by computing the entailment between two consecutive sentences and discarding the entailed ones. The identification of these entailment relations helps to avoid incorporating redundant information in summaries.

Code quantity principle (*cqp*): this is a linguistic principle which proves the existence of a proportional relation between how important the information is, and the number of coding elements it has (Givón, 1990). In this approach we assume that sentences containing longer noun-phrases are more relevant.

The aforementioned techniques are combined together taking always into account the term-frequency, leading to different summarisation strategies (*tf*, *te+tf*, *cqp+tf*, *te+cqp+tf*). Finally, the resulting summary is produced by extracting the highest scored sentences up to the desired length, according the techniques explained.

5.2 Query-focused Summarisation

Through adapting the generic summarisation approach into a query-focused one, we could benefit from obtaining more specific sentences with regard to the topic of the review. As a preliminary work, we are going to assume that a review is about a bank, and as a consequence, the name of the bank is considered to be the topic. It is worth mentioning that a person can refer to a specific bank in different ways. For example, in the case of *"The National Westmin-*

ster Bank", it can be referred to as *"National Westminster"* or *"NatWest"*. Such different denominations were manually identified and they were used to biased the content of the generated summaries, employing the same techniques of *tf*, *te* and the *cqp* combined together. One limitation of this approach is that we do not directly deal with the coreference problem, so for example, sentences containing pronouns referring also to the bank, will not be taken into consideration in the summarisation process. We are aware of this limitation and for future work it would be necessary to run a coreference algorithm to identify all occurrences of a bank within a review. However, since the main goal of this paper is to carry out a preliminary analysis of the usefulness of summaries in contrast to whole reviews in the rating-inference problem, we did not take this problem into account at this stage of the research. In addition, when we do query-focused summarisation only we rely on the SUMMA toolkit (Saggion, 2008) to produce a query similarity value for each sentence in the review which in turn is used to rank sentences for an extractive summary (*qf*). This similarity value is the cosine similarity between a sentence vector (terms and weights) and a query vector (terms and weigths) and where the query is the name of the entity being reviewed (e.g. *National Westminster*).

5.3 Opinion-oriented Summarisation

Since reviews are written by people who want to express their opinion and experience with regard to a bank, in this particular case, either generic or query-focused summaries can miss including some important information concerning their sentiments and feelings towards this particular entity. Therefore, a sentiment classification system similar to the one used in (Balahur-Dobrescu et al., 2009) is used together with the summarisation approach, in order to generate opinion-oriented summaries. First of all, the sentences containing opinions are identified, assigning each of them a polarity (positive and negative) and a numerical value corresponding to the polarity strength (the higher the negative score, the more negative the sentence and similarly, the higher the positive score, the more positive the sentence). Sentences containing a polarity value of 0 are considered neutral and are not taken into account. Once the sentences are classified into positives, negatives and neutrals, they are grouped together according to its type. Further on, the same combination of techniques as for previously explained summarisation approaches are then used.

Additionally, a summary containing only the most positive and negative sentences is also generated (we have called this type of summaries *sent*) in order to check whether the polarity strength on its own could be a relevant feature for the summarisation process.

6 Evaluation Environment

In this Section we are going to describe in detail all the experimental set-up. Firstly, we will explain the corpus we used together with some figures regarding some statistics computed. Secondly, we will describe in-depth all the experiments we ran and the results obtained. Finally, an extensive discussion will be given in order to analyse all the results and draw some conclusions.

6.1 Experiments and Results

The main objective of the paper is to investigate the influence of summaries in contrast to full reviews for the rating-inference problem.

The purpose of the experiments is to analyse the performance of the different suggested text summarisation approaches and compare them to the performance of the full review. Therefore, the experiments conducted were the following: for each proposed summarisation approach, we experimented with five different types of compression rates for summaries (ranging from 10% to 50%). Apart from the full review, we dealt with 14 different summarisation approaches (4 for generic, 5 for query-focused and 5 for opinion-oriented summarisation), as well as 2 baselines (*lead* and *final*, taking the first or the last sentences according to a specific compression rate, respectively). Each experiment consisted of predicting the correct star of a review, either with the review as a whole or with one of the summarisation approaches. As we previously said in Section 4, for predicting the correct star-rating, we used machine learning techniques. In particular, different features were used to train a SVM classifier with 10-fold cross validation[4], using the whole review:

[4]The classifier used was the one integrated within the GATE framework: http://gate.ac.uk/

the *root* of each word, its *category*, and the calculated value employing the *SentiWordNet* lexicon, as well as their combinations. As a baseline for the full document we took into account a totally uninformed approach with respect to the class with higher number of reviews, i.e. considering all documents as if they were scored with 4 stars. The different results according different features can be seen in Table 3.

Feature	$F_{\beta=1}$
baseline	0.300
root	0.378
category	0.367
sentiWN	0.333
root+category	0.356
root+sentiWN	0.333
category+sentiWN	0.389
root+category+sentiWN	**0.413**

Table 3: F-measure results using the full review for classification

Regarding the features for training the summaries, it is worth mentioning that the best performing feature when no sentiment-based features are taken into account is the one using the root of the words. Consequently, this feature was used to train the summaries. Moreover, since the best results using the full review were obtained using the combination of the all the features (*root+category+sentiWN*), we also selected this combination to train the SVM classifier with our summaries. Conducting both experiments, we could analyse to what extent the sentiment-based feature benefit the classification process.

The results obtained are shown in Table 4 and Table 5, respectively. These tables show the F-measure value obtained for the classification task, when features extracted from summaries are used instead from the full review. On the one hand, results using the *root* feature extracted from summaries can be seen in Table 4. On the other hand, Table 5 shows the results when the combination of all the linguistic and sentiment-based features (*root+category+sentiWN*), that has been extracted from summaries, are used for training the SVM classifier.

We also performed two statistical tests in order to measure the significance for the results obtained. The tests we performed were the one-way Analysis of Variance (ANOVA) and the t-test (Spiegel and Castellan, 1998). Given a group of experiments, we first run ANOVA for analysing the difference between their means. In case some differences are found, we run the t-test between those pairs.

6.2 Discussion

A first analysis derived from the results obtained in Table 3 makes us be aware of the difficulty associated to the rating-inference task. As can be seen, a baseline without any information from the document at all, is performing around 30%, which compared to the remaining approaches is not a very bad number. However, we assumed that dealing with some information contained in documents, the classification algorithm will do better in finding the correct star associated to a review. This was the reason why we experimented with different features alone or in combination. From these experiments, we obtained that the combination of linguistic and semantic-based features leads to the best results, obtaining a F-measure value of 41%. If sentiment-based features are not taken into account, the best feature is the root of the word on its own. Furthermore, in order to analyse further combinations, we ran some experiments with bigrams. However, the results obtained did not improve the ones we already had, so they are not reported in this paper.

As far as the results is concerned comparing the use of summaries to the full document, it is worth mentioning that when using specific summarisation approaches, such as query-focused summaries combined with term-frequency, we get better results than using the full document with a 90% confidence interval, according to a t-test. In particular, *qf* for 10% is significant with respect to the full document, using only root as feature for training. For the results regarding the combination of *root*, *category* and *SentiWordNet*, *qf* for 10% and *qf+tf* for 10% and 20% are significant with respect to the full document.

Concerning the different summarisation approaches, it cannot be claimed a general tendency about which ones may lead to the best results. We also performed some significance tests between different strategies, and in most of the cases, the t-test and the ANOVA did not report significance over 95%. Only a few approaches were significant at a 95% confidence level, for instance, *te+cqp+tf* and *sent+te+cqp+tf* with respect to *sent+cqp+tf*

Approach		Compression Rate				
Summarisation method		**10%**	**20%**	**30%**	**40%**	**50%**
lead	$F_{\beta=1}$	0.411	0.378	0.367	0.311	0.322
final	$F_{\beta=1}$	0.322	0.389	0.300	**0.467**	**0.456**
tf	$F_{\beta=1}$	0.400	0.344	0.400	0.367	0.367
te+tf	$F_{\beta=1}$	0.367	0.422	0.411	0.389	0.322
cqp+tf	$F_{\beta=1}$	0.300	0.344	0.311	0.300	0.256
te+cqp+tf	$F_{\beta=1}$	0.422	0.356	0.333	0.300	0.322
qf	$F_{\beta=1}$	0.513	0.388	0.375	0.363	0.363
qf+tf	$F_{\beta=1}$	**0.567**	**0.467**	0.311	0.367	0.389
qf+te+tf	$F_{\beta=1}$	0.389	0.367	0.411	0.378	0.333
qf+cqp+tf	$F_{\beta=1}$	0.300	0.356	0.378	0.378	0.333
qf+te+cqp+tf	$F_{\beta=1}$	0.322	0.322	0.367	0.367	0.356
sent	$F_{\beta=1}$	0.344	0.380	0.391	0.290	0.336
sent+tf	$F_{\beta=1}$	0.378	0.425	**0.446**	0.303	0.337
sent+te+tf	$F_{\beta=1}$	0.278	0.424	0.313	0.369	0.347
sent+cqp+tf	$F_{\beta=1}$	0.333	0.300	0.358	0.358	0.324
sent+te+cqp+tf	$F_{\beta=1}$	0.446	0.334	0.358	0.292	0.369

Table 4: Classification results (F-measure) for summaries using *root* (*lead* = first sentences; *final* = last sentences; *tf* = term frequency; *te* = textual entailment; *cqp* = code quantity principle with noun-phrases; *qf* = query-focused summaries; and *sent* = opinion-oriented summaries)

for 10%; *sent+tf* in comparison to *sent+cqp+tf* for 20%; or *sent* with respect to *cqp+tf* for 40% and 50% compression rates. Other examples of the approaches that were significant at a 90% level of confidence are *qf* for 10% with respect to *sent+te+cqp+tf*. Due to the wide range of summarisation strategies tested in the experiments, the results obtained vary a lot and, due to the space limitations, it is not possible to report all the tables. What it seems to be clear from the results is that the code quantity principle (see Section 5) is not contributing much to the summarisation process, thus obtaining poor results when it is employed. Intuitively, this can be due to the fact that after the first mention of the bank, there is a predominant use of pronouns, and as a consequence, the accuracy of the tool that identifies noun-phrases could be affected. The same reason could be affecting the term-frequency calculus, as it is computed based on the lemmas of the words, not taking into account the pronouns that refer also to them.

7 Conclusion and Future Work

This paper presented a preliminary study of inference-rating task. We have proposed here a new framework for comparison and extrinsic evaluation of summaries in a text-based classification task. In our research, text summaries generated using different strategies were used for training a SVM classifier instead of full reviews. The aim of this task was to correctly predict the category of a review within a 1 to 5 star-scale. For the experiments, we gathered 89 bank reviews from the Internet and we generated 16 summaries of 5 different compression rates for each of them (80 different summaries for each review, having generated in total 7,120 summaries). We also experimented with several linguistic and sentiment-based features for the classifier. Although the results obtained are not significant enough to state that summaries really help the rating-inference task, we have shown that in some cases the use of summaries (e.g. query/entity-focused summaries) could offer competitive advantage over the use of full documents and we have also shown that some summarisation techniques do not degrade the performance of a rating-inference algorithm when compared to the use of full documents. We strongly believe that this preliminary study could serve as a starting point for future developments.

Although we have carried out extensive experimentation with different summarisation techniques, compression rates, and document/summary features, there are many issues that we have not explored. In the future, we plan to investigate whether the results could be affected by the class distribution of the reviews, and in this line we would like to see the distribution of the documents using clustering tech-

Approach		Compression Rate				
Summarisation method		10%	20%	30%	40%	50%
lead	$F_{\beta=1}$	0.275	0.422	0.422	0.378	0.322
final	$F_{\beta=1}$	0.275	0.378	0.333	0.344	0.400
tf	$F_{\beta=1}$	0.411	0.422	0.411	0.378	0.378
te+tf	$F_{\beta=1}$	0.411	0.344	0.344	0.344	0.378
cqp+tf	$F_{\beta=1}$	0.358	0.267	0.333	0.222	0.289
te+cqp+tf	$F_{\beta=1}$	0.444	0.411	0.411	0.311	0.322
qf	$F_{\beta=1}$	**0.563**	**0.488**	0.400	0.375	0.350
qf+tf	$F_{\beta=1}$	0.444	0.411	**0.433**	0.367	0.356
qf+te+tf	$F_{\beta=1}$	0.322	0.367	0.356	0.344	0.344
qf+cqp+tf	$F_{\beta=1}$	0.292	0.322	0.367	0.333	0.356
qf+te+cqp+tf	$F_{\beta=1}$	0.356	0.378	0.356	0.367	0.356
sent	$F_{\beta=1}$	0.322	0.370	0.379	**0.412**	**0.414**
sent+tf	$F_{\beta=1}$	0.378	0.446	0.359	0.380	0.402
sent+te+tf	$F_{\beta=1}$	0.333	0.414	0.404	0.380	0.381
sent+cqp+tf	$F_{\beta=1}$	0.300	0.333	0.347	0.358	0.296
sent+te+cqp+tf	$F_{\beta=1}$	0.436	0.413	0.425	0.359	0.324

Table 5: Classification results (F-measure) for summaries using *root*, *category* and *SentiWordNet* (*lead* = first sentences; *final* = last sentences; *tf* = term frequency; *te* = textual entailment; *cqp* = code quantity principle with noun-phrases; *qf* = query-focused summaries; and *sent* = opinion-oriented summaries)

niques. Moreover, we would also like to investigate what it would happen if we consider the values of the star-rating scale as ordinal numbers, and not only as labels for categories. We will replicate the experiments presented here using as evaluation measure the "mean square error" which has been pinpointed as a more appropriate measure for categorisation in an ordinal scale. Finally, in the medium to long-term we plan to extent the experiments and analysis to other available datasets in different domains, such as movie or book reviews, in order to see if the results could be influenced by the nature of the corpus, allowing also further results for comparison with other approaches and assessing the difficulty of the task from a perspective of different domains.

Acknowledgments

This research has been supported by the project PROMETEO "Desarrollo de Técnicas Inteligentes e Interactivas de Minería de Textos" (2009/119) from the Valencian Government. Moreover, Elena Lloret is funded by the FPI program (BES-2007-16268) from the Spanish Ministry of Science and Innovation under the project TEXT-MESS (TIN2006-15265-C06-01), and Horacio Saggion is supported by a Ramón y Cajal Fellowship from the Ministry of Science and Innovation, Spain. The authors would also like to thank Alexandra Balahur for helping to process the dataset with her Opinion Mining approach.

References

S. Baccianella, A. Esuli, and F. Sebastiani. 2009. Multi-facet Rating of Product Reviews. In *Proceedings of the 31th European Conference on IR Research on Advances in Information Retrieval*, pages 461–472.

A. Bagga and B. Baldwin. 1998. Entity-Based Cross-Document Coreferencing Using the Vector Space Model. In *Proceedings of the COLING-ACL*, pages 79–85.

A. Balahur-Dobrescu, M. Kabadjov, J. Steinberger, R. Steinberger, and A. Montoyo. 2009. Summarizing Opinions in Blog Threads. In *Proceedings of the Pacific Asia Conference on Language, INformation and Computation Conference*, pages 606–613.

S. Chakraborti, R. Mukras, R. Lothian, N. Wiratunga, S. Watt, and D Harper. 2007. Supervised Latent Semantic Indexing using Adaptive Sprinkling. In *Proceedings of IJCAI-07*, pages 1582–1587.

H. Cunningham, D. Maynard, K. Bontcheva, and V. Tablan. 2002. GATE: A Framework and Graphical Development Environment for Robust NLP Tools and Applications. In *Proceedings of the ACL*.

A. Devitt and K. Ahmad. 2007. Sentiment Polarity Identification in Financial News: A Cohesion-based Approach. In *Proceedings of the ACL*, pages 984–991.

W. Du and S. Tan. 2009. An Iterative Reinforcement Approach for Fine-Grained Opinion Mining. In *Proceedings of the NAACL*, pages 486–493.

A. Esuli and F. Sebastiani. 2006. SENTIWORDNET: A Publicly Available Lexical Resource for Opinion Mining. In *Proceedings of LREC*, pages 417–422.

C. Fellbaum. 1998. *WordNet: An Electronical Lexical Database*. The MIT Press, Cambridge, MA.

O. Ferrández, D. Micol, R. Muñoz, and M. Palomar. 2007. A Perspective-Based Approach for Solving Textual Entailment Recognition. In *Proceedings of the ACL-PASCAL Workshop on Textual Entailment and Paraphrasing*, pages 66–71, June.

S. Ferrari, T. Charnois, Y. Mathet, F. Rioult, and D. Legallois. 2009. Analyse de Discours Évaluatif, Modèle Linguistique et Applications. In *Fouille de données d'opinion*, volume E-17, pages 71–93.

T. Givón, 1990. *Syntax: A functional-typological introduction, II*. John Benjamins.

C. Grouin, M. Hurault-Plantet, P. Paroubek, and J. B. Berthelin. 2009. DEFT'07 : Une Campagne d'Avaluation en Fouille d'Opinion. In *Fouille de données d'opinion*, volume E-17, pages 1–24.

Y. Hu, W. Li, and Q. Lu. 2008. Developing Evaluation Model of Topical Term for Document-Level Sentiment Classification. In *Proceedings of the 10th Pacific Rim International Conference on Artificial Intelligence*, pages 175–186.

H. Isozaki and H. Kazawa. 2002. Efficient Support Vector Classifiers for Named Entity Recognition. In *Proceedings of the 19th International Conference on Computational Linguistics*, pages 390–396.

M. A. Kumar and M. Gopal. 2009. Text Categorization Using Fuzzy Proximal SVM and Distributional Clustering of Words. In *Proceedings of the 13th Pacific-Asia Conference on Advances in Knowledge Discovery and Data Mining*, pages 52–61.

S. Latif and M. McGee Wood. 2009. A Novel Technique for Automated Linguistic Quality Assessment of Students' Essays Using Automatic Summarizers. *Computer Science and Information Engineering, World Congress on*, 5:144–148.

C. W. K. Leung, S. C. F. Chan, and F. L. Chung. 2006. Integrating Collaborative Filtering and Sentiment Analysis: A Rating Inference Approach. In *Proceedings of The ECAI 2006 Workshop on Recommender Systems*, pages 62–66.

Y. Li, K. Bontcheva, and H. Cunningham. 2009. Adapting SVM for Data Sparseness and Imbalance: A Case Study in Information Extraction. *Natural Language Engineering*, 15(2):241–271.

E. Lloret, A. Balahur, M. Palomar, and A. Montoyo. 2009. Towards Building a Competitive Opinion Summarization System: Challenges and Keys. In *Proceedings of the NAACL. Student Research Workshop and Doctoral Consortium*, pages 72–77.

I. Mani, D. House, G. Klein, L. Hirshman, L. Obrst, T. Firmin, M. Chrzanowski, and B. Sundheim. 1998. The TIPSTER SUMMAC Text Summarization Evaluation. Technical report, The Mitre Corporation.

I. Mani. 2001. *Automatic Text Summarization*. John Benjamins Publishing Company.

R. McDonald, K. Hannan, T. Neylon, M. Wells, and J. Reynar. 2007. Structured Models for Fine-to-Coarse Sentiment Analysis. In *Proceedings of the ACL*, pages 432–439.

R. Mukras, N. Wiratunga, R. Lothian, S. Chakraborti, and D. Harper. 2007. Information Gain Feature Selection for Ordinal Text Classification using Probability Redistribution. In *Proceedings of the Textlink workshop at IJCAI-07*.

A. Nenkova, L. Vanderwende, and K. McKeown. 2006. A Compositional Context Sensitive Multi-document Summarizer: Exploring the Factors that Influence Summarization. In *Proceedings of the ACM SIGIR conference on Research and development in information retrieval*, pages 573–580.

B. Pang and L. Lee. 2005. Seeing Stars: Exploiting Class Relationships for Sentiment Categorization with Respect to Rating Scales. In *Proceedings of the ACL*, pages 115–124.

B. Pang and L. Lee. 2008. Opinion Mining and Sentiment Analysis. *Foundations and Trends in Information Retrieval*, 2(1-2):1–135.

H. Saggion and A. Funk. 2009. Extracting Opinions and Facts for Business Intelligence. *RNTI*, E-17:119–146.

H. Saggion. 2008. SUMMA: A Robust and Adaptable Summarization Tool. *Traitement Automatique des Languages*, 49:103–125.

K. Shimada and T. Endo. 2008. Seeing Several Stars: A Rating Inference Task for a Document Containing Several Evaluation Criteria. In *Proceedings of the 12th Pacific-Asia Conference on Advances in Knowledge Discovery and Data Mining*, pages 1006–1014.

S. Spiegel and N. J. Castellan, Jr. 1998. *Nonparametric Statistics for the Behavioral Sciences*. McGraw-Hill International.

V. Stoyanov and C. Cardie. 2006. Toward Opinion Summarization: Linking the Sources. In *Proceedings of the Workshop on Sentiment and Subjectivity in Text*, pages 9–14.

P. D. Turney. 2002. Thumbs Up or Thumbs Down?: Semantic Orientation Applied to Unsupervised Classification of Reviews. In *Proceedings of the ACL*, pages 417–424.

T. Wilson, J. Wiebe, and P. Hoffmann. 2005. Recognizing Contextual Polarity in Phrase-level Sentiment Analysis. In *Proceedings of the EMNLP*, pages 347–354.

L. Zhuang, F. Jing, and X. Y. Zhu. 2006. Movie Review Mining and Summarization. In *Proceedings of the 15th ACM international conference on Information and knowledge management*, pages 43–50.

Recognizing Stances in Ideological On-Line Debates

Swapna Somasundaran
Dept. of Computer Science
University of Pittsburgh
Pittsburgh, PA 15260
swapna@cs.pitt.edu

Janyce Wiebe
Dept. of Computer Science and
The Intelligent Systems Program
University of Pittsburgh
Pittsburgh, PA 15260
wiebe@cs.pitt.edu

Abstract

This work explores the utility of sentiment and arguing opinions for classifying stances in ideological debates. In order to capture arguing opinions in ideological stance taking, we construct an arguing lexicon automatically from a manually annotated corpus. We build supervised systems employing sentiment and arguing opinions and their targets as features. Our systems perform substantially better than a distribution-based baseline. Additionally, by employing both types of opinion features, we are able to perform better than a unigram-based system.

1 Introduction

In this work, we explore if and how ideological stances can be recognized using opinion analysis. Following (Somasundaran and Wiebe, 2009), *stance*, as used in this work, refers to an overall position held by a person toward an object, idea or proposition. For example, in a debate "Do you believe in the existence of God?," a person may take a for-existence of God stance or an against existence of God stance. Similarly, being pro-choice, believing in creationism, and supporting universal healthcare are all examples of ideological stances.

Online web forums discussing ideological and political hot-topics are popular.[1] In this work, we are interested in dual-sided debates (there are two possible polarizing sides that the participants can take). For example, in a healthcare debate, participants can take a for-healthcare stance or an against-healthcare stance. Participants generally pick a side (the websites provide a way for users to tag their stance) and post an argument/justification supporting their stance.

Personal opinions are clearly important in ideological stance taking, and debate posts provide outlets for expressing them. For instance, let us consider the following snippet from a universal healthcare debate. Here the writer is expressing a negative sentiment[2] regarding the government (the opinion spans are highlighted in bold and their *targets*, what the opinions are about, are highlighted in italics).

(1) *Government* is a **disease** pretending to be its own cure. [side: against healthcare]

The writer's negative sentiment is directed toward the government, the initiator of universal healthcare. This negative opinion reveals his against-healthcare stance.

We observed that *arguing*, a less well explored type of subjectivity, is prominently manifested in ideological debates. As used in this work, *arguing* is a type of linguistic subjectivity, where a person is arguing for or against something or expressing a belief about what is true, should be true or should be done

[1] http://www.opposingviews.com, http://wiki.idebate.org, http://www.createdebate.com and http://www.forandagainst.com are examples of such debating websites.

[2] As used in this work, *sentiment* is a type of linguistic subjectivity, specifically positive and negative expressions of emotions, judgments, and evaluations (Wilson and Wiebe, 2005; Wilson, 2007; Somasundaran et al., 2008).

Proceedings of the NAACL HLT 2010 Workshop on Computational Approaches to Analysis and Generation of Emotion in Text, pages 116–124,
Los Angeles, California, June 2010.

in his or her view of the world (Wilson and Wiebe, 2005; Wilson, 2007; Somasundaran et al., 2008).

For instance, let us consider the following snippet from a post supporting an against-existence of God stance.

(2) **Obviously** that hasn't happened, and to be completely objective (as all scientists **should be**) **we must** lean on the side of **greatest evidence** which at the present time is for evolution. [side: against the existence of God]

In supporting their side, people not only express their sentiments, but they also argue about what is true (e.g., this is prominent in the existence of God debate) and about what should or should not be done (e.g., this is prominent in the healthcare debate).

In this work, we investigate whether sentiment and arguing expressions of opinion are useful for ideological stance classification. For this, we explore ways to capture relevant opinion information as machine learning features into a supervised stance classifier. While there is a large body of resources for sentiment analysis (e.g., the sentiment lexicon from (Wilson et al., 2005)), arguing analysis does not seem to have a well established lexical resource. In order to remedy this, using a simple automatic approach and a manually annotated corpus,[3] we construct an arguing lexicon. We create features called *opinion-target pairs*, which encode not just the opinion information, but also what the opinion is about, its target. Systems employing sentiment-based and arguing-based features alone, or both in combination, are analyzed. We also take a qualitative look at features used by the learners to get insights about the information captured by them.

We perform experiments on four different ideological domains. Our results show that systems using both sentiment and arguing features can perform substantially better than a distribution-based baseline and marginally better than a unigram-based system. Our qualitative analysis suggests that opinion features capture more insightful information than using words alone.

The rest of this paper is organized as follows: We first describe our ideological debate data in Section 2. We explain the construction of our arguing lexicon in Section 3 and our different systems in Section 4. Experiments, results and analyses are presented in Section 5. Related work is in Section 6 and conclusions are in Section 7.

[3]MPQA corpus available at http://www.cs.pitt.edu/mpqa.

2 Ideological Debates

Political and ideological debates on hot issues are popular on the web. In this work, we analyze the following domains: Existence of God, Healthcare, Gun Rights, Gay Rights, Abortion and Creationism. Of these, we use the first two for development and the remaining four for experiments and analyses. Each domain is a political/ideological issue and has two polarizing stances: for and against.

Table 2 lists the domains, examples of debate topics within each domain, the specific sides for each debate topic, and the domain-level stances that correspond to these sides. For example, consider the Existence of God domain in Table 2. The two stances in this domain are *for*-existence of God and *against*-existence of God. "Do you believe in God", a specific debate topic within this domain, has two sides: "Yes!!" and "No!!". The former corresponds to the for-existence of God stance and the latter maps to the against-existence of God stance. The situation is different for the debate "God Does Not Exist". Here, side "against" corresponds to the for-existence of God stance, and side "for" corresponds to the against-existence of God stance.

In general, we see in Table 2 that, while specific debate topics may vary, in each case the two sides for the topic correspond to the domain-level stances. We download several debates for each domain and manually map debate-level stances to the stances for the domain. Table 2 also reports the number of debates, and the total number of posts for each domain. For instance, we collect 16 different debates in the healthcare domain which gives us a total of 336 posts. All debate posts have user-reported debate-level stance tags.

2.1 Observations

Preliminary inspection of development data gave us insights which shaped our approach. We discuss some of our observations in this section.

Arguing Opinion

We found that arguing opinions are prominent when people defend their ideological stances. We

Domain/Topics	$stance_1$	$stance_2$
Healthcare (16 debates, 336 posts)	*for*	*against*
Should the US have universal healthcare	Yes	No
Debate: Public insurance option in US health care	Pro	Con
Existence of God (7 debates, 486 posts)	*for*	*against*
Do you believe in God	Yes!!	No!!
God Does Not Exist	against	for
Gun Rights (18 debates, 566 posts)	*for*	*against*
Should Guns Be Illegal	against	for
Debate: Right to bear arms in the US	Yes	No
Gay Rights (15 debates, 1186 posts)	*for*	*against*
Are people born gay	Yes	No
Is homosexuality a sin	No	Yes
Abortion (13 debates, 618 posts)	*for*	*against*
Should abortion be legal	Yes	No
Should south Dakota pass the abortion ban	No	Yes
Creationism (15 debates, 729 posts)	*for*	*against*
Evolution Is A False Idea	for	against
Has evolution been scientifically proved	It has not	It has

Table 1: Examples of debate topics and their stances

saw an instance of this in Example 2, where the participant argues against the existence of God. He argues for what (he believes) is right (**should be**), and is imperative (**we must**). He employs "**Obviously**" to draw emphasis and then uses a superlative construct (**greatest**) to argue for evolution.

Example 3 below illustrates arguing in a healthcare debate. The spans **most certainly believe** and **has or must do** reveal arguing (**ESSENTIAL, IMPORTANT** are sentiments).

(3) ... I **most certainly believe** that there are some **ESSENTIAL, IMPORTANT** things that the government **has or must do** [side: for healthcare]

Observe that the text spans revealing arguing can be a single word or multiple words. This is different from sentiment expressions that are more often single words.

Opinion Targets

As mentioned previously, a target is what an opinion is about. Targets are vital for determining stances. Opinions by themselves may not be as informative as the *combination* of opinions and targets. For instance, in Example 1 the writer supports an against-healthcare stance using a negative sentiment. There is a negative sentiment in the example below (Example 4) too. However, in this case the writer supports a for-healthcare stance. It is by understanding *what* the opinion is about, that we can recognize the stance.

(4) Oh, **the answer is GREEDY** insurance companies that buy your Rep & Senator. [side: for healthcare]

We also observed that targets, or in general items that participants from either side choose to speak about, by themselves may not be as informative as opinions in conjunction with the targets. For instance, Examples 1 and 3 both speak about the government but belong to opposing sides. Understanding that the former example is negative toward the government and the latter has a positive arguing about the government helps us to understand the corresponding stances.

Examples 1, 3 and 4 also illustrate that there are a variety of ways in which people support their stances. The writers express opinions about government, the initiator of healthcare and insurance companies, and the parties hurt by government run healthcare. Participants group government and healthcare as essentially the *same* concept, while they consider healthcare and insurance companies as *alternative* concepts. By expressing opinions regarding a variety of items that are same or alternative to main topic (healthcare, in these examples), they are, in effect, revealing their stance (Somasundaran et al., 2008).

3 Constructing an Arguing Lexicon

Arguing is a relatively less explored category in subjectivity. Due to this, there are no available lexicons with arguing terms (clues). However, the MPQA corpus (Version 2) is annotated with arguing subjectivity (Wilson and Wiebe, 2005; Wilson, 2007). There are two arguing categories: *positive arguing* and *negative arguing*. We use this corpus to generate a ngram (up to trigram) arguing lexicon.

The examples below illustrate MPQA arguing annotations. Examples 5 and 7 illustrate positive arguing annotations and Example 6 illustrates negative arguing.

(5) Iran **insists its nuclear program is purely for peaceful purposes**.

(6) Officials in Panama **denied that Mr. Chavez or any of his family members had asked for asylum**.

(7) Putin remarked that the events in Chechnia "**could be interpreted only in the context of the struggle against international terrorism**."

Inspection of these text spans reveal that arguing annotations can be considered to be comprised of two pieces of information. The first piece of information is what we call the *arguing trigger expression*. The trigger is an indicator that an arguing is taking place, and is the primary component that anchors the arguing annotation. The second component is the expression that reveals more about the argument, and can be considered to be secondary for the purposes of detecting arguing. In Example 5, "insists", by itself, conveys enough information to indicate that the speaker is arguing. It is quite likely that a sentence of the form "X insists Y" is going to be an arguing sentence. Thus, "insists" is an arguing trigger.

Similarly, in Example 6, we see *two* arguing triggers: "denied" and "denied that". Each of these can independently act as arguing triggers (For example, in the constructs "X denied that Y" and "X denied Y"). Finally, in Example 7, the arguing annotation has the following independent trigger expressions "could be * only", "could be" and "could". The wild card in the first trigger expression indicates that there could be zero or more words in its place.

Note that MPQA annotations do not provide this primary/secondary distinction. We make this distinction to create general arguing clues such as "insist". Table 3 lists examples of arguing annotations from the MPQA corpus and what we consider as their arguing trigger expressions.

Notice that trigger words are generally at the beginning of the annotations. Most of these are unigrams, bigrams or trigrams (though it is possible for these to be longer, as seen in Example 7). Thus, we can create a lexicon of arguing trigger expressions

Positive arguing annotations	Trigger Expr.
actually reflects Israel's determination ...	**actually**
am convinced that improving ...	**am convinced**
bear witness that Mohamed is his ...	**bear witness**
can only rise to meet it by making ...	**can only**
has always seen usama bin ladin's ...	**has always**

Negative Arguing Annotations	Trigger Expr.
certainly not a foregone conclusion	**certainly not**
has never been any clearer	**has never**
not too cool for kids	**not too**
rather than issuing a letter of ...	**rather than**
there is no explanation for	**there is no**

Table 2: Arguing annotations from the MPQA corpus and their corresponding trigger expressions

by extracting the starting n-grams from the MPQA annotations. The process of creating the lexicon is as follows:

1. Generate a $candidate\ Set$ from the annotations in the corpus. Three candidates are extracted from the stemmed version of each annotation: the first word, the bigram starting at the first word, and the trigram starting at the first word. For example, if the annotation is "can only rise to meet it by making some radical changes", the following candidates are extracted from it: "can", "can only" and "can only rise".

2. Remove the candidates that are present in the sentiment lexicon from (Wilson et al., 2005) (as these are already accounted for in previous research). For example, "actually", which is a trigger word in Table 3, is a neutral subjectivity clue in the lexicon.

3. For each candidate in the $candidate\ Set$, find the likelihood that it is a reliable indicator of positive or negative arguing *in the MPQA corpus*. These are likelihoods of the form: $P(positive\ arguing|candidate) = \frac{\#candidate\ is\ in\ a\ positive\ arguing\ span}{\#candidate\ is\ in\ the\ corpus}$ and $P(negative\ arguing|candidate) = \frac{\#candidate\ is\ in\ a\ negative\ arguing\ span}{\#candidate\ is\ in\ the\ corpus}$

4. Make a lexicon entry for each candidate consisting of the stemmed text and the two probabilities described above.

This process results in an arguing lexicon with 3762 entries, where 3094 entries have

$P(positive\ arguing|candidate) > 0$; and 668 entries have $P(negative\ arguing|candidate) > 0$. Table 3 lists select interesting expressions from the arguing lexicon.

Entries indicative of Positive Arguing
be important to, would be better, would need to, be just the, be the true, my opinion, the contrast, show the, prove to be, only if, on the verge, ought to, be most, youve get to, render, manifestation, ironically, once and for, no surprise, overwhelming evidence, its clear, its clear that, it be evident, it be extremely, it be quite, it would therefore
Entries indicative of Negative Arguing
be not simply, simply a, but have not, can not imagine, we dont need, we can not do, threat against, ought not, nor will, never again, far from be, would never, not completely, nothing will, inaccurate and, inaccurate and, find no, no time, deny that

Table 3: Examples of positive arguing ($P(positive\ arguing|candidate) > P(negative\ arguing|candidate)$) and negative arguing ($P(negative\ arguing|candidate) > P(positive\ arguing|candidate)$)from the arguing lexicon

4 Features for Stance Classification

We construct opinion target pair features, which are units that capture the combined information about opinions and targets. These are encoded as binary features into a standard machine learning algorithm.

4.1 Arguing-based Features

We create arguing features primarily from our arguing lexicon. We construct additional arguing features using modal verbs and syntactic rules. The latter are motivated by the fact that modal verbs such as "must", "should" and "ought" are clear cases of arguing, and are often involved in simple syntactic patterns with clear targets.

4.1.1 Arguing-lexicon Features

The process for creating features for a post using the arguing lexicon is simple. For each sentence in the post, we first determine if it contains a positive or negative arguing expression by looking for trigram, bigram and unigram matches (in that order) with the arguing lexicon. We prevent the same text span from matching twice – once a trigram match is found, a substring bigram (or unigram) match with the same text span is avoided. If there are multiple arguing expression matches found within a sentence, we determine the most prominent arguing polarity by adding up the positive arguing probabilities and negative arguing probabilities (provided in the lexicon) of all the individual expressions.

Once the prominent arguing polarity is determined for a sentence, the prefix ap (arguing positive) or an (arguing negative) is attached to all the content words in that sentence to construct opinion-target features. In essence, all content words (nouns, verbs, adjectives and adverbs) in the sentence are assumed to be the target. Arguing features are denoted as *ap-target* (positive arguing toward *target*) and *an-target* (negative arguing toward $target$).

4.1.2 Modal Verb Features for Arguing

Modals words such as "must" and "should" are usually good indicators of arguing. This is a small closed set. Also, the target (what the arguing is about) is syntactically associated with the modal word, which means it can be relatively accurately extracted by using a small set of syntactic rules.

For every modal detected, three features are created by combining the modal word with its subject and object. Note that all the different modals are replaced by "should" while creating features. This helps to create more general features. For example, given a sentence "They must be available to all people", the method creates three features "they should", "should available" and "they should available". These patterns are created independently of the arguing lexicon matches, and added to the feature set for the post.

4.2 Sentiment-based Features

Sentiment-based features are created independent of arguing features. In order to detect sentiment opinions, we use a sentiment lexicon (Wilson et al., 2005). In addition to positive ($^+$) and negative ($^-$) words, this lexicon also contains subjective words that are themselves neutral ($^=$) with respect to polarity. Examples of neutral entries are "absolutely", "amplify", "believe", and "think".

We find the sentiment polarity of the entire sentence and assign this polarity to each content word in the sentence (denoted, for example, as $target^+$). In order to detect the sentence polarity, we use the Vote and Flip algorithm from Choi and Cardie (2009). This algorithm essentially counts the number of positive, negative and neutral lexicon hits in a given expression and accounts for negator words. The algorithm is used as is, except for the default polarity assignment (as we do not know the most prominent polarity in the corpus). Note that the Vote and Flip algorithm has been developed for expressions but we employ it on sentences. Once the polarity of a sentence is determined, we create sentiment features for the sentence. This is done for all sentences in the post.

5 Experiments

Experiments are carried out on debate posts from the following four domains: Gun Rights, Gay Rights, Abortion, and Creationism. For each domain, a corpus with equal class distribution is created as follows: we merge all debates and sample instances (posts) from the majority class to obtain equal numbers of instances for each stance. This gives us a total of 2232 posts in the corpus: 306 posts for the Gun Rights domain, 846 posts for the Gay Rights domain, 550 posts for the Abortion domain and 530 posts for the Creationism domain.

Our first baseline is a distribution-based baseline, which has an accuracy of 50%. We also construct *Unigram*, a system based on unigram content information, but no explicit opinion information. Unigrams are reliable for stance classification in political domains (as seen in (Lin et al., 2006; Kim and Hovy, 2007)). Intuitively, evoking a particular topic can be indicative of a stance. For example, a participant who chooses to speak about "child" and "life" in an abortion debate is more likely from an against-abortion side, while someone speaking about "woman", "rape" and "choice" is more likely from a for-abortion stance.

We construct three systems that use opinion information: The *Sentiment* system that uses only the sentiment features described in Section 4.2, the *Arguing* system that uses only arguing features constructed in Section 4.1, and the *Arg+Sent* system that uses both sentiment and arguing features.

All systems are implemented using a standard implementation of SVM in the Weka toolkit (Hall et al., 2009). We measure performance using the accuracy metric.

5.1 Results

Table 4 shows the accuracy averaged over 10 fold cross-validation experiments for each domain. The first row (Overall) reports the accuracy calculated over all 2232 posts in the data.

Overall, we notice that all the supervised systems perform better than the distribution-based baseline. Observe that Unigram has a better performance than Sentiment. The good performance of Unigram indicates that what participants choose to speak about is a good indicator of ideological stance taking. This result confirms previous researchers' intuition that, in general, political orientation is a function of "authors' attitudes over multiple issues rather than positive or negative sentiment with respect to a single issue" (Pang and Lee, 2008). Nevertheless, the Arg+Sent system that uses both arguing and sentiment features outperforms Unigram.

We performed McNemar's test to measure the difference in system behaviors. The test was performed on all pairs of supervised systems using all 2232 posts. The results show that there is a significant difference between the classification behavior of Unigram and Arg+Sent systems ($p < 0.05$). The difference between classifications of Unigram and Arguing approaches significance ($p < 0.1$). There is no significant difference in the behaviors of all other system pairs.

Moving on to detailed performance in each domain, we see that Unigram outperforms Sentiment for all domains. Arguing and Arg+Sent outperform Unigram for three domains (Guns, Gay Rights and Abortion), while the situation is reversed for one domain (Creationism). We carried out separate t-tests for each domain, using the results from each test fold as a data point. Our results indicate that the performance of Sentiment is significantly different from all other systems for all domains. However there is no significant difference between the performance of the remaining systems.

5.2 Analysis

On manual inspection of the top features used by the classifiers for discriminating the stances, we found that there is an overlap between the content words used by Unigram, Arg+Sent and Arguing. For

Domain (#posts)	Distribution	Unigram	Sentiment	Arguing	Arg+Sent
Overall (2232)	50	62.50	55.02	62.59	63.93
Guns Rights (306)	50	66.67	58.82	69.28	70.59
Gay Rights (846)	50	61.70	52.84	62.05	63.71
Abortion (550)	50	59.1	54.73	59.46	60.55
Creationism (530)	50	64.91	56.60	62.83	63.96

Table 4: Accuracy of the different systems

example, in the Gay Rights domain, "understand" and "equal" are amongst the top features in Unigram, while "ap-understand" (positive arguing for "understand") and "ap-equal" are top features for Arg+Sent.

However, we believe that Arg+Sent makes finer and more insightful distinctions based on polarity of opinions toward the same set of words. Table 5 lists some interesting features in the Gay Rights domain for Unigram and Arg+Sent. Depending on whether positive or negative attribute weights were assigned by the SVM learner, the features are either indicative of for-gay rights or against-gay rights. Even though the features for Unigram are intuitive, it is not evident if a word is evoked as, for example, a pitch, concern, or denial. Also, we do not see a clear separation of the terms (for e.g., "bible" is an indicator for against-gay rights while "christianity" is an indicator for for-gay rights)

The arguing features from Arg+Sent seem to be relatively more informative – positive arguing about "christianity", "corinthians", "mormonism" and "bible" are all indicative of against-gay rights stance. These are indeed beliefs and concerns that shape an against-gay rights stance. On the other hand, negative arguings with these same words denote a for-gay rights stance. Presumably, these occur in refutations of the concerns influencing the opposite side. Likewise, the appeal for equal rights for gays is captured positive arguing about "liberty", "independence", "pursuit" and "suffrage".

Interestingly, we found that our features also capture the ideas of opinion variety and *same* and *alternative* targets as defined in previous research (Somasundaran et al., 2008) – in Table 5, items that are similar (e.g., "christianity" and "corinthians") have similar opinions toward them for a given stance (for e.g., ap-christianity and ap-corinthians belong to against-gay rights stance while an-christianity and an-corinthians belong to for-gay rights stance). Additionally, items that are *alternatives* (e.g. "gay" and "heterosexuality") have opposite polarities associated with them for a given stance, that is, positive arguing for "heterosexuality" and negative arguing for "gay" reveal the the same stance.

In general, unigram features associate the choice of topics with the stances, while the arguing features can capture the concerns, defenses, appeals or denials that signify each side (though we do not explicitly encode these fine-grained distinctions in this work). Interestingly, we found that sentiment features in Arg+Sent are not as informative as the arguing features discussed above.

6 Related Work

Generally, research in identifying political viewpoints has employed information from words in the document (Malouf and Mullen, 2008; Mullen and Malouf, 2006; Grefenstette et al., 2004; Laver et al., 2003; Martin and Vanberg, 2008; Lin et al., 2006; Lin, 2006). Specifically, Lin et al. observe that people from opposing perspectives seem to use words in differing frequencies. On similar lines, Kim and Hovy (2007) use unigrams, bigrams and trigrams for election prediction from forum posts. In contrast, our work specifically employs sentiment-based and arguing-based features to perform stance classification in political debates. Our experiments are focused on determining how different opinion expressions reinforce an overall political stance. Our results indicate that while unigram information is reliable, further improvements can be achieved in certain domains using our opinion-based approach. Our work is also complementary to that by Greene and Resnik (2009), which focuses on syntactic packaging for recognizing perspectives.

For Gay Rights	Against Gay Rights
Unigram Features	
constitution, fundamental, rights, suffrage, pursuit, discrimination, government, happiness, shame, wed, gay, heterosexuality, chromosome, evolution, genetic, christianity, mormonism, corinthians, procreate, adopt	pervert, hormone, liberty, fidelity, naval, retarded, orientation, private, partner, kingdom, bible, sin, bigot
Arguing Features from Arg+Sent	
ap-constitution, ap-fundamental, ap-rights, ap-hormone, ap-liberty, ap-independence, ap-suffrage, ap-pursuit, ap-discrimination, an-government, ap-fidelity, ap-happiness, an-pervert, an-naval, an-retarded, an-orientation, an-shame, ap-private, ap-wed, ap-gay, an-heterosexuality, ap-partner, ap-chromosome, ap-evolution, ap-genetic, an-kingdom, an-christianity, an-mormonism, an-corinthians, an-bible, an-sin, an-bigot, an-procreate, ap-adopt,	an-constitution, an-fundamental, an-rights, an-hormone, an-liberty, an-independence, an-suffrage, an-pursuit, an-discrimination, ap-government, an-fidelity, an-happiness, ap-pervert, ap-naval, ap-retarded, ap-orientation, ap-shame, an-private, an-wed, an-gay, ap-heterosexuality, an-partner, an-chromosome, an-evolution, an-genetic, ap-kingdom, ap-christianity, ap-mormonism, ap-corinthians, ap-bible, ap-sin, ap-bigot, ap-procreate, an-adopt

Table 5: Examples of features associated with the stances in Gay Rights domain

Discourse-level participant relation, that is, whether participants agree/disagree has been found useful for determining political side-taking (Thomas et al., 2006; Bansal et al., 2008; Agrawal et al., 2003; Malouf and Mullen, 2008). Agreement/disagreement relations are not the main focus of our work. Other work in the area of polarizing political discourse analyze co-citations (Efron, 2004) and linking patterns (Adamic and Glance, 2005). In contrast, our focus is on document content and opinion expressions.

Somasundaran et al. (2007b) have noted the usefulness of the arguing category for opinion QA. Our tasks are different; they use arguing to retrieve relevant answers, but not distinguish stances. Our work is also different from related work in the domain of product debates (Somasundaran and Wiebe, 2009) in terms of the methodology.

Wilson (2007) manually adds positive/negative arguing information to entries in a sentiment lexicon from (Wilson et al., 2005) and uses these as arguing features. Our arguing trigger expressions are separate from the sentiment lexicon entries and are derived from a corpus. Our n-gram trigger expressions are also different from manually created regular expression-based arguing lexicon for speech data (Somasundaran et al., 2007a).

7 Conclusions

In this paper, we explore recognizing stances in ideological on-line debates. We created an arguing lexicon from the MPQA annotations in order to recognize arguing, a prominent type of linguistic subjectivity in ideological stance taking. We observed that opinions or targets in isolation are not as informative as their combination. Thus, we constructed opinion target pair features to capture this information.

We performed supervised learning experiments on four different domains. Our results show that both unigram-based and opinion-based systems perform better than baseline methods. We found that, even though our sentiment-based system is able to perform better than the distribution-based baseline, it does not perform at par with the unigram system. However, overall, our arguing-based system does as well as the unigram-based system, and our system that uses both arguing and sentiment features obtains further improvement. Our feature analysis suggests that arguing features are more insightful than unigram features, as they make finer distinctions that reveal the underlying ideologies.

References

Lada A. Adamic and Natalie Glance. 2005. The political blogosphere and the 2004 u.s. election: Divided they blog. In *LinkKDD*.

Rakesh Agrawal, Sridhar Rajagopalan, Ramakrishnan Srikant, and Yirong Xu. 2003. Mining newsgroups using networks arising from social behavior. In *WWW*.

Mohit Bansal, Claire Cardie, and Lillian Lee. 2008. The power of negative thinking: Exploiting label disagreement in the min-cut classification framework. In

Proceedings of the 22nd International Conference on Computational Linguistics (COLING-2008).

Yejin Choi and Claire Cardie. 2009. Adapting a polarity lexicon using integer linear programming for domain-specific sentiment classification. In *Proceedings of the 2009 Conference on Empirical Methods in Natural Language Processing*, pages 590–598, Singapore, August. Association for Computational Linguistics.

Miles Efron. 2004. Cultural orientation: Classifying subjective documents by cocitation analysis. In *AAAI Fall Symposium on Style and Meaning in Language, Art, and Music*.

Stephan Greene and Philip Resnik. 2009. More than words: Syntactic packaging and implicit sentiment. In *Proceedings of Human Language Technologies: The 2009 Annual Conference of the North American Chapter of the Association for Computational Linguistics*, pages 503–511, Boulder, Colorado, June. Association for Computational Linguistics.

Gregory Grefenstette, Yan Qu, James G. Shanahan, and David A. Evans. 2004. Coupling niche browsers and affect analysis for an opinion mining application. In *Proceeding of RIAO-04*, Avignon, FR.

Mark Hall, Eibe Frank, Geoffrey Holmes, Bernhard Pfahringer, Peter Reutemann, and Ian H. Witten. 2009. The weka data mining software: An update. In *SIGKDD Explorations, Volume 11, Issue 1*.

Soo-Min Kim and Eduard Hovy. 2007. Crystal: Analyzing predictive opinions on the web. In *Proceedings of the 2007 Joint Conference on Empirical Methods in Natural Language Processing and Computational Natural Language Learning (EMNLP-CoNLL)*, pages 1056–1064.

Michael Laver, Kenneth Benoit, and John Garry. 2003. Extracting policy positions from political texts using words as data. *American Political Science Review*, 97(2):311–331.

Wei-Hao Lin, Theresa Wilson, Janyce Wiebe, and Alexander Hauptmann. 2006. Which side are you on? Identifying perspectives at the document and sentence levels. In *Proceedings of the 10th Conference on Computational Natural Language Learning (CoNLL-2006)*, pages 109–116, New York, New York.

Wei-Hao Lin. 2006. Identifying perspectives at the document and sentence levels using statistical models. In *Proceedings of the Human Language Technology Conference of the NAACL, Companion Volume: Doctoral Consortium*, pages 227–230, New York City, USA, June. Association for Computational Linguistics.

Robert Malouf and Tony Mullen. 2008. Taking sides: Graph-based user classification for informal online political discourse. *Internet Research*, 18(2).

Lanny W. Martin and Georg Vanberg. 2008. A robust transformation procedure for interpreting political text. *Political Analysis*, 16(1):93–100.

Tony Mullen and Robert Malouf. 2006. A preliminary investigation into sentiment analysis of informal political discourse. In *AAAI 2006 Spring Symposium on Computational Approaches to Analysing Weblogs (AAAI-CAAW 2006)*.

Bo Pang and Lillian Lee. 2008. Opinion mining and sentiment analysis. *Foundations and Trends in Information Retrieval*, Vol. 2(1-2):pp. 1–135.

Swapna Somasundaran and Janyce Wiebe. 2009. Recognizing stances in online debates. In *Proceedings of the Joint Conference of the 47th Annual Meeting of the ACL and the 4th International Joint Conference on Natural Language Processing of the AFNLP*, pages 226–234, Suntec, Singapore, August. Association for Computational Linguistics.

Swapna Somasundaran, Josef Ruppenhofer, and Janyce Wiebe. 2007a. Detecting arguing and sentiment in meetings. In *SIGdial Workshop on Discourse and Dialogue*, Antwerp, Belgium, September.

Swapna Somasundaran, Theresa Wilson, Janyce Wiebe, and Veselin Stoyanov. 2007b. Qa with attitude: Exploiting opinion type analysis for improving question answering in on-line discussions and the news. In *International Conference on Weblogs and Social Media*, Boulder, CO.

Swapna Somasundaran, Janyce Wiebe, and Josef Ruppenhofer. 2008. Discourse level opinion interpretation. In *Proceedings of the 22nd International Conference on Computational Linguistics (Coling 2008)*, pages 801–808, Manchester, UK, August.

Matt Thomas, Bo Pang, and Lillian Lee. 2006. Get out the vote: Determining support or opposition from congressional floor-debate transcripts. In *Proceedings of the 2006 Conference on Empirical Methods in Natural Language Processing*, pages 327–335, Sydney, Australia, July. Association for Computational Linguistics.

Theresa Wilson and Janyce Wiebe. 2005. Annotating attributions and private states. In *Proceedings of ACL Workshop on Frontiers in Corpus Annotation II: Pie in the Sky*.

Theresa Wilson, Janyce Wiebe, and Paul Hoffmann. 2005. Recognizing contextual polarity in phrase-level sentiment analysis. In *hltemnlp2005*, pages 347–354, Vancouver, Canada.

Theresa Wilson. 2007. *Fine-grained Subjectivity and Sentiment Analysis: Recognizing the Intensity, Polarity, and Attitudes of private states*. Ph.D. thesis, Intelligent Systems Program, University of Pittsburgh.

NewsViz:
Emotional Visualization of News Stories

Eva Hanser, Paul Mc Kevitt, Tom Lunney and Joan Condell
School of Computing & Intelligent Systems
Faculty of Computing & Engineering
University of Ulster, Magee
Derry/Londonderry, BT48 7JL
Northern Ireland
hanser-e@email.ulster.ac.uk,
{p.mckevitt, tf.lunney, j.condell}@ulster.ac.uk

Abstract

The NewsViz system aims to enhance news reading experiences by integrating 30 seconds long Flash-animations into news article web pages depicting their content and emotional aspects. NewsViz interprets football match news texts automatically and creates abstract 2D visualizations. The user interface enables animators to further refine the animations. Here, we focus on the emotion extraction component of NewsViz which facilitates subtle background visualization. NewsViz detects moods from news reports. The original text is part-of-speech tagged and adjectives and/or nouns, the word types conveying most emotional meaning, are filtered out and labeled with an emotion and intensity value. Subsequently reoccurring emotions are joined into longer lasting moods and matched with appropriate animation presets. Different linguistic analysis methods were tested on NewsViz: word-by-word, sentence-based and minimum threshold summarization, to find a minimum number of occurrences of an emotion in forming a valid mood. NewsViz proved to be viable for the fixed domain of football news, grasping the overall moods and some more detailed emotions precisely. NewsViz offers an efficient technique to cater for the production of a large number of daily updated news stories. NewsViz bypasses the lack of information for background or environment depiction encountered in similar applications. Further development may refine the detection of emotion shifts through summarization with the full implementation of football and common linguistic knowledge.

1 Introduction

News reports are regarded as objective facts, commonly delivered in an objective, unbiased manner and represented in a neutral and formal format: typically a static headline, a summarizing paragraph with one image and eventually the body text with one to three more images. Even though reporters find the content of news stories worth mentioning for emotional reasons and the content often affects readers emotionally, story brevity, scarce background information and poor combination of visual and verbal information hinders learning and feeling by viewers. In order to reach the audience emotionally, to educate and to entertain, emphasis on visual elements is important as they tend to be more memorable than verbal ones. The emphasis of NewsViz lies on expression, impacting on the reader's understanding of the article and making it more memorable. The software prototype, NewsViz, automatically creates animations from news articles. Abstract design elements show emotions conveyed in the stories. The main objective of NewViz remains information provision and thus our focus is emotion extraction which is universally applicable and without opinion bias. NewsViz is an efficient software tool for designers to be able to build daily updated animations. Input for NewsViz is natural language text. Multimodal systems automatically mapping text to visuals face challenges in interpreting human language which is variable, ambiguous, imprecise and relies on the communicative partners possessing common knowledge. Enabling a machine to understand a natural language text involves feeding the

Proceedings of the NAACL HLT 2010 Workshop on Computational Approaches to Analysis and Generation of Emotion in Text, pages 125–130,
Los Angeles, California, June 2010.

machine with grammatical structures, e.g. part-of-speech, semantic relations, e.g. emotion value and intensity, and visual descriptions, e.g. colors and motion direction, to match suitable graphics.

2 Background and Related Research

Text-to-visual mapping relates to the areas of natural language processing (NLP) and multimodal storytelling which attempt to enable computers to interpret and generate natural human language and mental images. Text-to-visual mapping starts with linguistic analysis of the text. Despite variability, ambiguity and imprecision, syntactic analysis tools achieve mostly reliable results, such as trainable part-of-speech tagger software tools which identify parts of speech with 97% accuracy. For example, Qtag (Mason, 2003) attaches a tag to each word labeling it as noun, verb, adjective or other.

Semantic interpretation and actual understanding of the meaning of a text is more difficult, because it depends largely on commonsense knowledge. Commonsense knowledge and mental images need to be structured, related through logical rules and entered into databases before computational text interpretation is possible. WordNet (Miller, 1995) determines semantic relations between words and is an extended dictionary specifying word relations such as similarity, part-of relations, hierarchy or manner. Story segmentation is performed by e.g. SeLeCT (Stokes, 2003), an example application based on semantic analysis to find story or subtopic changes within a text. Groups of semantically related words called cohesive 'lexical chains' are extracted from a text. They are determined through WordNet's semantic relations and additionally through statistically acquired co-occurrences (e.g. Diego Maradonna, Hand of God). Their starting and end points indicate topical unit boundaries.

Sensing emotions from multimodal input has mainly been investigated with the objective of developing human-like agents. The football commentary system, Byrne (Binsted and Luke, 1999), includes a commentator with emotions influenced by his personality and intentions. SOCCER (Retz-Schmidt, 1988) analyses football scenes visually in order to simultaneously add linguistic descriptions of the events. SOBA (Buitelaar et al., 2006) extracts information from soccer match reports, annotates relevant expressions (e.g. players, teams, goals.) and generates knowledge base entities. The collected football knowledge can set preconditions and context to consequently evaluate current events and assign appropriate emotions. The MoodNews website (Mitchell, 2005) demonstrates a very simple linguistic method to distinguish positive, negative and neutral content in BBC news headlines. It effectively ranks them on a color scale between good to bad. The three kinds of emotions are appointed through keyword scoring based on a small vocabulary of 160 words and phrases. The Emotion Sensitive News Agent (ESNA) (Shaikh et al., 2007) chategorizes news stories from different RSS sources into eight emotion categories according to their emotional content, determined through a cognitive evaluation and user preferences.

Automated story visualization systems deliver initial results for object and action depiction, as in WordsEye (Coyne and Sproat, 2001), creating static 3D images from written descriptions. Additionally, automated camera and character animation, interaction and speech synthesis is realized in CONFUCIUS (Ma, 2006). ScriptViz (Liu and Leung, 2006) renders 3D scenes from NL screenplays immediately during the writing process, extracting verbs and adverbs to interpret events and states in sentences. The Unseen Video (Scheibel and Weinrother, 2005), is a good example of abstract mood visualization. Local weather data is automatically retrieved from news websites and influences the look and feel of the Flash animation through shapes, colors and images. The Story Picturing Engine (Joshi et al., 2004) visualizes texts selecting and matching pictures and their annotations from image databases.

The work discussed here demonstrates that sufficient subsets of the English language can be mapped to computer understandable language for the visualization of stories.

3 The NewsViz System

NewsViz takes online news articles as input and outputs animations reflecting the content of these news stories. NewViz consists of three main components: the linguistic analysis, the animation composer and an interface for editing text and animations (Figure

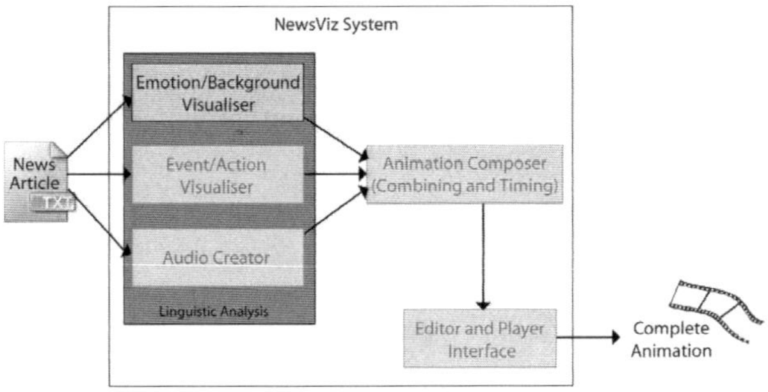

Figure 1: NewsViz System Architecture.

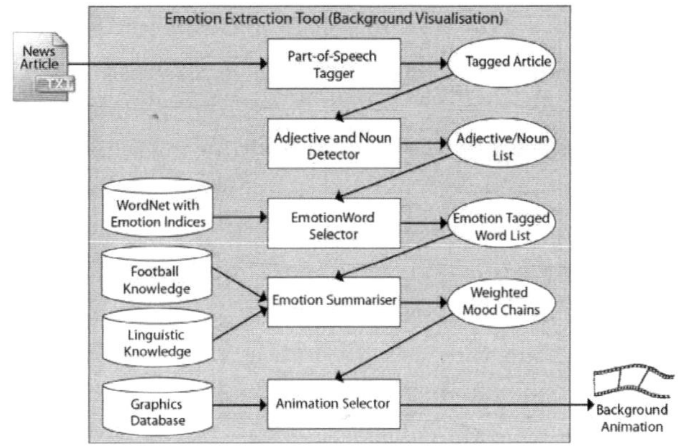

Figure 2: Emotion Extraction Component.

1). The *linguistic component* constructs three elements of the animation in different processes. The *emotion extraction tool* creates atmospheric background visuals, the *action visualizer* depicts people, objects and their actions and the *audio creator* selects music and sound effects. The *composer* synchronizes the different outputs. Here, we focus on the emotion extraction component (Figure 2) developed in Flash MX and Photoshop. Emotional aspects within the news story are identified and linked to appropriate presets of background animations.

3.1 Emotion Extraction

The first step in processing the text is to tag parts of speech for all words. The part-of-speech tagger, Qtag (Mason, 2003), attaches tags to nouns, verbs, adjectives and other parts of speech. The tagged text is sent on to the adjective and noun detector. These two types of words are selected for further processing because they are most central to conveying emotional meaning and sufficient for the visualisation of the emotional content. Nouns and adjectives are the parts of speech which represent the highest number of affective words as found in WordNet-Affect (Strapparava and Valitutti, 2004). Verbs and adverbs will be addressed in future work to increase sensitivity and precision, but their impact on the resulting animations may not be as significant. Next, the emotion word selector checks the adjectives and nouns in the emotion dictionary and attaches emotion tags indicating their kind of emotion and intensity. The dictionary holds manually created emotion-indices and default intensity values of all affective words.

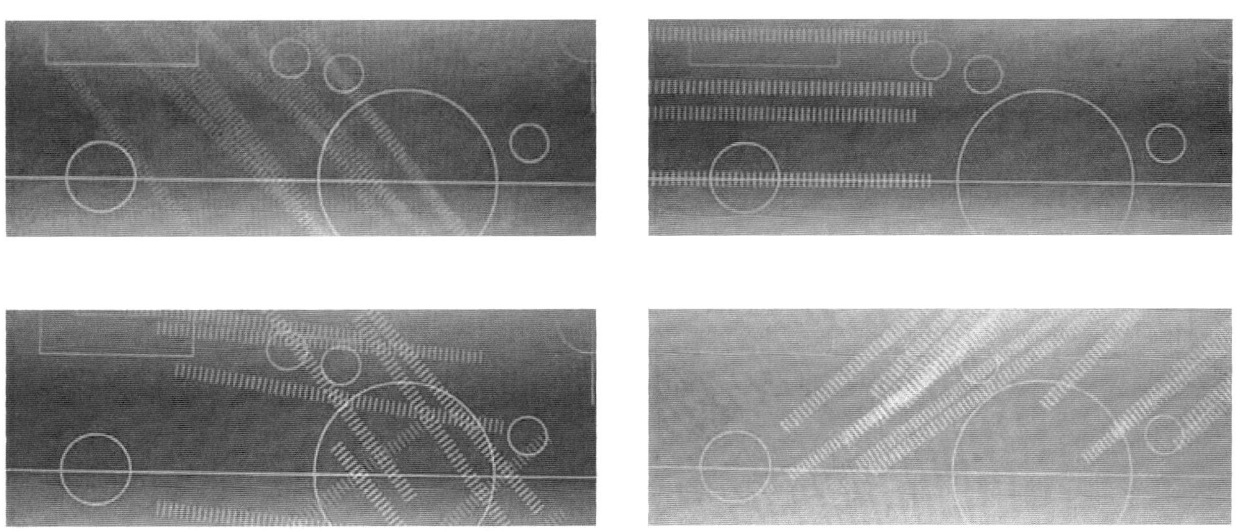

Figure 3: Animations for Sadness (blue), Boredom (green), Tension (red) and Happiness (yellow).

Four emotions have been found relevant in relation to football matches - happiness, sadness, tension and boredom. Words with a neutral emotion index do not describe football relevant emotions. To achieve a coherent course of emotion and animation, neutral phrases are replaced by the previous mood with decreasing intensity. The list of emotion tagged words is handed to the emotion summarizer. During the summarization process subsequent emotions of the same type are combined to form one longer-lasting mood. Each mood is labeled with its type, average intensity and display duration. With the 'word-by-word' summarization method mood boundaries appear as soon as the emotion type of the next word differs. In order to reduce error and excessive mood swings, the minimum threshold method sets a minimum number of words required to represent a mood. Alternatively, the sentence-based method assumes that one sentence conveys one idea and consequently one emotion. Hence, it calculates an average emotion for each sentence, before combining identical emotions. A chronological list of mood chunks is created.

3.2 Animation Construction

The animation selection component loads the individual animation elements from the graphics database and combines them in a 30 seconds long animation. The graphics database contains prefabricated graphics sorted by an emotion index which are combined and adjusted according to mood intensities. Based on the weighted mood list, the emotion sequence order, the type of graphic element, its display duration, and the background color are determined. The intensity value specifies the element size and the number of objects loaded. An emotion change causes the current animation elements to fade out and to load different elements. Animation examples are shown in Figure 3.

3.3 User Interface

NewsViz provides users with options to load or type news stories into the text editor. The options menu offers different emotion extraction and mood summarization methods. By pressing the 'run' button the visualization can be watched in the preview window. The text processing runs 'on the fly' in the background. If the user is satisfied they can save the animation. If the user prefers to alter the animation manually, they have the option to edit the original text or the animation elements frame by frame. Figure 4 shows the user interface with animation player. The final animations are integrated at the top of the news article's internet page (Figure 5).

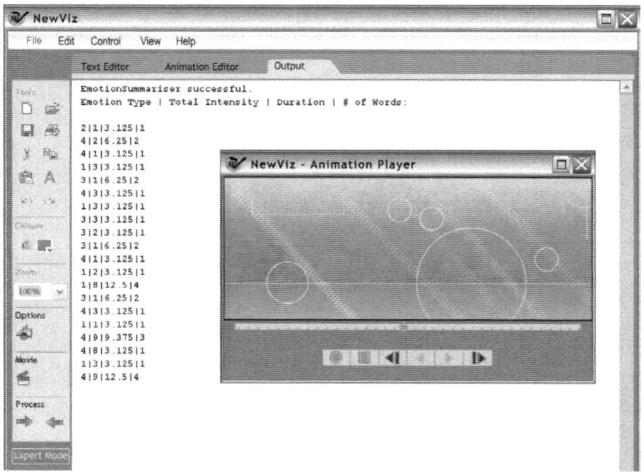

Figure 4: NewsViz User Interface.

Figure 5: Animation Integrated into Website.

4 Evaluation and Testing

NewsViz was tested on a set of four news articles related to the same news domain - football match reports. The articles were taken from BBC and FIFA online describing the same two World Cup 2006 matches. The three different emotion extraction methods, word-by-word, sentence-based and

Method / Wordtype	Word by Word		Sentence based		Threshold 2		Threshold 3		total
	correct	grain	correct	grain	correct	grain	correct	grain	
adjectives	3.125	12	3.25	7.5	2.375	5	1.25	2.3	**2.5**
nouns	3.875	31	2.625	9.3	2.875	14	2	4.8	**2.844**
both	4	33	2.75	9.5	3.5	18	1.5	10	**2.938**
total	**3.667**	**25**	**2.875**	**8.8**	**2.917**	**12**	**1.583**	**5.7**	

Figure 6: Results Analysis of all Test Texts.

threshold were run on these news stories with varying word types or word type combinations. The output of NewsViz is evaluated against two forms of human interpretation of the articles. A short manual description outlines the general course of emotion of a match as reported in each article naming three to five emotions. A second more fine grained interpretation assigns one (or two) emotions to each sentence. In correspondence to Beeferman's probabilistic error metric (Beeferman et al., 1999) three types of emotion extraction error are distinguished. Falsely detected emotions are rated with zero points. Missing emotions were assessed depending on their significance in the text. If the overall feeling of the match was represented, two to three points would be given, but if the main emotions were missing, no points were assigned. Very close, but not exact emotions, got a value of four. A correct representation of the course of emotion received five points. The grain counts the number of the extracted emotions per text. The results for correctness of emotional findings and amount of emotions detected (grain) of each method run on each part-of-speech or word type combination are presented in Figure 6.

The results analysis shows that the effectiveness of adjectives or nouns varies from text to text, but generally the best results are achieved with the extraction of both kinds of words. On average the word-by-word method produces emotion sequences with the closest correctness, but unfortunately its output is too fine grained for visualization. Thirty second long animations are best visualized with two to ten mood swings. This means that some form of summarization is needed. Combining emotions of logically structured chunks of text, namely sentences, in the sentence-based summarization method achieved better results than the minimum subsequent occurrence of two or three emotions with the threshold method. The sentence-based summarizaion as well as the threshold method with a minimum value of 3 produce the most appropriate grain/number of emotions. Some misinterpretation is due to false part-of-speech tagging by Qtag which has particular trouble with proper nouns. More accuracy can be achieved through training Qtag on football reports. Overall the results for NewsViz are satisfactory and it demonstrates that it is possible to extract emotions from news texts. The generally different sensations of the two described football matches are distinguishable. Three of the four test texts show good results, but for one article the extracted emotions do not seem to match the human sensation.

5 Relation to Other Work

NewsViz uses natural human language as input to create animated output. NewsViz aims to solely reflect emotions as they are mentioned in the news article to keep the objective and formal character of news reporting. Therefore, NewsViz applies a reduced, universal and 'personality-free' version of existing concepts for emotion and mood construction. Instead of facial expressions and gestures NewsViz combines and illustrates emotions with design principles. NewsViz offers manual reediting of the automatically created animations.

6 Conclusion and Future Work

NewsViz extracts emotion-bearing words from online football news reports based on an extended dictionary with emotion-indices assigned to each entry. The extracted emotions are processed and illustrated in abstract background animations. Results from initial testing demonstrate that this automated process has satisfactory performance. Technologically, NewsViz is viable for the fixed domain of football reports and offers a sound basis for more affective text-to-visual mapping. Future work will aim to improve the linguistic and semantic processing of emotions. This involves the extension of the parts of speech selection to include verbs and adverbs, assuming that more input data will lead to better results. Rules for common and linguistic knowledge will be integrated. Linguistic knowledge identifies emotions in context applying language rules to emotion interpretation, i.e. it solves negation by inverting emotions. With the integration of a dependency parser, which relates words according to their sentence structure, emotions of related words can be found and their average emotion determined. Domain-specific knowledge (e.g. football) provides background information including match statistics, players' and teams' names, team colors and league tables. It also accommodates game rules or match situations with their emotional consequences. The mood list is refined through moods discovered with commonsense knowledge and football facts which set pre-conditions and context representing long-term moods influencing current event-based emotions. Future work will reveal whether NewsViz is feasible when extended to different domains. The emotion database could be extended through the WordNet-Affect dictionary (Strapparava and Valitutti, 2004). NewsViz enriches standard news websites with attractive and informative animations and can track emotional aspects of people's views on world events. NewsViz brings news reported on the internet closer to readers, making it more easily understood and memorized which is much appreciated by online users overloaded with information. NewsViz assists animation designers in the production of daily updated visualizations creating initial scenes.

References

D. Beeferman, A. Berger and J. Lafferty. 1999. Statistical models for text segmentation. *Machine Learning*, 34:177–210. Springer Netherlands.

K. Binsted and S. Luke. 1999. Character Design for Soccer Commentary. *Lecture Notes in Computer Science. RoboCup-98: Robot Soccer World Cup II*, 1604:22–33. Springer-Verlag, London, UK.

P. Buitelaar, T. Eigner, G. Gulrajani, A. Schutz, M. Siegel, N. Weber, P. Cimiano, G. Ladwig, M. Mantel, H. Zhu. 2006. Generating and Visualizing a Soccer Knowledge Base. *Proceedings of the EACL06 Demo Session*, 4/2006:123–126.

B. Coyne and R. Sproat. 2001. WordsEye: an automatic text-to-scene conversion system. *Proceedings of the 28th Annual Conference on Computer Graphics and Interactive Techniques*, 487–496. ACM Press, Los Angeles, USA.

D. Joshi, J. Z. Wang and J. Li. 2004. The Story Picturing Engine: Finding Elite Images to Illustrate a Story Using Mutual Reinforcement. *Proceedings of the 6th ACM SIGMM International Workshop on Multimedia Information Retrieval*, 119–126. ACM Press, New York, USA.

Z. Liu and K. Leung. 2006. Script visualization (ScriptViz): a smart system that makes writing fun. *Soft Computing*, 10(1), 34–40. Springer Berlin/Heidelberg, Germany.

Minhua Ma. 2006. Automatic Conversion of Natural Language to 3D Animation. *Ph.D. Thesis*. School of Computing and Intelligent Systems, University of Ulster, UK.

O. Mason. 2003. Qtag. `http://phrasys.net/uob/om/software`.

G. A. Miller. 1995. WordNet: a lexical database for English. *Communications of the ACM*, 38(11):39–41.

Davy Mitchell. 2005. MoodNews. `http://www.latedecember.com/sites/moodnews`.

G. Retz-Schmidt. 1988. A REPLAI of SOCCER Recognizing intensions in the domain of soccer games. *Proc. European Conf. AI (ECAI-88)*, 8:455-457.

Daniel Scheibel and Ferdinand Weinrother. 2005. The Unseen Video. `http://www.theunseenvideo.com`.

Mostafa Al Masum Shaikh, Helmut Prendinger and Mitsuru Ishizuka. 2007. Emotion Sensitive News Agent: An Approarch Towards User Centric Emotion Sensing from the News. *Proceedings 2007 IEEE/WIC/ACM International Conference on Web Intelligence (WI07)*, 614–620. Silicon Valley, USA.

N. Stokes. 2003. Spoken and Written News Story Segmentation Using Lexical Chains. *Proceedings of HTL-NAACL 2003*, 49–54. Edmonton, Canada.

C. Strapparava and A. Valitutti. 2004. WordNet-Affect: an Affective Extension of WordNet. *Proceedings of the 4th International Conference on Language Resources and Evaluation (LREC 2004)*, 1083–1086.

Sentiment Classification using Automatically Extracted Subgraph Features

Shilpa Arora, Elijah Mayfield, Carolyn Penstein-Rosé and Eric Nyberg
Language Technologies Institute
Carnegie Mellon University
5000 Forbes Avenue, Pittsburgh, PA 15213
{shilpaa, emayfiel, cprose, ehn}@cs.cmu.edu

Abstract

In this work, we propose a novel representation of text based on patterns derived from linguistic annotation graphs. We use a subgraph mining algorithm to automatically derive features as frequent subgraphs from the annotation graph. This process generates a very large number of features, many of which are highly correlated. We propose a genetic programming based approach to feature construction which creates a fixed number of strong classification predictors from these subgraphs. We evaluate the benefit gained from evolved structured features, when used in addition to the bag-of-words features, for a sentiment classification task.

1 Introduction

In recent years, the topic of sentiment analysis has been one of the more popular directions in the field of language technologies. Recent work in supervised sentiment analysis has focused on innovative approaches to feature creation, with the greatest improvements in performance with features that insightfully capture the essence of the linguistic constructions used to express sentiment, e.g. (Wilson et al., 2004), (Joshi and Rosé, 2009)

In this spirit, we present a novel approach that leverages subgraphs automatically extracted from linguistic annotation graphs using efficient subgraph mining algorithms (Yan and Han, 2002). The difficulty with automatically deriving complex features comes with the increased feature space size. Many of these features are highly correlated and do not provide any new information to the model. For example, a feature of type *unigram_POS* (e.g. *"camera_NN"*) doesn't provide any additional information beyond the *unigram* feature (e.g. *"camera"*), for words that are often used with the same part of speech. However, alongside several redundant features, there are also features that provide new information. It is these features that we aim to capture.

In this work, we propose an evolutionary approach that constructs complex features from subgraphs extracted from an annotation graph. A constant number of these features are added to the unigram feature space, adding much of the representational benefits without the computational cost of a drastic increase in feature space size.

In the remainder of the paper, we review prior work on features commonly used for sentiment analysis. We then describe the annotation graph representation proposed by Arora and Nyberg (2009). Following this, we describe the frequent subgraph mining algorithm proposed in Yan and Han (2002), and used in this work to extract frequent subgraphs from the annotation graphs. We then introduce our novel feature evolution approach, and discuss our experimental setup and results. Subgraph features combined with the feature evolution approach gives promising results, with an improvement in performance over the baseline.

2 Related Work

Some of the recent work in sentiment analysis has shown that structured features (features that capture syntactic patterns in text), such as n-grams, dependency relations, etc., improve performance beyond

Proceedings of the NAACL HLT 2010 Workshop on Computational Approaches to Analysis and Generation of Emotion in Text, pages 131–139,
Los Angeles, California, June 2010.

the bag of words approach. Arora et al. (2009) show that deep syntactic scope features constructed from transitive closure of dependency relations give significant improvement for identifying types of claims in product reviews. Gamon (2004) found that using deep linguistic features derived from phrase structure trees and part of speech annotations yields significant improvements on the task of predicting satisfaction ratings in customer feedback data. Wilson et al. (2004) use syntactic clues derived from dependency parse tree as features for predicting the intensity of opinion phrases[1].

Structured features that capture linguistic patterns are often hand crafted by domain experts (Wilson et al., 2005) after careful examination of the data. Thus, they do not always generalize well across datasets and domains. This also requires a significant amount of time and resources. By automatically deriving structured features, we might be able to learn new annotations faster.

Matsumoto et al. (2005) propose an approach that uses frequent sub-sequence and sub-tree mining approaches (Asai et al., 2002; Pei et al., 2004) to derive structured features such as word sub-sequences and dependency sub-trees. They show that these features outperform bag-of-words features for a sentiment classification task and achieve the best performance to date on a commonly-used movie review dataset. Their approach presents an automatic procedure for deriving features that capture long distance dependencies without much expert intervention.

However, their approach is limited to sequences or tree annotations. Often, features that combine several annotations capture interesting characteristics of text. For example, Wilson et al. (2004), Gamon (2004) and Joshi and Rosé (2009) show that a combination of dependency relations and part of speech annotations boosts performance. The annotation graph representation proposed by Arora and Nyberg (2009) is a formalism for representing several linguistic annotations together on text. With an annotation graph representation, instances are represented as graphs from which frequent subgraph patterns may be extracted and used as features for learning new annotations.

[1] Although, in this work we are classifying sentences and not phrases, similar clues may be used for sentiment classification in sentences as well

In this work, we use an efficient frequent subgraph mining algorithm (gSpan) (Yan and Han, 2002) to extract frequent subgraphs from a linguistic annotation graph (Arora and Nyberg, 2009). An annotation graph is a general representation for arbitrary linguistic annotations. The annotation graph and subgraph mining algorithm provide us a quick way to test several alternative linguistic representations of text. In the next section, we present a formal definition of the annotation graph and a motivating example for subgraph features.

3 Annotation Graph Representation and Feature Subgraphs

Arora and Nyberg (2009) define the annotation graph as a quadruple: $G = (N, E, \Sigma, \lambda)$, where N is the set of nodes, E is the set of edges, s.t. $E \subset N \times N$, and $\Sigma = \Sigma_N \cup \Sigma_E$ is the set of labels for nodes and edges. $\lambda : N \cup E \rightarrow \Sigma$ is the labeling function for nodes and edges. Examples of node labels (Σ_N) are *tokens (unigrams)* and annotations such as *part of speech*, *polarity* etc. Examples of edge labels (Σ_E) are *leftOf*, *dependency type* etc. The *leftOf* relation is defined between two adjacent nodes. The *dependency type* relation is defined between a head word and its modifier.

Annotations may be represented in an annotation graph in several ways. For example, a dependency triple annotation 'good_amod_movie', may be represented as a *d_amod* relation between the head word 'movie' and its modifier 'good', or as a node *d_amod* with edges *ParentOfGov* and *ParentOfDep* to the head and the modifier words. An example of an annotation graph is shown in Figure 1.

The instance in Figure 1 describes a movie review comment, *'interesting, but not compelling.'*. The words 'interesting' and 'compelling' both have positive prior polarity, however, the phrase expresses negative sentiment towards the movie. Heuristics for special handling of *negation* have been proposed in the literature. For example, Pang et al. (2002) append every word following a negation, until a punctuation, with a 'NOT' . Applying a similar technique to our example gives us two sentiment bearing features, one positive (*'interesting'*) and one negative (*'NOT-compelling'*), and the model may not be as sure about the predicted label, since there is both positive and negative sentiment present.

In Figure 2, we show three discriminating subgraph features derived from the annotation graph in Figure 1. These subgraph features capture the negative sentiment in our example phrase. The first feature in 2(a) captures the pattern using dependency relations between words. A different review comment may use the same linguistic construction but with a different pair of words, for example *"a pretty good, but not excellent story."* This is the same linguistic pattern but with different words the model may not have seen before, and hence may not classify this instance correctly. This suggests that the feature in 2(a) may be too specific.

In order to mine general features that capture the rhetorical structure of language, we may add prior polarity annotations to the annotation graph, using a lexicon such as Wilson et al. (2005). Figure 2(b) shows the subgraph in 2(a) with polarity annotations. If we want to generalize the pattern in 2(a) to any positive words, we may use the feature subgraph in Figure 2(c) with X wild cards on words that are polar or negating. This feature subgraph captures the negative sentiment in both phrases *'interesting, but not compelling.'* and *"a pretty good, but not excellent story."*. Similar generalization using wild cards on words may be applied with other annotations such as part of speech annotations as well. By choosing where to put the wild card, we can get features similar to, but more powerful than, the dependency back-off features in Joshi and Rosé (2009).

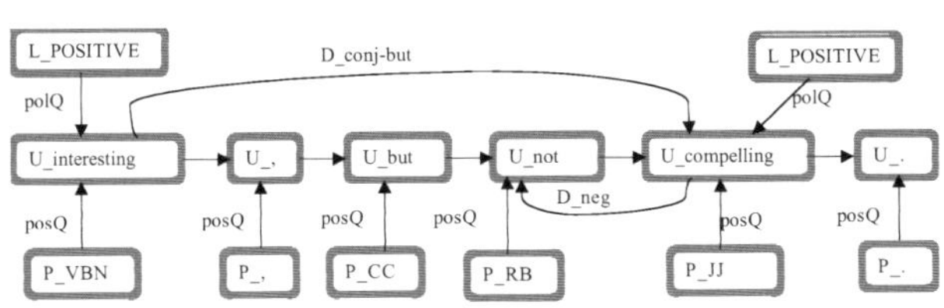

Figure 1: Annotation graph for sentence *'interesting, but not compelling.'* . Prefixes: 'U' for unigrams (tokens), 'L' for polarity, 'D' for dependency relation and 'P' for part of speech. Edges with no label encode the 'leftOf' relation between words.

4 Subgraph Mining Algorithms

In the previous section, we demonstrated that subgraphs from an annotation graph can be used to identify the rhetorical structure used to express sentiment. The subgraph patterns that represent general linguistic structure will be more frequent than surface level patterns. Hence, we use a frequent subgraph mining algorithm to find frequent subgraph patterns, from which we construct features to use in the supervised learning algorithm.

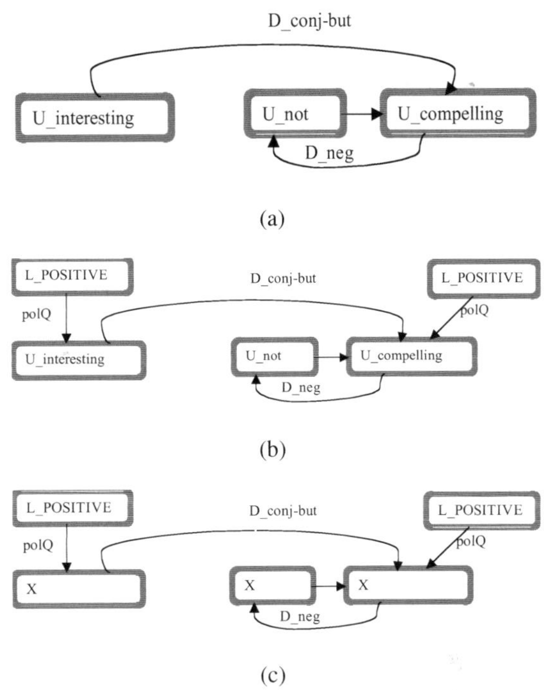

Figure 2: Subgraph features from the annotation graph in Figure 1

The goal in frequent subgraph mining is to find frequent subgraphs in a collection of graphs. A graph G' is a subgraph of another graph G if there exists a subgraph isomorphism[2] from G' to G, denoted by $G' \sqsubseteq G$.

Earlier approaches in frequent subgraph mining (Inokuchi et al., 2000; Kuramochi and Karypis, 2001) used a two-step approach of first generating the candidate subgraphs and then testing their frequency in the graph database. The second step involves a subgraph isomorphism test, which is NP-complete. Although efficient isomorphism testing algorithms have been developed making it practical to use, with lots of candidate subgraphs to test, it can

[2] http://en.wikipedia.org/wiki/Subgraph_isomorphism_problem

still be very expensive for real applications.

gSpan (Yan and Han, 2002) uses an alternative pattern growth based approach to frequent subgraph mining, which extends graphs from a single subgraph directly, without candidate generation. For each discovered subgraph G, new edges are added recursively until all frequent supergraphs of G have been discovered. gSpan uses a depth first search tree (DFS) and restricts edge extension to only vertices on the rightmost path. However, there can be multiple DFS trees for a graph. gSpan introduces a set of rules to select one of them as representative. Each graph is represented by its unique canonical DFS code, and the codes for two graphs are equivalent if the graphs are isomorphic. This reduces the computational cost of the subgraph mining algorithm substantially, making gSpan orders of magnitude faster than other subgraph mining algorithms. With several implementations available [3], gSpan has been commonly used for mining frequent subgraph patterns (Kudo et al., 2004; Deshpande et al., 2005). In this work, we use gSpan to mine frequent subgraphs from the annotation graph.

5 Feature Construction using Genetic Programming

A challenge to overcome when adding expressiveness to the feature space for any text classification problem is the rapid increase in the feature space size. Among this large set of new features, most are not predictive or are very weak predictors, and only a few carry novel information that improves classification performance. Because of this, adding more complex features often gives no improvement or even worsens performance as the feature space's signal is drowned out by noise.

Riloff et al. (2006) propose a feature subsumption approach to address this issue. They define a hierarchy for features based on the information they represent. A complex feature is only added if its discriminative power is a delta above the discriminative power of all its simpler forms. In this work, we use a Genetic Programming (Koza, 1992) based approach which evaluates interactions between features and evolves complex features from them. The advantage of the genetic programing based approach over feature subsumption is that it allows us to evaluate a feature using multiple criteria. We show that this approach performs better than feature subsumption.

A lot of work has considered this genetic programming problem (Smith and Bull, 2005). The most similar approaches to ours are taken by Krawiec (2002) and Otero et al. (2002), both of which use genetic programming to build tree feature representations. None of this work was applied to a language processing task, though there has been some similar work to ours in that community, most notably (Hirsch et al., 2007), which built search queries for topic classification of documents. Our prior work (Mayfield and Rosé, 2010) introduced a new feature construction method and was effective when using unigram features; here we extend our approach to feature spaces which are even larger and thus more problematic.

The Genetic Programming (GP) paradigm is most advantageous when applied to problems where there is not a correct answer to a problem, but instead there is a gradient of partial solutions which incrementally improve in quality. Potential solutions are represented as trees consisting of functions (non-leaf nodes in the tree, which perform an action given their child nodes as input) and terminals (leaf nodes in the tree, often variables or constants in an equation). The tree (an individual) can then be interpreted as a program to be executed, and the output of that program can be measured for fitness (a measurement of the program's quality). High-fitness individuals are selected for reproduction into a new generation of candidate individuals through a breeding process, where parts of each parent are combined to form a new individual.

We apply this design to a language processing task at the stage of feature construction - given many weakly predictive features, we would like to combine them in a way which produces a better feature. For our functions we use boolean statements AND and XOR, while our terminals are selected randomly from the set of all unigrams and our new, extracted subgraph features. Each leaf's value, when applied to a single sentence, is equal to 1 if that subgraph is present in the sentence, and 0 if the subgraph is not

[3] `http://www.cs.ucsb.edu/~xyan/software/gSpan.htm`, `http://www.kyb.mpg.de/bs/people/nowozin/gboost/`

present.

The tree in Figure 3 is a simplified example of our evolved features. It combines three features, a unigram feature 'too' (centre node) and two subgraph features: 1) the subgraph in the leftmost node occurs in collocations containing *"more than"* (e.g., *"nothing more than"* or *"little more than"*), 2) the subgraph in the rightmost node occurs in negative phrases such as *"opportunism at its most glaring"* (JJS is a superlative adjective and PRP$ is a possessive pronoun). A single feature combining these weak indicators can be more predictive than any part alone.

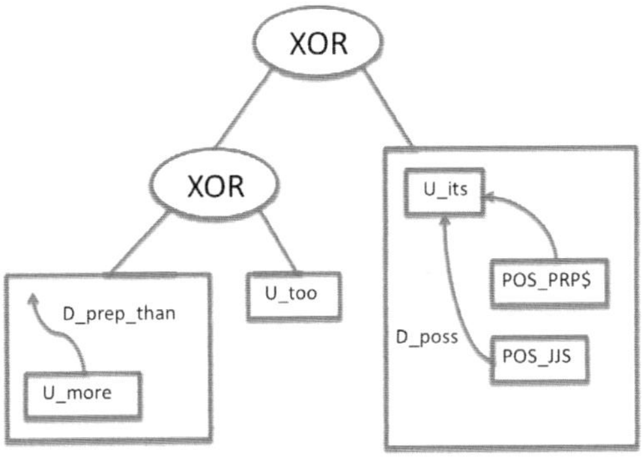

Figure 3: A tree constructed using subgraph features and GP (Simplified for illustrative purposes)

In the rest of this section, we first describe the feature construction process using genetic programming. We then discuss how fitness of an individual is measured for our classification task.

5.1 Feature Construction Process

We divide our data into two sets, training and test. We again divide our training data in half, and train our GP features on only one half of this data[4] This is to avoid overfitting the final SVM model to the GP features. In a single GP run, we produce one feature to match each class value. For a sentiment classification task, a feature is evolved to be predictive of the positive instances, and another feature is evolved to be predictive of the negative documents. We repeat this procedure a total of 15 times (using different seeds for random selection of features), producing a total of 30 new features to be added to the feature space.

[4]For genetic programming we used the ECJ toolkit (`http://cs.gmu.edu/~eclab/projects/ecj/`).

5.2 Defining Fitness

Our definition of fitness is based on the concepts of precision and recall, borrowed from information retrieval. We define our set of documents as being comprised of a set of positive documents $P_0, P_1, P_2, ...P_u$ and a set of negative documents $N_0, N_1, N_2, ...N_v$. For a given individual I and document D, we define $hit(I, D)$ to equal 1 if the statement I is true of that document and 0 otherwise. Precision and recall of an individual feature for predicting positive documents[5] is then defined as follows:

$$Prec(I) = \frac{\sum_{i=0}^{u} hit(I, P_i)}{\sum_{i=0}^{u} hit(I, P_i) + \sum_{i=0}^{v} hit(I, N_i)} \quad (1)$$

$$Rec(I) = \frac{\sum_{i=0}^{u} hit(I, P_i)}{u} \quad (2)$$

We then weight these values to give significantly more importance to precision, using the F_β measure, which gives the harmonic mean between precision and recall:

$$F_\beta(I) = \frac{(1+\beta^2) \times (Prec(I) \times Rec(I))}{(\beta^2 \times Prec(I)) + Rec(I)} \quad (3)$$

In addition to this fitness function, we add two penalties to the equation. The first penalty applies to prevent trees from becoming overly complex. One option to ensure that features remain moderately simple is to simply have a maximum depth beyond which trees cannot grow. Following the work of Otero et al. (2002), we penalize trees based on the number of nodes they contain. This discourages bloat, i.e. sections of trees which do not contribute to overall accuracy. This penalty, known as parsimony pressure, is labeled *PP* in our fitness function.

The second penalty is based on the correlation between the feature being constructed, and the subgraphs and unigrams which appear as nodes within that individual. Without this penalty, a feature may

[5]Negative precision and recall are defined identically, with obvious adjustments to test for negative documents instead of positive.

often be redundant, taking much more complexity to represent the same information that is captured with a simple unigram. We measure correlation using Pearson's product moment, defined for two vectors X, Y as:

$$\rho_{x,y} = \frac{E[(X - \mu_X)(Y - \mu_Y)]}{\sigma_X \sigma_Y} \tag{4}$$

This results in a value from 1 (for perfect alignment) to -1 (for inverse alignment). We assign a penalty for any correlation past a cutoff. This function is labeled *CC* (correlation constraint) in our fitness function.

Our fitness function therefore is:

$$\text{Fitness} = F_{\frac{1}{8}} + PP + CC \tag{5}$$

6 Experiments and Results

We evaluate our approach on a sentiment classification task, where the goal is to classify a movie review sentence as expressing positive or negative sentiment towards the movie.

6.1 Data and Experimental Setup

Data: The dataset consists of snippets from Rotten Tomatoes (Pang and Lee, 2005) [6]. It consists of 10662 snippets/sentences total with equal number positive and negative sentences (5331 each). This dataset was created and used by Pang and Lee (2005) to train a classifier for identifying positive sentences in a full length review. We use the first 8000 (4000 positive, 4000 negative) sentences as training data and evaluate on remaining 2662 (1331 positive, 1331 negative) sentences. We added part of speech and dependency triple annotations to this data using the Stanford parser (Klein and Manning, 2003).

Annotation Graph: For the annotation graph representation, we used *Unigrams (U)*, *Part of Speech (P)* and *Dependency Relation Type (D)* as labels for the nodes, and *ParentOfGov* and *ParentOfDep* as labels for the edges. For a dependency triple such as "amod_good_movie", five nodes are added to the annotation graph as shown in Figure 4(a). *ParentOfGov* and *ParentOfDep* edges are added from the

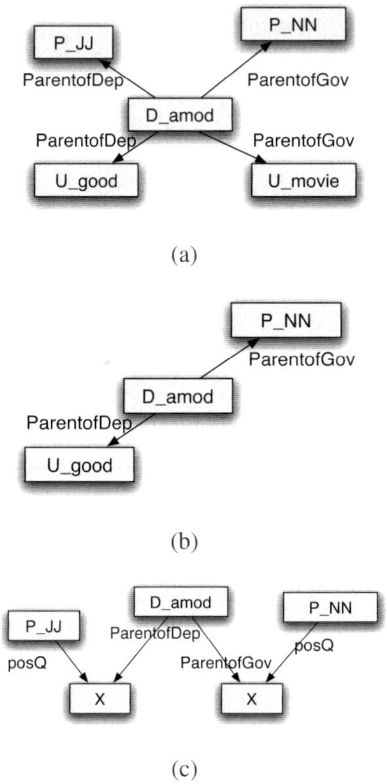

Figure 4: Annotation graph and a feature subgraph for dependency triple annotation "amod_good_camera". (c) shows an alternative representation with wild cards

dependency relation node *D_amod* to the unigram nodes *U_good* and *U_movie*. These edges are also added for the part of speech nodes that correspond to the two unigrams in the dependency relation, as shown in Figure 4(a). This allows the algorithm to find general patterns, based on a dependency relation between two part of speech nodes, two unigram nodes or a combination of the two. For example, a subgraph in Figure 4(b) captures a general pattern where *good* modifies a noun. This feature exists in "amod_good_movie", "amod_good_camera" and other similar dependency triples. This feature is similar to the the dependency back-off features proposed in Joshi and Rosé (2009).

The extra edges are an alternative to putting wild cards on words, as proposed in section 3. On the other hand, putting a wild card on every word in the annotation graph for our example (Figure 4(c)), will only give features based on dependency relations between part of speech annotations. Thus, the wild card based approach is more restrictive than

[6] `http://www.cs.cornell.edu/people/pabo/movie-review-data/rt-polaritydata.tar.gz`

adding more edges. However, with lots of edges, the complexity of the subgraph mining algorithm and the number of subgraph features increases tremendously.

Classifier: For our experiments we use Support Vector Machines (SVM) with a linear kernel. We use the SVM-light[7] implementation of SVM with default settings.

Parameters: The *gSpan* algorithm requires setting the minimum support threshold ($minsup$) for the subgraph patterns to extract. Support for a subgraph is the number of graphs in the dataset that contain the subgraph. We experimented with several values for minimum support and $minsup = 2$ gave us the best performance.

For Genetic Programming, we used the same parameter settings as described in Mayfield and Rosé (2010), which were tuned on a different dataset[8] than one used in this work, but it is from the same movie review domain. We also consider one alteration to these settings. As we are introducing many new and highly correlated features to our feature space through subgraphs, we believe that a stricter constraint must be placed on correlation between features. To accomplish this, we can set our correlation penalty cutoff to 0.3, lower than the 0.5 cutoff used in prior work. Results for both settings are reported.

Baselines: To the best of our knowledge, there is no supervised machine learning result published on this dataset. We compare our results with the following baselines:

- *Unigram-only Baseline:* In sentiment analysis, unigram-only features have been a strong baseline (Pang et al., 2002; Pang and Lee, 2004). We only use unigrams that occur in at least two sentences of the training data same as Matsumoto et al. (2005). We also filter out stop words using a small stop word list[9].

- χ^2 *Baseline:* For our training data, after filtering infrequent unigrams and stop words, we get 8424 features. Adding subgraph features increases the total number of features to $44,161$, a factor of 5 increase in size. Feature selection can be used to reduce this size by selecting the most discriminative features. χ^2 feature selection (Manning et al., 2008) is commonly used in the literature. We compare two methods of feature selection with χ^2, one which rejects features if their χ^2 score is not significant at the 0.05 level, and one that reduces the number of features to match the size of our feature space with GP.

- *Feature Subsumption (FS):* Following the idea in Riloff et al. (2006), a complex feature C is discarded if $IG(S) \geq IG(C) - \delta$, where IG is Information Gain and S is a simple feature that *representationally subsumes* C, i.e. the text spans that match S are a superset of the text spans that match C. In our work, complex features are subgraph features and simple features are unigram features contained in them. For example, $(D\_amod)\_Edge\_ParentOfDep\_(U\_bad)$ is a complex feature for which U_bad is a simple feature. We tried same values for $\delta \in \{0.002, 0.001, 0.0005\}$, as suggested in Riloff et al. (2006). Since all values gave us same number of features, we only report a single result for feature subsumption.

- *Correlation (Corr):* As mentioned earlier, some of the subgraph features are highly correlated with unigram features and do not provide new knowledge. A correlation based filter for subgraph features can be used to discard a complex feature C if its absolute correlation with its simpler feature (unigram feature) is more than a certain threshold. We use the same threshold as used in the GP criterion, but as a hard filter instead of a penalty.

6.2 Results and Discussion

In Table 1, we present our results. As can be seen, subgraph features when added to the unigrams, without any feature selection, decrease the performance. χ^2 feature selection with fixed feature space size provides a very small gain over unigrams. All other feature selection approaches perform worse

[7] `http://svmlight.joachims.org/`

[8] Full movie review data by Pang et al. (2002)

[9] `http://nlp.stanford.edu/IR-book/html/htmledition/dropping-common-terms-stop-words-1.html` (with one modification: removed 'will', added 'this')

Settings	#Features	Acc.	Δ
Uni	8424	75.66	-
Uni + Sub	44161	75.28	-0.38
Uni + Sub, χ^2 sig.	3407	74.68	-0.98
Uni + Sub, χ^2 size	8454	75.77	+0.11
Uni + Sub, (FS)	18234	75.47	-0.19
Uni + Sub, (Corr)	18980	75.24	-0.42
Uni + GP (U) †	8454	76.18	+0.52
Uni + GP (U+S) ‡	8454	76.48	+0.82
Uni + GP (U+S) †	8454	**76.93**	+1.27

Table 1: Experimental results for feature spaces with unigrams, with and without subgraph features. Feature selection with 1) fixed significance level (χ^2 sig.), 2) fixed feature space size (χ^2 size), 3) Feature Subsumption (FS) and 4) Correlation based feature filtering (Corr)). GP features for unigrams only {GP(U)}, or both unigrams and subgraph features {GP(U+S)}. Both the settings from Mayfield and Rosé (2010) (‡) and more stringent correlation constraint (†) are reported. $\#Features$ is the number of features in the training data. Acc is the accuracy and Δ is the difference from unigram only baseline. Best performing feature configuration is highlighted in bold.

than the unigram-only approach. With GP, we observe a marginally significant gain ($p < 0.1$) in performance over unigrams, calculated using one-way ANOVA. Benefit from GP is more when subgraph features are used in addition to the unigram features, for constructing more complex pattern features. Additionally, our performance is improved when we constrain the correlation more severely than in previously published research, supporting our hypothesis that this is a helpful way to respond to the problem of redundancy in subgraph features.

A problem that we see with χ^2 feature selection is that several top ranked features may be highly correlated. For example, the top 5 features based on χ^2 score are shown in Table 2; it is immediately obvious that the features are highly redundant.

With GP based feature construction, we can consider this relationship between features, and construct new features as a combination of selected unigram and subgraph features. With the correlation criterion in the evolution process, we are able to build combined features that provide new information compared to unigrams.

The results we present are for the best performing parameter configuration that we tested, after a series of experiments. We realize that this places us in danger of overfitting to the particulars of this data set, however, the data set is large enough to partially mitigate this concern.

(D_advmod)_Edge_ParentOfDep _(U_too)
U_too
U_bad
U_movie
(D_amod)_Edge_ParentOfDep _(U_bad)

Table 2: Top features based on χ^2 score

7 Conclusion and Future Work

We have shown that there is additional information to be gained from text beyond words, and demonstrated two methods for increasing this information - a subgraph mining approach that finds common syntactic patterns that capture sentiment-bearing rhetorical structure in text, and a feature construction technique that uses genetic programming to combine these more complex features without the redundancy, increasing the size of the feature space only by a fixed amount. The increase in performance that we see is small but consistent.

In the future, we would like to extend this work to other datasets and other problems within the field of sentiment analysis. With the availability of several off-the-shelf linguistic annotators, we may add more linguistic annotations to the annotation graph and richer subgraph features may be discovered. There is also additional refinement that can be performed on our genetic programming fitness function, which is expected to improve the quality of our features.

Acknowledgments

This work was funded in part by the DARPA Machine Reading program under contract FA8750-09-C-0172, and in part by NSF grant DRL-0835426. We would like to thank Dr. Xifeng Yan and Marisa Thoma for the gSpan code.

References

Shilpa Arora, Mahesh Joshi and Carolyn P. Rosé. 2009. *Identifying Types of Claims in Online Customer Re-*

views. Proceedings of the HLT/NAACL.

Shilpa Arora and Eric Nyberg. 2009. *Interactive Annotation Learning with Indirect Feature Voting*. Proceedings of the HLT/NAACL (Student Research Workshop).

Tatsuya Asai, Kenji Abe, Shinji Kawasoe, Hiroshi Sakamoto and Setsuo Arikawa. 2002. *Efficient substructure discovery from large semi-structured data*. Proceedings of SIAM Int. Conf. on Data Mining (SDM).

Mukund Deshpande , Michihiro Kuramochi , Nikil Wale and George Karypis. 2005. *Frequent Substructure-Based Approaches for Classifying Chemical Compounds*. IEEE Transactions on Knowledge and Data Engineering.

Michael Gamon. 2004. *Sentiment classification on customer feedback data: noisy data, large feature vectors, and the role of linguistic analysis*, Proceedings of COLING.

Laurence Hirsch, Robin Hirsch and Masoud Saeedi. 2007. *Evolving Lucene Search Queries for Text Classification*. Proceedings of the Genetic and Evolutionary Computation Conference.

Mahesh Joshi and Carolyn P. Rosé. 2009. *Generalizing Dependency Features for Opinion Mining*. Proceedings of the ACL-IJCNLP Conference (Short Papers).

Akihiro Inokuchi, Takashi Washio and Hiroshi Motoda. 2000. *An Apriori-based Algorithm for Mining Frequent Substructures from Graph Data*. Proceedings of PKDD.

Dan Klein and Christopher D. Manning. 2003. *Accurate unlexicalized parsing*. Proceedings of the main conference of the ACL.

John Koza. 1992. *Genetic Programming: On the Programming of Computers by Means of Natural Selection*. MIT Press.

Krzysztof Krawiec. 2002. *Genetic programming-based construction of features for machine learning and knowledge discovery tasks*. Genetic Programming and Evolvable Machines.

Taku Kudo, Eisaku Maeda and Yuji Matsumoto. 2004. *An Application of Boosting to Graph Classification*. Proceedings of NIPS.

Michihiro Kuramochi and George Karypis. 2002. *Frequent Subgraph Discovery*. Proceedings of ICDM.

Christopher D. Manning, Prabhakar Raghavan and Hinrich Schtze. 2008. *Introduction to Information Retrieval*. Proceedings of PAKDD.

Shotaro Matsumoto, Hiroya Takamura and Manabu Okumura. 2005. *Sentiment Classification Using Word Sub-sequences and Dependency Sub-trees*. Proceedings of PAKDD.

Elijah Mayfield and Carolyn Penstein-Rosé. 2010. *Using Feature Construction to Avoid Large Feature Spaces in Text Classification*. Proceedings of the Genetic and Evolutionary Computation Conference.

Fernando Otero, Monique Silva, Alex Freitas and Julio Nievola. 2002. *Genetic Programming for Attribute Construction in Data Mining*. Proceedings of the Genetic and Evolutionary Computation Conference.

Bo Pang, Lillian Lee and Shivakumar Vaithyanathan. 2002. *Thumbs up? Sentiment Classication using Machine Learning Techniques*. Proceedings of EMNLP.

Bo Pang and Lillian Lee. 2004. *A Sentimental Education: Sentiment Analysis Using Subjectivity Summarization Based on Minimum Cuts*. Proceedings of the main conference of ACL.

Bo Pang and Lillian Lee. 2005. *Seeing stars: Exploiting class relationships for sentiment categorization with respect to rating scales*. Proceedings of the main conference of ACL.

Jian Pei, Jiawei Han, Behzad Mortazavi-asl, Jianyong Wang, Helen Pinto, Qiming Chen, Umeshwar Dayal and Mei-chun Hsu. 2004. *Mining Sequential Patterns by Pattern-Growth: The PrefixSpan Approach*. Proceedings of IEEE Transactions on Knowledge and Data Engineering.

Ellen Riloff, Siddharth Patwardhan and Janyce Wiebe. 2006. *Feature Subsumption for Opinion Analysis*. Proceedings of the EMNLP.

Matthew Smith and Larry Bull. 2005. *Genetic Programming with a Genetic Algorithm for Feature Construction and Selection*. Genetic Programming and Evolvable Machines.

Theresa Wilson, Janyce Wiebe and Rebecca Hwa. 2004. *Just How Mad Are You? Finding Strong and Weak Opinion Clauses*. Proceedings of AAAI.

Theresa Wilson, Janyce Wiebe and Paul Hoffmann. 2005. *Recognizing Contextual Polarity in Phrase-Level Sentiment Analysis*. Proceedings of HLT/EMNLP.

Xifeng Yan and Jiawei Han. 2002. *gSpan: Graph-Based Substructure Pattern Mining*. UIUC Technical Report, UIUCDCS-R-2002-2296 (shorter version in ICDM'02).

Hierarchical versus Flat Classification of Emotions in Text

Diman Ghazi [(a)], Diana Inkpen [(a)], Stan Szpakowicz [(a, b)]

[(a)] School of Information Technology and Engineering, University of Ottawa

[(b)] Institute of Computer Science, Polish Academy of Sciences

{dghaz038,diana,szpak}@site.uottawa.ca

Abstract

We explore the task of automatic classification of texts by the emotions expressed. Our novel method arranges neutrality, polarity and emotions hierarchically. We test the method on two datasets and show that it outperforms the corresponding "flat" approach, which does not take into account the hierarchical information. The highly imbalanced structure of most of the datasets in this area, particularly the two datasets with which we worked, has a dramatic effect on the performance of classification. The hierarchical approach helps alleviate the effect.

1 Introduction

Computational approaches to emotion analysis have focused on various emotion modalities, but there was only limited effort in the direction of automatic recognition of emotion in text (Aman, 2007).

Oleveres et al.(1998), as one of the first works in emotion detection in text, uses a simple Natural Language Parser for keyword spotting, phrase length measurement and emoticon identification.

They apply a rule-based expert system to construct emotion scores based on the parsed text and contextual information. However their simple word-level analysis system is not sufficient when the emotion is expressed by more complicated phrases and sentences.

More advanced systems for textual emotion recognition performed sentence-level analysis. Liu et al. (2003), proposed an approach aimed at understanding the underlying semantics of language using large-scale real-world commonsense knowledge to classify sentences into "basic" emotion categories. They developed a commonsense affect model enabling the analysis of the affective qualities of text in a robust way.

In SemEval 2007, one of the tasks was carried out in an unsupervised setting and the emphasis was on the study of emotion in lexical semantics (Strapparava and Mihalcea, 2008; Chaumartin, 2007; Kozareva *et al.*, 2007; Katz *et al.*, 2007). Neviarouskaya et al.(2009) applied a rule-based approach to affect recognition from a blog text. However, statistical and machine learning approaches have became a method of choice for constructing a wide variety of NLP applications (Wiebe et al., 2005).

There has been previous work using statistical methods and supervised machine learning, including (Aman, 2007; Katz *et al.*, 2007; Alm, 2008; Wilson et al., 2009). Most of that research concentrated on feature selections and applying lexical semantics rather than on different learning schemes. In particular, only *flat* classification has been considered.

According to Kiritchenko *et al.* (2006), "Hierarchical categorization deals with categorization problems where categories are organized in hierarchies". Hierarchical text categorization places new items into a collection with a predefined hierarchical structure. The categories are partially ordered, usually from more generic to more specific.

Koller and Sahami (1997) carried out the first proper study of a hierarchical text categorization problem in 1997. More work in hierarchical text categorization has been reported later. Keshtkar and Inkpen (2009) applied a hierarchical approach to mood classification: classifying blog posts into 132 moods. The connection with our work is only indirect, because – even though moods and emotions may seem similar – their hierarchy structure and the classification task are quite different. The work reported in (Kiritchenko *et al.*, 2006) is more general. It explores two main aspects of hierarchic-

Proceedings of the NAACL HLT 2010 Workshop on Computational Approaches to Analysis and Generation of Emotion in Text, pages 140–146,
Los Angeles, California, June 2010.

al text categorization: learning algorithms and performance evaluation.

In this paper, we extend our preliminary work (Ghazi *et al.*, 2010) on hierarchical classification. Hierarchical classification is a new approach to emotional analysis, which considers the relation between neutrality, polarity and emotion of a text. The main idea is to arrange these categories and their interconnections into a hierarchy and leverage it in the classification process.

We categorize sentences into six basic emotion classes; there also may, naturally, be no emotion in a sentence. The emotions are *happiness*, *sadness*, *fear*, *anger*, *disgust*, and *surprise* (Ekman, 1992). In one of the datasets we applied, we did consider the class *non-emotional*.

For these categories, we have considered two forms of hierarchy for classification, with two or three levels. In the two-level method, we explore the effect of neutral instances on one dataset and the effect of polarity on the other dataset. In the three-level hierarchy, we consider neutrality and polarity together.

Our experiments on data annotated with emotions show performance which exceeds that of the corresponding flat approach.

Section 2 of this paper gives an overview of the datasets and feature sets. Section 3 describes both hierarchical classification methods and their evaluation with respect to flat classification results. Section 4 discusses future work and presents a few conclusions.

2 Data and Feature Sets

2.1 Datasets

The statistical methods typically require training and test corpora, manually annotated with respect to each language-processing task to be learned (Wiebe *et al.*, 2005). One of the datasets in our experiments is a corpus of blog sentences annotated with Ekman's emotion labels (Aman, 2007). The second dataset is a sentence-annotated corpus resource divided into three parts for large-scale exploration of affect in children's stories (Alm, 2008).

In the first dataset, each sentence is tagged by a dominant emotion in the sentence, or labelled as non-emotional. The dataset contains 173 weblog posts annotated by two judges. Table 1 shows the details of the dataset.

In the second dataset, two annotators have annotated 176 stories. The affects considered are the same as Ekman's six emotions, except that the *surprise* class is subdivided into *positive surprise* and *negative surprise*. We run our experiments on only sentences with high agreement- sentences with the same affective labels annotated by both annotators. That is the version of the dataset which merged *angry* and *disgusted* instances and combined the positive and negative *surprise* classes. The resulting dataset, therefore, has only five classes (Alm, 2008). Table 1 presents more details about the datasets, including the range of frequencies for the class distribution (Min is the proportion of sentences with the most infrequent class, Max is the proportion for sentences with the most frequent class.) The proportion of the most frequent class also gives us a baseline for the accuracies of our classifiers (since the poorest baseline classifier could always choose the most frequent class).

Table 1. Datasets specifications.

	Domain	*Size*	*# classes*	*Min-Max%*
Aman's Data set	Weblogs	2090	7	6-38 %
Alm's Data set	Stories	1207	5	9-36%

2.2 Feature sets

In (Ghazi *et al.*, 2010), three sets of features – one corpus-based and two lexically-based – are compared on Aman's datasets. The first experiment is a corpus-based classification which uses unigrams (bag-of-words). In the second experiment, classification was based on features derived from the *Prior-Polarity* lexicon[1] (Wilson *et al.* 2009); the features were the tokens common between the prior-polarity lexicon and the chosen dataset. In the last experiment, we used a combination of the emotional lists of words from *Roget's Thesaurus*[2] (Aman and Szpakowicz, 2008) and *WordNet Affect*[3] (Strapparava and Valitutti, 2004); we call it the *polarity feature set*.

[1] www.cs.pitt.edu/mpqa

[2] The 1987 Penguin's Roget's Thesaurus was used.

[3] www.cse.unt.edu/~rada/affective text/data/WordNetAffectEmotioLists.tar.gz

Based on the results and the discussion in (Ghazi *et al.*, 2010), we decided to use the polarity feature set in our experiments. This feature set has certain advantages. It is quite a bit smaller than the unigram features, and we have observed that they appear to be more meaningful. For example, the unigram features include (inevitably non-emotional) names of people and countries. It is also possible to have misspelled tokens in unigrams, while the prior-polarity lexicon features are well-defined words usually considered as polar. Besides, lexical features are known to be more domain- and corpus-independent. Last but not least, our chosen feature set significantly outperforms the third set.

2.3 Classification

As a classification algorithm, we use the support vector machines (SVM) algorithm with tenfold cross-validation as a testing option. It is shown that SVM obtains good performance in text classification: it scales well to the large numbers of features (Kennedy and Inkpen, 2006; Aman, 2007).

We apply the same settings at each level of the hierarchy for our hierarchical approach classification.

In hierarchical categorization, categories are organized into levels (Kiritchenko *et al.*, 2006). We use the hierarchical categories to put more knowledge into our classification method as the category hierarchies are carefully composed manually to represent our knowledge of the subject. We will achieve that in two forms of hierarchy. A two-level hierarchy represents the relation of emotion and neutrality in text, as well as the relation of positive and negative polarity. These two relations are examined in two different experiments, each on a separate dataset.

A three-level hierarchy is concerned with the relation between polarity and emotions along with the relation between neutrality and emotion. We assume that, of Ekman's six emotions, *happiness* belongs to the positive polarity class, while the other five emotions have negative polarity. This is quite similar to the three-level hierarchy of affect labels used by Alm (2008). In her diagram, she considers happiness and positive surprise as positive, and the rest as negative emotions. She has not, however, used this model in the classification approach: classification experiments were only run at three separate affect levels. She also considers positive and negative surprise as one *Surprise* class.

For each level of our proposed hierarchy, we run two sets of experiments. In the first set, we assume that all the instances are correctly classified at the preceding levels, so we only need to be concerned with local mistakes. Because we do not have to deal with instances misclassified at the previous level, we call these results *reference results*.

In the second set of experiments, the methodology is different than in (Ghazi *et al.* 2010). In that work both training and testing of subsequent levels is based on the results of preceding levels. A question arises, however: once we have good data available, why train on incorrect data which result from mistakes at the preceding level? That is why we decided to train on correctly-labelled data and when testing, to compute global results by cumulating the mistakes from all the levels of the hierarchical classification. In other words, classification mistakes at one level of the hierarchy carry on as mistakes at the next levels. Therefore, we talk of *global results* because we compute the accuracy, precision, recall and F-measure globally, based on the results at all levels. These results characterize the hierarchical classification approach when testing on new sentences: the classifiers are applied in a pipeline order: level 1, then level 2 on the results of the previous level (then level 3 if we are in the three-level setting).

In the next section, we show the experiments and results on our chosen datasets.

3 Results and discussions

3.1 Two-level classification

This section has two parts. The main goal of the first part is to find out how the presence of neutral instances affects the performance of features for distinguishing between emotional classes in Aman's dataset. This was motivated by a similar work in polarity classification (Wilson *et al.*, 2009).

In the second part, we discuss the effect of considering positive and negative polarity of emotions for five affect classes in Alm's dataset.

Table 2. Two-level emotional classification on Aman's dataset (the highest precision, recall, and F-measure values for each class are shown in bold). The results of the flat classification are repeated for convenience.

		Two-level classification			Flat classification		
		Precision	Recall	F-measure	Precision	Recall	F-measure
1st level	*emo*	0.88	0.85	0.86	--	--	--
	non-emo	**0.88**	0.81	**0.84**	0.54	**0.87**	0.67
2nd level reference results	*happiness*	0.59	**0.95**	**0.71**	**0.74**	0.60	0.66
	sadness	**0.77**	**0.49**	**0.60**	0.69	0.42	0.52
	fear	**0.91**	**0.49**	**0.63**	0.82	**0.49**	0.62
	surprise	**0.75**	**0.32**	**0.45**	0.64	0.27	0.38
	disgust	0.66	**0.35**	**0.45**	**0.68**	0.31	0.43
	anger	**0.72**	**0.33**	**0.46**	0.67	0.26	0.38
Accuracy			**68.32%**			61.67%	
2-level experiment global results	*non-emo*	**0.88**	0.81	**0.84**	0.54	**0.87**	0.67
	happiness	0.56	**0.86**	**0.68**	**0.74**	0.60	0.66
	sadness	0.64	**0.42**	0.51	**0.69**	**0.42**	**0.52**
	fear	0.75	0.43	0.55	**0.82**	**0.49**	**0.62**
	surprise	0.56	**0.29**	**0.38**	**0.64**	0.27	**0.38**
	disgust	0.52	0.29	0.37	**0.68**	**0.31**	**0.43**
	anger	0.55	**0.27**	0.36	**0.67**	0.26	**0.38**
Accuracy			**65.50%**			61.67%	

3.1.1 Neutral-Emotional

At the first level, emotional versus non-emotional classification tries to determine whether an instance is neutral or emotional. The second step takes all instances which level 1 classified as emotional, and tries to classify them into one of Ekman's six emotions. Table 2 presents the result of experiments and, for comparison, the flat classification results. A comparison of the results in both experiments with flat classification shows that in both cases the accuracy of two-level approach is significantly better than the accuracy of flat classification.

One of the results worth discussing further is the precision of the non-emotional class: it increases while recall decreases. We will see the same pattern in further experiments. This happens to the classes which used to dominate in flat classification but they no longer dominate in hierarchical classification. Classifiers tends to give priority to a dominant class, so more instances are placed in this class; thus, classification achieves low precision and high recall. Hierarchical methods tend to produce higher precision.

The difference between precision and recall of the *happiness* class in the flat approach and the two-level approach cannot be ignored. It can be explained as follows: at the second level there are no more non-emotional instances, so the happiness class dominates, with 42% of all the instances. As explained before, this gives high recall and low precision for the happiness class. We hope to address this big gap between precision and recall of the happiness class in the next experiments, three-level classification. It separates happiness from the other five emotions, so it makes the number of instances of each level more balanced.

Our main focus is comparing hierarchical and flat classification, assuming all the other parameters are fixed. We mention, however, the best previous results achieved by Aman (2007) on the same dataset. Her best result was obtained by combining corpus-based unigrams, features derived from emotional lists of words from *Roget's Thesaurus* (explained in 2.2) and common words between the dataset and *WordNetAffect*. She also applied SVM with tenfold cross validation. The results appear in Table 3.

Table 3. Aman's best results on her data set.

	Precision	Recall	F-Measure
happiness	0.813	0.698	0.751
sadness	0.605	0.416	0.493
fear	0.868	0.513	0.645
surprise	0.723	0.409	0.522
disgust	0.672	0.488	0.566
anger	0.650	0.436	0.522
non-emo	0.587	0.625	0.605

Table 4. Two-level emotional classification on Alm's dataset (the highest precision, recall, and F-measure values for each class are shown in bold).

		Two-level classification			Flat classification		
		Precision	Recall	F-measure	Precision	Recall	F-measure
1st level	*neg*	0.81	0.93	0.87	--	--	--
	pos	**0.84**	0.64	**0.72**	0.56	**0.86**	0.68
2nd level reference results	*sadness*	0.65	**0.68**	**0.66**	**0.67**	0.53	0.59
	fear	**0.59**	**0.40**	**0.47**	**0.59**	0.38	0.46
	surprise	**0.45**	**0.21**	**0.29**	0.35	0.10	0.16
	anger	0.49	**0.73**	**0.59**	**0.54**	0.43	0.48
Accuracy			59.07%			57.41%	
2-level experiment global results	*happiness*	**0.84**	0.64	**0.72**	0.56	**0.86**	0.68
	sadness	0.55	**0.61**	0.58	**0.67**	0.53	**0.59**
	fear	0.45	**0.39**	0.42	**0.59**	0.38	**0.46**
	surprise	0.27	**0.21**	**0.19**	**0.35**	0.10	0.16
	anger	0.43	**0.68**	**0.53**	**0.54**	0.43	0.48
Accuracy			56.57%			57.41%	

By comparing the reference results in Table 2 with Aman's result shown in Table 3, our results on two classes, *non-emo* and sadness are significantly better. Even though recall of our experiments is higher for *happiness* class, the precision makes the F-measure to be lower. The reason behind the difference between the precisions is the same as their difference between in our hierarchical and flat comparisons. As it was also mentioned there we hope to address this problem in three-level classification. Both precision and recall of the *sadness* in our experiments is higher than Aman's results. We have a higher precision for *fear,* but recall is slightly lower. For the last three classes our precision is higher while recall is significantly lower.

The size of these three classes, which are the smallest classes in the dataset, appears to be the reason. It is possible that the small set of features that we are using will recall fewer instances of these classes comparing to the bigger feature sets used by Aman (2007).

3.1.2 Negative-Positive polarity

These experiments have been run on Alm's dataset with five emotion classes. This part is based on the assumption that the *happiness* class is positive and the remaining four classes are negative.

At the first level, positive versus negative classification tries to determine whether an instance bears a positive emotion. The second step takes all instances which level 1 classified as negative, and tries to classify them into one of the four negative classes, namely *sadness*, *fear*, *surprise* and *anger-disgust*. The results show a higher accuracy in *reference results* while it is slightly lower for global results. In terms of precision and recall, however, there is a high increase in precision of positive (*happiness*) class while the recall decreases.

The results show a higher accuracy in *reference results* while it is slightly lower for global results. In terms of precision and recall, however, there is a high increase in precision of positive (*happiness*) class while the recall decreases.

We also see a higher F-measure for all classes in the reference results. That confirms the consistency between the result in Table 2 and Table 4.

In the global measurements, recall is higher for all the classes at the second level, but the F-measure is higher only for three classes.

Here we cannot compare our results with the best previous results achieved by Alm (2008), because the datasets and the experiments are not the same. She reports the accuracy of the classification results for three sub-corpora separately. She randomly selected neutral instances from the annotated data and added them to the dataset, which makes it different than the data set we used in our experiments.

3.2 Three-level classification

In this approach, we go even further: we break the seven-class classification task into three levels. The first level defines whether the instance is emotional. At the second level the instances defined as emotional by the first level will be classified on their polarity. At the third level, we assume that the instances of *happiness* class have positive polarity and the other five emotions negative polarity. That is why we take the negative instances from the second level and classify them into the five negative emotion classes. Table 5 presents the results of this classification. The results show that the accuracy of both reference results and global results are higher than flat classification, but the accuracy of the global results is not significantly better.

At the first and second level, the F-measure of *no-emotion* and *happiness* classes is significantly better. At the third level, except in the class *disgust*, we see an increase in the F-measure of all classes in comparison with both the two-level and flat classification.

Table 5. Three-level emotional classification on Aman's dataset (the highest precision, recall, and F-measure values for each class are shown in bold)

		Three-level Classification		
		Precision	Recall	F
1st level	*emo*	0.88	0.85	0.86
	non-emo	**0.88**	0.81	**0.84**
2nd level reference results	*positive*	**0.89**	**0.65**	**0.75**
	negative	0.79	0.94	0.86
3rd level reference results	*sadness*	0.63	**0.54**	**0.59**
	fear	**0.88**	**0.52**	**0.65**
	surprise	**0.79**	**0.37**	**0.50**
	disgust	0.42	**0.38**	0.40
	anger	0.38	**0.71**	**0.49**
Accuracy			**65.5%**	
3 level experiment global results	*non-emo*	**0.88**	0.81	**0.84**
	happiness	**0.77**	**0.62**	**0.69**
	sadness	0.43	**0.49**	0.46
	fear	0.52	0.4	0.45
	surprise	0.46	**0.32**	**0.38**
	disgust	0.31	**0.31**	0.31
	anger	0.35	**0.55**	**0.43**
Accuracy			**62.2%**	

Also, as shown by the two-level experiments, the results of the second level of the reference results approach an increase in the precision of the *happiness* class. That makes the instances defined as *happiness* more precise.

By comparing the results with Table 3, which is the best previous results, we see an increase in the precision of *happiness* class and its F-measure consequently; therefore in these results we get a higher F-measure for three classes, *non-emo*, *sadness* and *fear*. We get the same F-measure for *happiness* and slightly lower F-measure for *surprise* but we still have a lower F-measure for the other two classes, namely, *disgust* and *anger*. The other difference is the high increase in the recall value for *fear*.

4 Conclusions and Future Work

The focus of this study was a comparison of the hierarchical and flat classification approaches to emotional analysis and classification. In the emotional classification we noticed that having a dominant class in the dataset degrades the results significantly. A classifier trained on imbalanced data gives biased results for the classes with more instances. Our results, based on a novel method, shows that the hierarchical classification approach is better at dealing with the highly imbalanced data. We also saw a considerable improvement in the classification results when we did not deal with the errors from previous steps and slightly better results when we evaluated the results globally.

In the future, we will consider different levels of our hierarchy as different tasks which could be handled differently. Each of the tasks has its own specification. We can, therefore, definitely benefit from analyzing each task separately and defining different sets of features and classification methods for each task rather than using the same method for every task.

References

Alm, C.: "Affect in text and speech", PhD dissertation, University of Illinois at Urbana-Champaign, Department of Linguistics (2008)

Aman, S.: "Identifying Expressions of Emotion in Text", Master's thesis, University of Ottawa, Ottawa, Canada (2007)

Aman, S., Szpakowicz, S.: "Using Roget's Thesaurus for Fine-grained Emotion Recognition". Proc. Conf. on Natural Language Processing (IJCNLP), Hyderabad, India, 296-302 (2008)

Chaumartin. F.: "Upar7: A knowledge-based system for headline sentiment tagging", Proc. SemEval-2007, Prague, Czech Republic, June (2007)

Ekman, P.: "An Argument for Basic Emotions", Cognition and Emotion, 6, 169-200 (1992)

Ghazi, D., Inkpen, D., Szpakowicz, S.: "Hierarchical approach to emotion recognition and classification in texts", A. Farzindar and V. Keselj (eds.), Proc. 23rd Canadian Conference on Artificial Intelligence, Ottawa, ON. Lecture Notes in Artificial Intelligence 6085, Springer Verlag, 40–50 (2010)

Katz, P., Singleton, M., Wicentowski, R.: "Swat-mp: the semeval-2007 systems for task 5 and task 14", Proc. SemEval-2007, Prague, Czech Republic, June (2007)

Kennedy, A., Inkpen, D.: "Sentiment classification of movie reviews using contextual valence shifter", Computational Intelligence 22. 110-125 (2006)

Keshtkar, F., Inkpen, D.: "Using Sentiment Orientation Features for Mood Classification in Blog Corpus", IEEE International Conf. on NLP and KE, Dalian, China, Sep. 24-27 (2009)

Kiritchenko, S., Matwin, S., Nock, R., Famili, F.: "Learning and Evaluation in the Presence of Class Hierarchies: Application to Text Categorization", Lecture Notes in Artificial Intelligence 4013, Springer, 395-406 (2006)

Koller, D., Sahami, M.: "Hierarchically Classifying Documents Using Very Few Words". Proc. International Conference on Machine Learning, 170-178 (1997)

Kozareva, Z., Navarro, B., Vazquez, S., Montoyo, A.: "UA-ZBSA: A headline emotion classification through web information", Proc. SemEval-2007, Prague, Czech Republic, June (2007)

Liu, H., Lieberman, H., Selker, T.: "A Model of Textual Affect Sensing using Real-World Knowledge". In Proc. IUI 2003, 125-132 (2003)

Neviarouskaya, A., Prendinger, H., and Ishizuka, M.: "Compositionality Principle in Recognition of Fine-Grained Emotions from Text", In: Proceedings of Third International Conference on Weblogs and Social Media (ICWSM'09), AAAI, San Jose, California, US, 278-281 (2009)

Olveres, J., Billinghurst, M., Savage, J., Holden, A.: "Intelligent, Expressive Avatars". In Proc. of the WECC'98, 47-55 (1998)

Strapparava, C., Mihalcea, R.: "SemEval-2007 Task 14: Affective Text" (2007)

Strapparava, C., Mihalcea, R.: "Learning to Identify Emotions in Text", Proc. ACM Symposium on Applied computing, Fortaleza, Brazil, 1556-1560 (2008)

Wilson, T., Wiebe, J., Hoffmann, P.: "Recognizing contextual polarity: an exploration of features for phrase-level sentiment analysis", Computational Linguistics 35(3), 399-433 (2009)

Wiebe, J., Wilson, T., Cardie, C.: "Annotating Expressions of Opinions and Emotions in Language", Language Resources and Evaluation 39, 165-210 (2005)

Author Index

Association for Computational Linguistics
209 N. Eighth Street
Stroudsburg, Pennsylvania 18360

CURRAN ASSOCIATES INC
proceedings
.com